what happened before the
big bang?

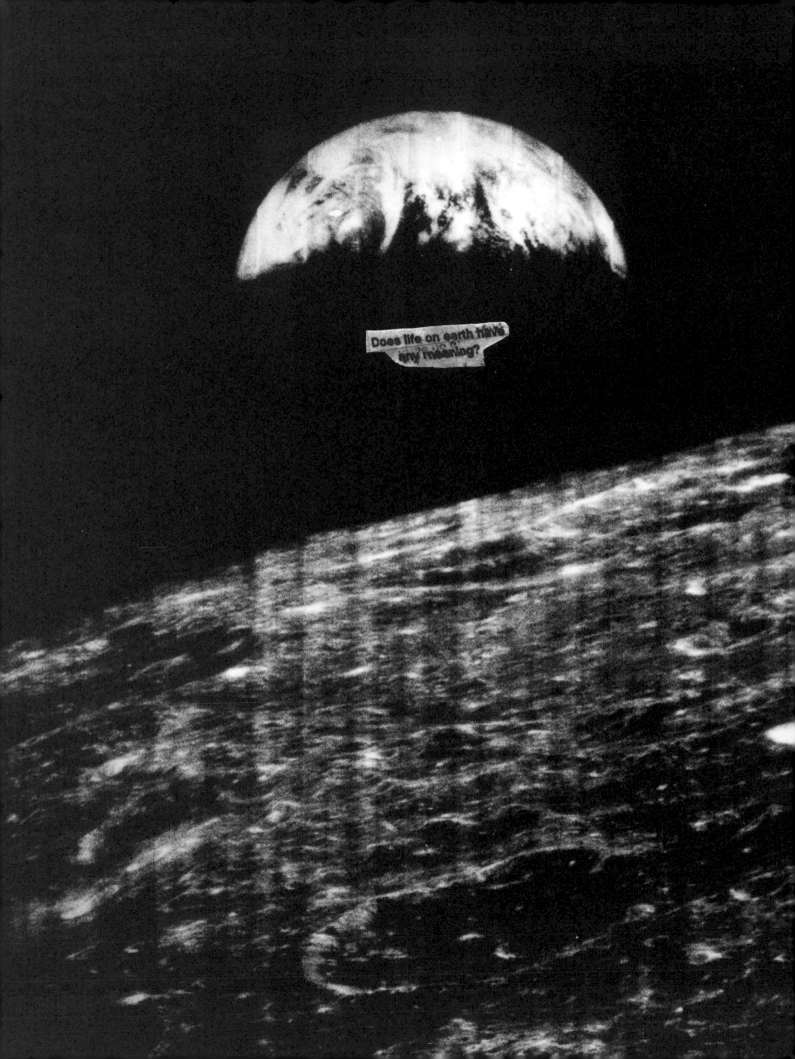

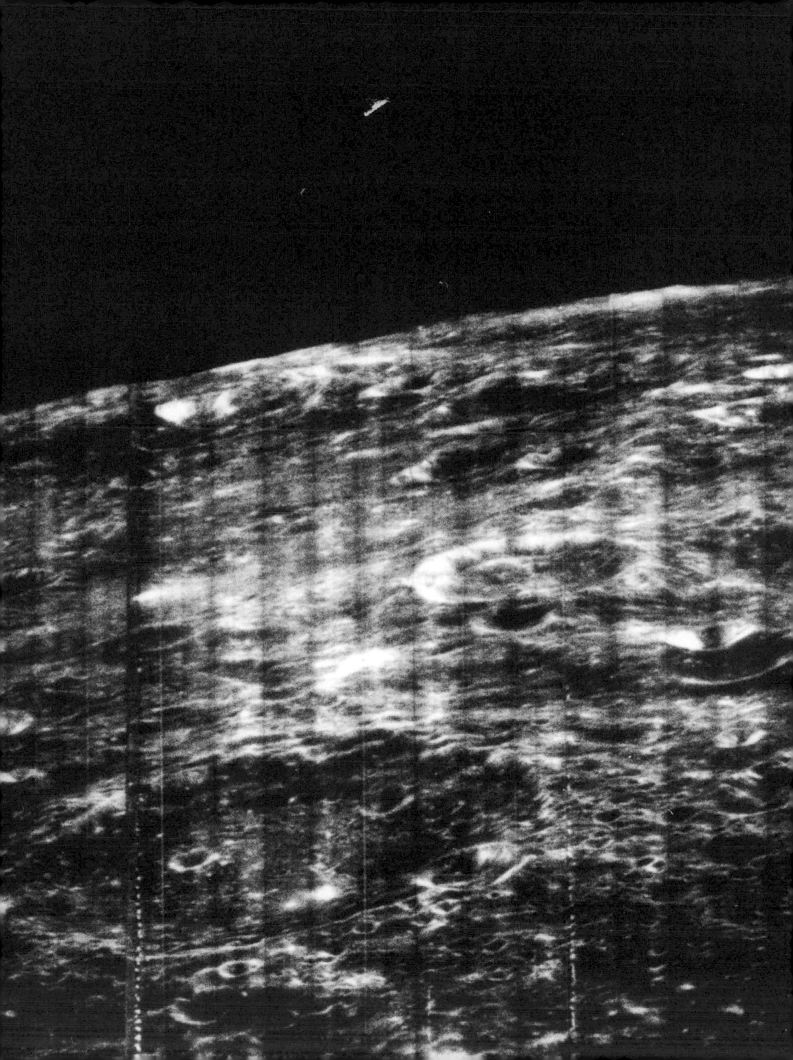

# World Population Growth

(billions)

7
6
5
4
3
2
1
0

0    500    1000    1500    2000

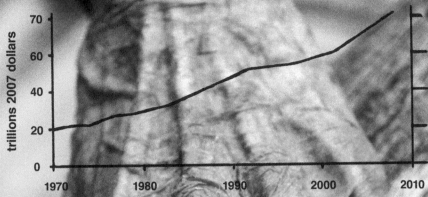

**Gross World Product**

trillions 2007 dollars

70

60

40

20

0

1970    1980    1990    2000    2010

# Species Extinction

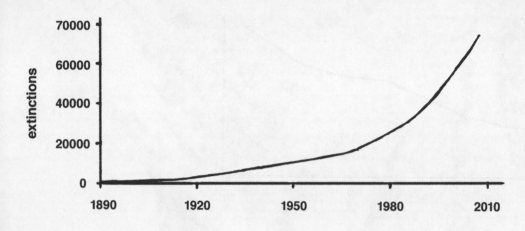

We can rewrite this definition by multiply
by $Q$:

$$\text{Profit} = (TR/Q - TC/Q) \times Q.$$

But note that $TR/Q$ is average revenue, w
total cost $ATC$. Therefore,

$$\text{Profit} = (P - ATC) \times Q.$$

This way of expressing the firm's profit al
Panel (a) of Figure 14-5 shows a fir
already discussed, the firm maximizes pr
price equals marginal cost. Now look at

SO YOU'RE TAKING ECONOMICS, HUH?

# MEME WARS

## THE CREATIVE DESTRUCTION OF NEOCLASSICAL ECONOMICS

A REAL WORLD ECONOMICS TEXTBOOK BY KALLE LASN

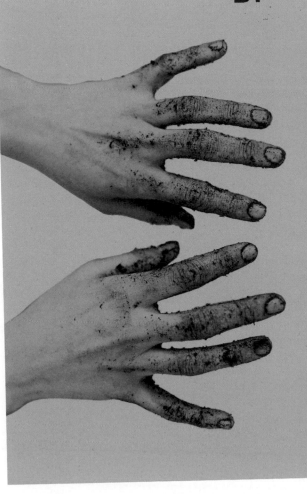

EDITED BY
DARREN FLEET

CREATIVE DIRECTOR
PEDRO INOUE

FEATURING
GEORGE AKERLOF
MARGARET ATWOOD
LOURDES BENERÍA
HERMAN DALY
MICHAEL HUDSON
STEVE KEEN
MANFRED MAX-NEEF
DAVID ORRELL
BILL REES
JOHN RALSTON SAUL
JOSEPH STIGLITZ

ART DIRECTOR
WILL BROWN

ASSISTANT ART DIRECTOR
ELLEN LEE

PRODUCTION MANAGER
LAUREN BERCOVITCH

AN ADBUSTERS
FIRST THINGS FIRST
P R O J E C T

SEVEN STORIES PRESS
140 WATTS STREET
NEW YORK, NY 10013
WWW.SEVENSTORIES.COM

COLLEGE PROFESSORS MAY ORDER EXAMINATION COPIES OF SEVEN STORIES PRESS TITLES FOR A FREE SIX-MONTH TRIAL
PERIOD. TO ORDER, VISIT WWW.SEVENSTORIES.COM/TEXTBOOK OR SEND A FAX ON SCHOOL LETTERHEAD TO (212) 226-1411.

BOOK DESIGN BY ADBUSTERS

LIBRARY OF CONGRESS CATALOGING-IN-PUBLICATION DATA

MEME WARS: THE CREATIVE DESTRUCTION OF NEOCLASSICAL ECONOMICS / EDITED BY KALLE LASN WITH ADBUSTERS. —1ST ED.
    p. cm.
    ISBN 978-1-60980-432-9
    1. ECONOMICS—PSYCHOLOGICAL ASPECTS. 2. OCCUPY WALL STREET (MOVEMENT) I. LASN, KALLE. II. MEDIA FOUNDATION (ORGANIZATION)
    HB74.P8M46 2012B
    330.1—DC23
    2012011119

PRINTED IN CHINA

9 8 7 6 5 4 3 2 1

ISBN: 978-1-60980-432-9

FOR
FRITZ SCHUMACHER,
GUY DEBORD,
HERMAN DALY

AND THE NEXT GENERATION OF ECONOMISTS
WHO WILL LEAVE NOTHING TO CHANCE.

Huddled alone outside the meditation tent, Occupy DC, McPherson Square, March 2012.

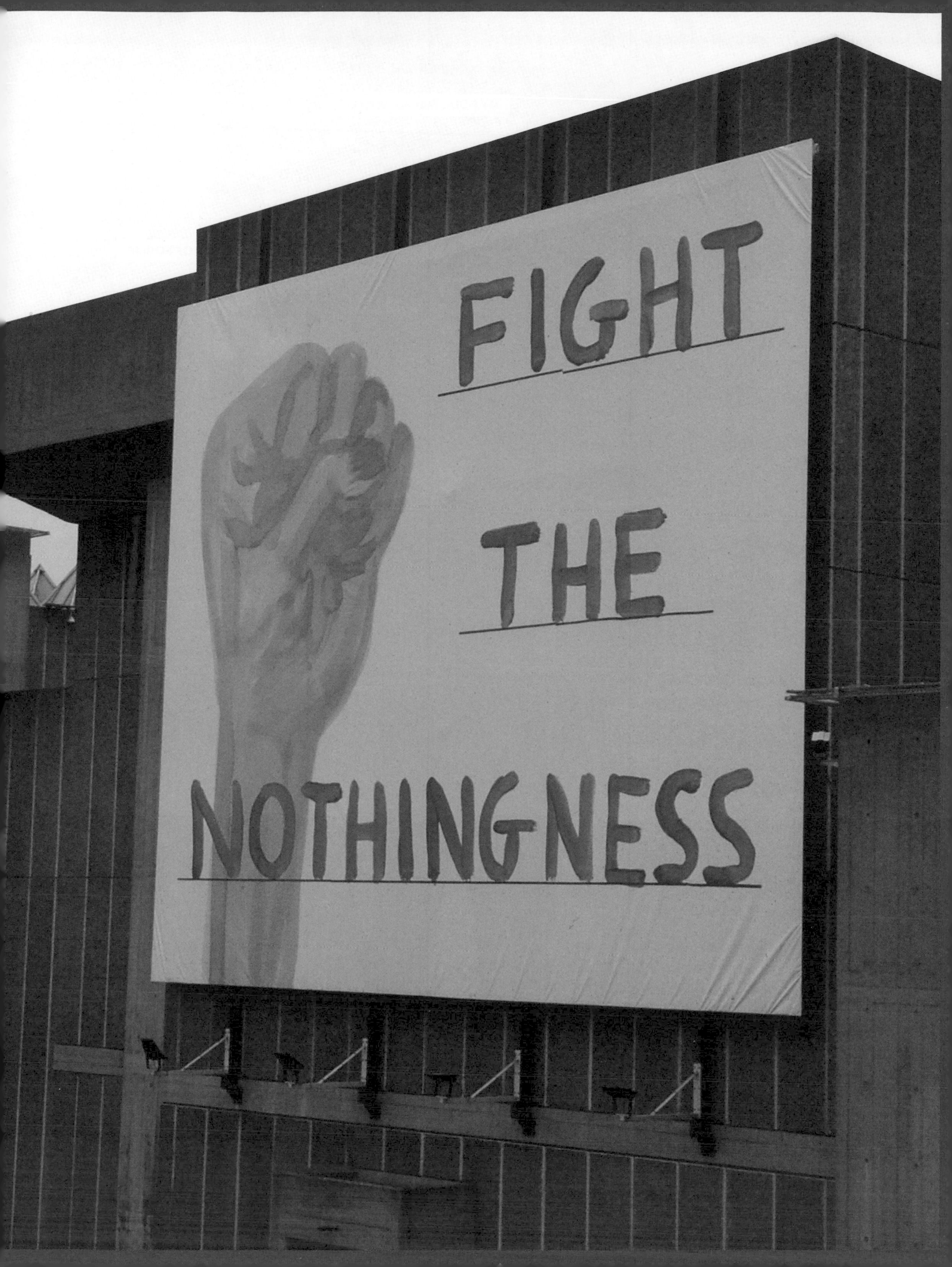
FIGHT
THE
NOTHINGNESS

MY SOUL WALKS WITH ME,

FORM OF FORMS.

TAKE ALL KEEP ALL

James Joyce

# Hey all you students out there,

You are entering university at a critical juncture. Capitalism is in crisis and the crisis is growing ever deeper. The inability of economists to incorporate externalities into their models and to account for phenomena such as species extinction, resource depletion and climate change—not to mention the 2008 financial meltdown that blindsided them all— has turned the profession into a target for derision and ridicule. And it's not just some academic joke— today even ordinary people look down their noses at the ineptitude of economics.

And yet as you delve into your textbooks, listen to the sensible, ordered tone of lectures and come to associate your professors with the accolades that hang on their walls, you may get the sense that economics is a science: A rigorous discipline with its own immutable laws, proven theories and crop of Nobel laureates. Far from it. You may be temporarily fooled by this façade, but you need only look beneath the surface to discover that economics is a highly contested field … a profession whose axioms and credibility are being questioned like never before. The prevailing neoclassical paradigm is crumbling and a new, more chaotic, more biologically and behaviorally based paradigm is struggling to emerge.

But your department, like most others around the world, is still marching in lockstep with the old guard. That's because generations of tenured professors have marginalized dissenters and eliminated competition. Your economics department operates very much like a police state … not a free marketplace of ideas in which innovation is acknowledged and rewarded. But outside your department, a vigorous heterodox economics thrives … there are social economists, feminist economists, interdisciplinary economists, behavioral economists, ecological economists and hundreds of intellectuals and maverick professors who are openly critical of the neoclassical regime and fighting to overthrow it.

So there are really two ways for you to approach your studies over the next few years: You can ignore all of the screaming inconsistencies, and accept the status quo. You can cross your fingers and hope the old paradigm has a generation or two left in it, enough for you to carve out a career. Or you can align yourself from the get-go with the mavericks. You can be an agitator, a provocateur, a meme warrior, an occupier, one of the students on campus who posts dissenting messages up on notice boards and openly challenges professors in class. You can bet your future on a paradigm shift.

All of us here at *Adbusters* hope this book fires up your imagination and inspires you to take the riskier, more exciting path.

Kalle Lasn, Summer 2012

I was sitting in a cold, drab Oxford lecture room in my first year of university waiting for my prof, Marxist thinker Erik Swyngedouw. He finally burst into the room with a cup of coffee in his hand and asked in his distinctive Belgian accent, "Can you see this coffee?" The obvious answer was, "Yes, of course I can see the cup." What, I wondered, was this guy getting at?

But it soon became clear that this wasn't going to be my usual dazed and drowsy experience wallowing at the back of the lecture theater. "You can see the coffee, but can you see the fields of Guatemala? Can you see the EU tariffs? Can you see the coffee workers' pay slips?" I soon realized what he was getting at. The world as it is didn't just happen. It is the way it is because of people, because of laws, because of attitudes.

Then Swyngedouw asked, "So, how many of you want to work in the Civil Service when you're older?" I thought for a second. The idea appealed, but my arms didn't leave my side. It was strange: As if by some magnetic force I was being kept in the system, the one that—for now—ruled the room. No other arms were raised; the question seemed absurd. "So, how many of you want to go work in the City: Invest, trade, move money and make money?" Arms shot up all around me. It all became painfully clear: Why, oh why, would anyone want to contribute to society when they could focus on making money?

I think Swyngedouw's aim was to show us we don't have to give in to the system, and the accumulation of money in our hands doesn't automatically lead to happiness. He told us the ratio of raised arms would have been reversed in the 1970s, but peoples' mindsets had changed. It seems that we're all looking out for ourselves, convinced somehow that profits will bring economic benefit to us all. Mind you, I don't see accumulating money in itself as an evil act. Work hard, make money, sure— but don't make it your idol. Don't screw everyone, don't screw up the planet, don't isolate yourself, don't become an island. We're in this life together.

Luke Sherlock
Oxford, UK

# REAL–WORLD
## CURRICULUM

Sentiment without action
is the ruin of the soul.

Edward Abbey

# I. BATTLE FOR

Anti-austerity protests erupt in
Barcelona, February 2012.

# THE SOUL OF ECONOMICS

## Hey you aspiring business leaders, investment bankers and policy wonks out there,

Economics is destiny!

Get it wrong: People revolt, ecosystems collapse, empires fall.

Get it right—even for a brief moment: A surge of optimism, creativity and enlightenment pulses through the land.

After sixty boom years, the economic destiny of the world has suddenly taken a major turn for the worse ... a surge of pessimism and depression is moving through the land. Food. Water. Oil. Pollution. Temperature. Everything seems to be reaching a peak, teetering on the edge of a long decline ahead.

In this first chapter, we take a romp through history and zero in on some of the evolutionary steps in economic thinking that got us into this current moment of existential angst. We go back to the early days of hunting, bartering, gift giving and cultural reciprocity ... we follow the increasingly sophisticated concepts of gain, trade and property ownership that emerged on the fringes of civilization until they exploded in the Renaissance ... through modes of money exchange and the birth of usury, interest and currency to the era of transatlantic slavery and colonial plunder ... and finally we arrive at this present moment in which our destiny seems to hang on the wild ups and downs of an incredibly complex system of ghost global financial flows, market algorithms, flash trading, mega banking and automated capitalism.

A battle is now underway for the soul of economics ... another evolutionary step in economic thinking is about to be taken. We don't know what it is yet, or in what direction it will go. But if we look back and understand where we came from, we may be able to figure it out.

A jaguar is sacrificed during an ancient Mayan ceremony.

# SACRIFICE

**No wisdom but in submission to the gods.**

—Antigone

All cultures have practiced sacrifice in one way or another, some cultures with more vehemence than others ... In a fundamental sense, and in modern terms, sacrifice is the "cost" in the cost-benefit analysis equation. Whatever that benefit may be, whether it be material or immaterial, whether it be survival or power, there is almost always a cost associated with benefit. Thus that "cost" or "sacrifice" is intrinsic to our existence.

Dr. Kathleen Cohen, *Sacrifices in Ancient Cultures*

# GIFT

**He who receives a benefit with gratitude repays the first installment on his debt.**

—Seneca the Younger

In these subsistence economies the basic operation was not getting, it was giving ... knowing that others would give to you. In other words the key economics mechanism was gift and reciprocity. In tribes, elaborate rules govern the giving and receiving, ensuring all are provided for. (No one in tribal society is poor or hungry, unless times are difficult for all.)

Ted Trainer, *The Radical Implications of a Zero Growth Economy*

Early Roman coins.

In his marvelous book *The Structures of Everyday Life: Civilization and Capitalism 15th–18th Century*, historian Fernand Braudel wrote of the gradual insinuation of the money economy into the lives of medieval peasants: "What did it actually bring? Sharp variations in prices of essential foodstuffs; incomprehensible relationships in which man no longer recognized either himself, his customs or his ancient values. His work became a commodity, himself a 'thing.'"

While early forms of money consisted of anything from sheep to shells, coins made of gold and silver gradually emerged as the most practical, universally accepted means of exchange, measure of value and store of value.

An early American fifty-five dollar note designed by Founding Father Benjamin Franklin, 1779.

# MONEY

Money's ease of storage enabled industrious individuals to accumulate substantial amounts of wealth. But this concentrated wealth also presented a target for thieves. Thievery was especially a problem for traders: While the portability of money enabled travel over long distances for the purchase of rare fabrics and spices, highwaymen often lurked along the way, ready to snatch a purse at knifepoint. These problems led to the invention of banking—a practice in which metalsmiths who routinely dealt with large amounts of gold and silver (and who were accustomed to keeping it in secure, well-guarded vaults) agreed to store other people's coins, offering storage receipts in return. Storage receipts could then be traded as money, thus making trade easier and safer.

Eventually, by the Middle Ages, goldsmith-bankers realized that they could issue these tradable receipts for more gold than they had in their vaults, without anyone being the wiser. They did this by making loans of the receipts, for which they charged a fee amounting to a percentage of the loan.

Richard Heinberg, *The End of Growth*

Cowrie shells were one of the first forms of currency used in ancient China, appearing during the Shang Dynasty (sixteenth century BCE–eleventh century BCE).

The island of Aegina was the first state in ancient Greece to mint coins, producing them as early as 700 BCE.

# GAIN

**The desert shall rejoice,
and blossom as the rose.**

—Isaiah 35:1

The idea of gain as positive social good is a relatively modern one. Throughout most of recorded history it has been conspicuous by its absence. Even our Pilgrim forefathers considered the notion of "buying cheap and selling dear" nothing short of satanic doctrine. Nonetheless, a genuine middle class appeared as a social force in the Mediterranean region during the course of the fourteenth century. Its development coincided with an increase of trade occasioned by two related discoveries: Tacking against the wind, a procedure that made sailing much less subject to the whims of nature, and the compass. Soon new trade routes opened up all over the world. Surplus capital came into existence and, with it, new

The busy port of Lisbon, painted in 1593. Portuguese sovereigns and sea captains once dominated trade in Latin America, Africa and the Far East.

it, new ambitions. By the beginning of the fifteenth century
a number of merchants had become wealthier than any
king. The fortune established by one of these, Giovanni de'
Medici (1360–1429), created what we know as the Florentine
Renaissance. The Medici became the bankers to all of Europe. Their home base, Florence, became a cultural center
to rank with the Athens of ancient Greece.

John Adkins Richardson, *Art: The Way It Is*

The mesmerizing gaze of our future.

The Syndics of the Clothmaker's Guild by Rembrandt, 1661. Guilds set prices, regulated quality and enforced the regulation of trade.

# USURY

And what do you benefit
if you gain the whole world
but lose your own soul?

—Mark 8:36

During the Christian era in Europe, wealth, privilege and power came with great moral costs. In frescoes, woodcuttings, architecture and murals, merchants, moneylenders, popes, cardinals and kings were depicted in shackles being carted off to hell under the watchful eyes of truncheon-wielding demons. The message to the illiterate population was clear—the rich and powerful have received their reward on Earth; best to be humble and poor, assured of a life in heaven after this one. Economic doctrines like the "just price" and taboos on debt dominated European markets. Normalization of interest and gain required an entirely new understanding of Christianity, a new aesthetic of wealth. Centered in Florence, a new crop of wealthy patrons began to hire artists to depict Christ and his followers, the Virgin Mary, the Pope, local elites and the like, lavished with opulence and wealth. The new idea was that riches and religion were symbiotic. The influential Dominican Friar Girolamo Savonarola led a short-lived resistance against such artistic revisionism. At the famed Bonfire of the Vanities in Florence, 1497, Savonarola oversaw the burning of religious and artistic masterworks done in this new opulent style. But he soon fell out of favor with the Florence elite and was burned alive himself in the same square a year later. On the ashes of his objections, the economic rebirth of Christianity began. The other great monotheistic religion, Islam, has maintained many of its rules forbidding usury into the modern age.

Darren Fleet

Jesus chasing the money traders from the temple in Jeruslem by El Greco. Nearly one half of Christ's parables deal directly with wealth and possessions.

Initially the church regarded the practice of profiting from loans as a sin—known as usury—but the bankers found a loophole in religious doctrine: It was permitted to charge for the reimbursement of expenses incurred in making the loan. This was termed interest. Gradually bankers widened the definition of "interest" to include what had formally been called "usury." The practice of loaning out receipts for gold that didn't really exist worked fine, unless many receipt-holders wanted to redeem paper notes for gold or silver all at once. Fortunately for the bankers, this happened so rarely that eventually the writing of receipts for more money than was on deposit became a perfectly respectable practice known as fractional reserve banking.

Richard Heinberg, *The End of Growth*

Christopher Columbus made four voyages to the New World. He claimed more than 1,700 Caribbean islands and their inhabitants for the Spanish Crown.

# PLUNDER

**Who can doubt that gunpowder against the infidels is incense for the Lord?**

—Gonzalo Fernández de Oviedo

In 1519 Cortés told Spain of the fabulous magnitude of Montezuma's Aztec treasure, and fifteen years later there arrived in Seville the gigantic ransom—a roomful of gold and two of silver—which Francisco Pizarro had made the Inca Atahualpa pay before strangling him. Years earlier the Crown had paid the sailors on Columbus's first voyage with gold carried off from the Antilles. The Caribbean island populations finally stopped paying tribute because they had disappeared: They were totally exterminated in the gold mines, in the deadly task of sifting auriferous sands with their bodies half submerged in water, or in breaking up the ground beyond the point of exhaustion, doubled up over the heavy cultivating tools brought from Spain. Many natives of Haiti anticipated the fate imposed by their white oppressors: They killed their children and committed mass suicide. The mid-sixteenth-century historian Fernández de Oviedo interpreted the Antillean holocaust thus: "Many of them, by way of diversion, took poison rather than work, and others hanged themselves with their own hands."

Eduardo Galeano, *Open Veins of Latin America: Five Centuries of the Pillage of a Continent*

Slaves for auction in Suriname. Over the span of four centuries, European traders and investors drained Africa of more than ten million human souls.

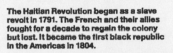

The Haitian Revolution began as a slave revolt in 1791. The French and their allies fought for a decade to regain the colony but lost. It became the first black republic in the Americas in 1804.

# PROPERTY

**Good fences make good neighbors.**

—Robert Frost

**Thomas Gainsborough's famous depiction of nobleman Robert Andrews on his estate in England. Painted in 1750, it represents the pride of ownership.**

Somewhere along the way, the idea of ownership changed. It used to be that land was held in common and home ownership was based on negotiation and need. In Europe, the seigneurial system allotted plots according to social order—lords and serfs—with an almighty God atop the pyramid as the ultimate owner. Humans were stewards in God's field. In Africa, kingdoms and chiefdoms governed vast territories dividing up homesteads according to rank, status and familial relations. In North America, indigenous groups based title on the concept of the ever-widening circle. An individual could no more own the land than they could own the sun or moon, and all inhabitants had a responsibility to respect the land for future generations.

The European enlightenment ushered in a new global tradition: Personal sovereignty, citizenship and private ownership. Alongside the expanding idea of citizen and individual rights, came the Greek-age political symbol of the property-owning subject. Settlers voyaging to the New World, with its promise of liberty, had no desire to continue Old World communal systems. Fences, divisions, deeds and markers were set into the ground and title became absolute, beyond society and time. On this new frontier, the human psyche flourished like a child pointing to all of the material items within its reach. God no longer owned the land, man did. It wasn't long before the Old World "ours" became the New World "mine."

**Darren Fleet**

*The Lincolnshire Ox* by George Stubbs, 1790. This painting captures the epoch wherein animals became livestock and landscape became property.

The British Enclosure Acts from the sixteenth to nineteenth centuries transferred nearly all public grazing lands into private tenured estates. Intended to improve the commons, the result was a rent system that pushed poor farmers off of public land, leaving wealthy landowners in possession of the countryside.

# DEBT

Man is born free, and
everywhere he is in chains.

—Jean Jacques Rousseau

English jails overflowed with debtors
in the eighteenth century. Those who
couldn't pay their loans were incarcer-
ated indefinitely until their debts were
repaid. Inmates had to pay for their own
keep and their families often resorted to
begging to get them out.

Credit has a history that goes back almost to the beginnings of civilization. For example, early banks (like the Bardi and Peruzzi banks of the tenth and thirteenth centuries) extended credit to monarchs so the latter could afford to go to war. But, during the past century, the extension of credit has become an overwhelmingly pervasive practice that reaches not just into every government and business, but nearly every household in the industrialized world.

Why this vast, recent expansion of credit? One word sums it up: Growth.

Credit gives us the ability to consume now and pay later. It is an expression of belief on the part of both borrower and lender that later the borrower will have a surplus with which to repay today's new debt, with interest, while still covering basic operating expenses. We will be better off in the future than we are today.

Modern economic theory treats debt as a neutral transfer between saver and consumer. In a world at the end of growth, it becomes anything other than neutral—as the "savers" will never be able to obtain their deferred consumption …

… The end of growth is the ultimate credit event, as everyone gradually comes to realize there will be no surplus later with which to repay interest on debt that is accruing now.

Richard Heinberg, *The End of Growth*

# EMPIRE

During the 350 years of the industrial age, a good fraction of Europe did consume more than it produced, by the simple expedient of owning most of the rest of the world and exploiting it for their own economic benefit. As late as 1914, the vast majority of the world's land surface was either ruled directly from a European capital, occupied by people of European descent, or dominated by European powers through some form of radically unequal treaty relationship. The accelerating drawdown of fossil fuels throughout that era shifted the process into overdrive, allowing the minority of the Earth's population who lived in Europe or the more privileged nations of the European diaspora—the United States the first among them—not only to adopt what were, by the standards of all other human societies, extravagantly lavish lifestyles, but to be able to expect that those lifestyles would become even more lavish in the future.

Only a tiny fraction of the people of the industrial world has begun to deal with the hard fact that those days are over. European domination of the globe came apart explosively in the four brutal decades between 1914, when the First World War broke out, and 1954, when the fall of French Indochina put a period on the age of European empire. The United States, which inherited what was left of Europe's imperial role, never achieved the level of global dominance that European nations took for granted until 1914—compare the British Empire, which directly ruled a quarter

**The rich take what they want and the poor grant what they must.**

—Thucydides

Colonial officials inspect African soldiers presenting arms. At the Berlin Conference in 1884, European statesman carved up plans to annex vast territories of Africa into their empires. No Africans were present.

of the Earth's land surface, with the hole-and-corner arrangements that allow America to maintain garrisons in other people's countries around the world.

Now the second and arguably more important source of Euro-American wealth and power—the exploitation of half a billion years of prehistoric sunlight in the form of fossil fuels—has peaked and entered its own decline, with consequences that bid fair to be at least as drastic as those that followed the shattering of the Pax Europa in 1914.

John Michael Greer, *The Wealth of Nature: Economics as if Survival Mattered*, New Society Publishers

Below: An Englishman gets a pedicure from an Indian servant during the Raj. Right: A wealthy couple after the hunt. Britain colonized the Indian subcontinent from 1858 to 1947.

# FINANCE

All money is a matter of belief.

—Adam Smith

When was the day that money became an idol instead of an instrument? Was it August 15, 1971, when to pay for the Vietnam War Nixon shocked the world by erasing the Gold Standard, thereby unilaterally making the value of the US dollar the reserve currency of the world economy? Or was it in the waning months of 2008, when the central banks of the industrialized nations purchased around $3 trillion of debt from certain corrupt institutions operating in the private sector? When was it, exactly, that money became the lifeblood of our civilization?

Matthew David Segall from *Cosmopolitical Reflections on Economy, Society, and Religion*

Five banks—J.P. Morgan, Bank of America, Citigroup Inc., Wells Fargo &
Co. and Goldman Sachs Group Inc. together held $8.5 trillion in assets at
the end of 2011, equal to 56 percent of the U.S. Economy. —*Bloomberg*

ASK YOUR PROFESSOR:

**What should the role of finance be in our society … what about the role of banks?**

# A PARABLE

During the sixth century BCE, the people of Athens fell slowly into troubled times. The city was dominated by the Eupatridae, the aristocracy of birth, who controlled the government, owned most of the land and used its power to drive poor farmers into debt during bad seasons. The Eupatridae acted as bankers. When the farmers were unable to meet their interest payments on their debts, they were reduced to the state of serfs on what had been their own land. Some were sold into slavery. A serf or a slave was, needless to say, no longer an Athenian citizen. This debt situation spun further and further out of control.

Faced by an impossible division between rich and poor, resulting in economic instability and the risk of revolution, the desperate Athenians called Solon into public office and gave him full powers. Twenty years earlier, he had already served as archon—the annual chief ruler. He was also Athens's leading poet. He used his poetry to set examples and to create political drive. His message was constant: Moderation and reform. He was as opposed to revolution as he was to tyranny. This sense of moderation is important to understand in light of what followed. Already the unpayable debts and the growing inequalities had pushed him to write:

> Public evil enters the house of each man, the gates of his courtyard cannot keep it out, it leaps over the high wall; let him flee to a corner of his bed chamber, it will certainly find him out.

The atmosphere in which he took power was not so very different from the one we know today. The same manic-depressive mood lay over the society. The Draconian financial/legal policies of the repressive rulers were based on Draco's original legal code. The manic counterweight revolved around the uncontrolled activities of the rich.

Solon's first act upon taking power was to redeem all the forfeited land and to free all the enslaved citizens. This he did by fiat. That is to say, he legislated immediate default. The Athenians called it the "shaking of burdens," but in practical terms what he had done amounted simply to ripping up the debt papers. In his own words, he had uprooted the mortgage stones that everywhere were planted and freed the fields that were enslaved before.

Having released both the people and the nation from their paper chains, he was able to reestablish the social balance. From there he went on to create a code of fair laws (in place of Draco's) and to lay the foundation for a democratic constitution. Athens immediately began its rise to glory, spewing out ideas, theater, sculpture and architecture, democratic concepts and concrete riches. All this eventually became the foundation of Roman and indeed Western civilization. Today we cannot move a step without some conscious or unconscious tribute to the genius of Solon of Athens—a genius unleashed by defaulting on debts.

John Ralston Saul, *Voltaire's Bastards*

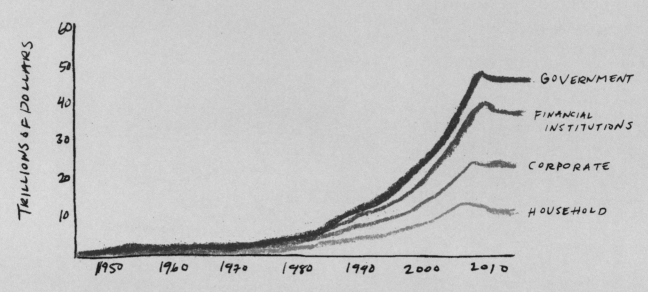

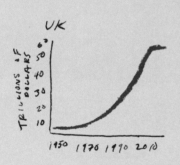

UK

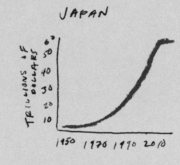

JAPAN

GERMANY

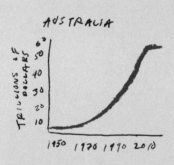

AUSTRALIA

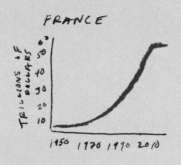

FRANCE

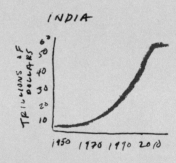

INDIA

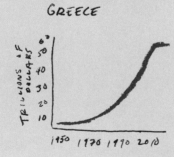

GREECE

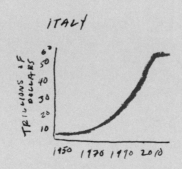

ITALY

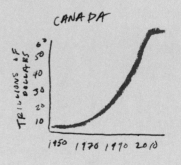

CANADA

# "DEBTS THAT CAN'T BE PAID, WON'T BE"

# MICHAEL HUDSON

Michael Hudson is president of the Institute for the Study of Long-Term Economic Trends (ISLET), a Wall Street financial analyst, Distinguished Research Professor of Economics at the University of Missouri and author of *Super-Imperialism: The Economic Strategy of American Empire* (1968 & 2003), and *Trade, Development and Foreign Debt* (1992 & 2009).

Book V of Aristotle's *Politics* describes the eternal transition of oligarchies making themselves into hereditary aristocracies—which end up being overthrown by tyrants or develop internal rivalries as some families decide to "take the multitude into their camp" and usher in democracy, within which an oligarchy emerges once again, followed by aristocracy, democracy, and so on throughout history.

Debt has been the main dynamic driving these shifts —always with new twists and turns. It polarizes wealth to create a creditor class, whose oligarchic rule is ended as new leaders ("tyrants" to Aristotle) win popular support by canceling the debts and redistributing property or taking its usufruct for the state.

Since the Renaissance, however, bankers have shifted their political support to democracies. This did not reflect egalitarian or liberal political convictions as such, but rather a desire for better security for their loans. As James Steuart explained in 1767, royal borrowings remained private affairs rather than truly public debts. For a sovereign's debts to become binding upon the entire nation, elected representatives had to enact the taxes to pay their interest charges.

By giving taxpayers this voice in government, the Dutch and British democracies provided creditors with much safer claims for payment than did kings and princes whose debts died with them. But the recent debt protests from Iceland to Greece and Spain suggest that creditors are shifting their support away from democracies. They are demanding fiscal austerity and even privatization sell-offs.

This is turning international finance into a new mode of warfare. Its objective is the same as military conquest in times past: To appropriate land and mineral resources, communal infrastructure and extract tribute. In response, democracies are demanding referendums over whether to pay creditors by selling off the public domain and raising taxes to impose unemployment, falling wages and economic depression. The alternative is to write down debts or even annul them, and to reassert regulatory control over the financial sector.

## NEAR EASTERN RULERS PROCLAIMED CLEAN SLATES TO PRESERVE ECONOMIC BALANCE

Charging interest on advances of goods or money was not originally intended to polarize economies. First administered early in the third millennium BCE as a contractual arrangement by Sumer's temples and palaces with merchants and entrepreneurs who typically worked in the royal bureaucracy, interest at 20 percent (doubling the principal in five years) was supposed to approximate a fair share of the returns from long-distance trade or leasing land and other public assets such as workshops, boats and ale houses.

As the practice was privatized by royal collectors of user fees and rents, "divine kingship" protected agrarian debtors. Hammurabi's laws (c. 1750 BCE) canceled their debts in times of flood or drought. All the rulers of his Babylonian dynasty began their first full year on the throne by canceling agrarian debts so as to clear out payment arrears by proclaiming a clean slate. Bondservants, land or crop rights and other pledges were returned to the debtors to "restore order" in an idealized "original" condition of balance. This practice survived in the Jubilee Year of Mosaic Law in Leviticus.

The logic was clear enough. Ancient societies needed to field armies to defend their land, and this required liberating indebted citizens from bondage. Hammurabi's laws protected charioteers and other fighters from being reduced to debt bondage, and blocked creditors from taking the crops of tenants on royal and other public lands and on communal land that owed manpower and military service to the palace.

In Egypt, the pharaoh Bakenranef (c. 720–715 BCE, "Bocchoris" in Greek) proclaimed a debt amnesty and abolished debt-servitude when faced with a military threat from Ethiopia. According to Diodorus of Sicily (writing in 40–30 BCE), he ruled that if a debtor contested the claim, the debt was nullified if the creditor could not back up his claim by producing a written contract. (It seems that creditors always have been prone to exaggerate the balances due). The pharaoh reasoned that "the bodies of citizens should belong to the state, to the end that it might avail itself of the services which its citizens owed it, in times of both war and peace. For he felt that it would be absurd for a soldier … to be haled to prison by his creditor for an unpaid loan, and that the greed of private citizens should in this way endanger the safety of all."

The fact that the main Near Eastern creditors were the palace, temples and their collectors made it politically easy to cancel the debts. It is always easy to annul debts owed to oneself. Even Roman emperors burned the tax records to prevent a crisis. But it was much harder to cancel debts owed to private creditors as the practice of charging interest spread westward to Mediterranean chiefdoms after about 750 BCE. Instead of enabling families to bridge gaps between income and outgo, debt became the major lever of land expropriation, polarizing communities between creditor oligarchies and indebted clients. In Judah, the prophet Isaiah (5:8–9) decried foreclosing creditors who "add house to house and join field to field till no space is left and you live alone in the land."

Creditor power and stable growth have rarely gone together. Most personal debts in this classical period were the product of small amounts of money lent to individuals living on the edge of subsistence who could not make ends meet. Forfeiture of land and assets—and personal liberty—forced debtors into bondage that became irreversible. By the seventh century BCE, "tyrants" (popular leaders) emerged to overthrow the aristocracies in Corinth and other wealthy Greek cities, gaining support by canceling the debts. In a less tyrannical manner, Solon founded the Athenian democracy in 594 BCE by banning debt bondage.

But oligarchies re-emerged and called in Rome when Sparta's kings Agis, Cleomenes and their successor Nabis sought to cancel debts late in the third century BCE. They were killed and their supporters were driven out. It has been a political constant of history since antiquity that creditor interests opposed both popular democracy and royal power able to limit the financial conquest of society—a conquest aimed at attaching interest-bearing debt claims for payment on as much of the economic surplus as possible.

When the Gracchi brothers and their followers tried to reform the credit laws in 133 BCE, the dominant Senatorial class acted with violence, killing them and inaugurating a century of Social War, resolved by the ascension of Augustus as emperor in 29 BCE.

## ROME'S CREDITOR OLIGARCHY WINS THE SOCIAL WAR, ENSERFS THE POPULATION AND BRINGS ON A DARK AGE

Matters were more bloody abroad. Aristotle did not mention empire building as part of his political schema, but foreign conquest has always been a major factor in imposing debts, and war debts have been the major cause of public debt in modern times. Antiquity's harshest debt levy was by Rome, whose creditors spread out to plague Asia Minor, its most prosperous province. The rule of law all but disappeared when the publican creditor "knights" arrived. Mithridates of Pontus led three popular revolts, and local populations in Ephesus and other cities rose up and killed a reported eighty thousand Romans in 88 BCE. The Roman army retaliated, and Sulla imposed war tribute of twenty thousand talents in 84 BCE. Charges for back interest multiplied this sum sixfold by 70 BCE.

Among Rome's leading historians, Livy, Plutarch and Diodorus blamed the fall of the Republic on creditor intransigence in waging the century-long Social War marked by political murder from 133 to 29 BCE. Populist leaders sought to gain a following by advocating debt cancelations (e.g., the Catiline conspiracy in 63–62 BCE). They were killed. By the second century CE about a quarter of the population was reduced to bondage. By the fifth century Rome's economy collapsed, stripped of money. Subsistence life reverted to the countryside as a Dark Age descended.

## CREDITORS FIND A LEGALISTIC REASON TO SUPPORT PARLIAMENTARY DEMOCRACY

When banking recovered after the Crusaders looted Byzantium and infused silver and gold to review Western European commerce, Christian opposition to charging interest was overcome by the combination of prestigious lenders (the Knights Templars and Hospitallers providing credit during the Crusades) and their major clients—kings, at first to pay the Church and increasingly to wage war. But royal debts went bad when kings died. The Bardi and Peruzzi went bankrupt in 1345 when Edward III repudiated his war debts. Banking families lost more on loans to the Habsburg and Bourbon despots on the thrones of Spain, Austria and France.

Matters changed with the Dutch democracy, seeking to win and secure its liberty from Habsburg Spain. The fact that their parliament was to contract permanent public debts on behalf of the state enabled the Low Countries to raise loans to employ mercenaries in an epoch when money and credit were the sinews of war. Access to credit "was accordingly their most powerful weapon in the struggle for their freedom," notes Ehrenberg. "Anyone who gave credit to a prince knew that the repayment of the debt depended only on his debtor's capacity and will to pay. The case was very different for the cities, which had power as overlords, but were also corporations, associations of individuals held in common bond. According to the generally accepted law each individual burgher was liable for the debts of the city both with his person and his property."

The financial achievement of parliamentary government was thus to establish debts that were not merely the personal obligations of princes, but were truly public and binding regardless of who occupied the throne. This is why the first two democratic nations, the Netherlands and Britain after its 1688 revolution, developed the most active capital markets and proceeded to become leading military powers. What is ironic is that it was the need for war financing that promoted democracy, forming a symbiotic trinity between war making, credit and parliamentary democracy in an epoch when money was still the sinews of war.

At this time "the legal position of the King qua borrower was obscure, and it was still doubtful whether his creditors had any remedy against him in case of default," Charles Wilson wrote. The more despotic Spain, Austria and France became, the greater the difficulty they found in financing their military adventures. By the end of the eighteenth century Austria was left "without credit, and consequently without much debt" the least credit-worthy and worst-armed country in Europe as James Steuart noted, fully dependent on British subsidies and loan guarantees by the time of the Napoleonic Wars.

## FINANCE ACCOMMODATES ITSELF TO DEMOCRACY, BUT THEN PUSHES FOR OLIGARCHY

While the nineteenth century's democratic reforms reduced the power of landed aristocracies to control parliaments, bankers moved flexibly to achieve a symbiotic relationship with nearly every form of government. In France, followers of Saint-Simon promoted the idea of banks acting like mutual funds, extending credit against equity shares in profit. The German state made an alliance with large banking and heavy industry. Marx wrote optimistically about how socialism would make finance productive rather than parasitic. In the United States, regulation of public utilities went hand in hand with guaranteed returns. In China, Sun-Yat-Sen wrote in 1922: "I intend to make all the national industries of China into a Great Trust owned by the Chinese people, and financed with international capital for mutual benefit."

World War I saw the United States replace Britain as the major creditor nation, and by the end of World War II it had cornered some 80 percent of the world's monetary gold. Its diplomats shaped the IMF and World Bank along creditor-oriented lines that financed trade dependency, mainly on the United States. Loans to finance trade and payments deficits were subject to "conditionalities" that shifted economic planning to client oligarchies and military dictatorships. The democratic response to resulting austerity plans squeezing out debt service was unable to go much beyond "IMF riots," until Argentina rejected its foreign debt.

A similar creditor-oriented austerity is now being imposed on Europe by the European Central Bank (ECB) and EU bureaucracy. Ostensibly social democratic governments have been directed to save the banks rather than reviving economic growth and employment. Losses on bad bank loans and speculations are taken onto the public balance sheet while scaling back public spending and even selling off infrastructure. The response of taxpayers stuck with the resulting debt has been to mount popular protests starting in Iceland and Latvia in 2009, and more widespread demonstrations in Greece and Spain to protest their governments' refusal to hold referendums on these fateful bailouts of foreign bondholders.

## SHIFTING PLANNING AWAY FROM ELECTED PUBLIC REPRESENTATIVES TO BANKERS

Every economy is planned. This traditionally has been the function of government. Relinquishing this role under the slogan of "free markets" leaves it in the hands of banks. Yet the planning privilege of credit creation and allocation turns out to be even more centralized than that of elected public officials. And to make matters worse, the financial time frame is short-term hit-and-run, ending up as asset stripping. By seeking their own gains, the banks tend to destroy the economy. The surplus ends up being consumed by interest and other financial charges, leaving no revenue for new capital investment or basic social spending.

This is why relinquishing policy control to a creditor class rarely has gone together with economic growth and rising living standards. The tendency for debts to grow faster than the population's ability to pay has been a basic constant throughout all recorded history. Debts mount up exponentially, absorbing the surplus and reducing much of the population to the equivalent of debt peonage. To restore economic balance, antiquity's cry for debt cancelation sought what the Bronze Age Near East achieved by royal fiat: To cancel the overgrowth of debts.

In more modern times, democracies have urged a strong state to tax rentier income and wealth, and when called for, to write down debts. This is done most readily when the state itself creates money and credit. It is done least easily when banks translate their gains into political power. When banks are permitted to be self-regulating and given veto power over government regulators, the economy is distorted to permit creditors to indulge in the speculative gambles and outright fraud that have marked the past decade. The fall of the Roman Empire demonstrates what happens when creditor demands are unchecked. Under these conditions the alternative to government planning and regulation of the financial sector becomes a road to debt peonage.

## FINANCE VS. GOVERNMENT; OLIGARCHY VS. DEMOCRACY

Democracy involves subordinating financial dynamics to serve economic balance and growth—and taxing rentier income or keeping basic monopolies in the public domain. Untaxing or privatizing property income "frees" it to be pledged to the banks, to be capitalized into larger loans. Financed by debt leveraging, asset-price inflation increases rentier wealth while indebting the economy at large. The economy shrinks, falling into negative equity.

The financial sector has gained sufficient influence to use such emergencies as an opportunity to convince governments that the economy will collapse if they do not "save the banks." In practice this means consolidating their control over policy,

which they use in ways that further polarize economies. The basic model is what occurred in ancient Rome, moving from democracy to oligarchy. In fact, giving priority to bankers and leaving economic planning to be dictated by the EU, ECB and IMF threatens to strip the nation-state of the power to coin or print money and levy taxes.

The resulting conflict is pitting financial interests against national self-determination. The idea of an independent central bank being "the hallmark of democracy" is a euphemism for relinquishing the most important policy decision—the ability to create money and credit—to the financial sector. Rather than leaving the policy choice to popular referendums, the rescue of banks organized by the EU and ECB now represents the largest category of rising national debt. The private bank debts taken onto government balance sheets in Ireland and Greece have been turned into taxpayer obligations. The same is true for America's $13 trillion added since September 2008 (including $5.3 trillion in Fannie Mae and Freddie Mac bad mortgages taken onto the government's balance sheet, and $2 trillion of Federal Reserve "cash-for-trash" swaps).

This is being dictated by financial proxies euphemized as technocrats. Designated by creditor lobbyists, their role is to calculate just how much unemployment and depression is needed to squeeze out a surplus to pay creditors for debts now on the books. What makes this calculation self-defeating is the fact that economic shrinkage—debt deflation—makes the debt burden even more unpayable.

Neither banks nor public authorities (or mainstream academics, for that matter) calculated the economy's realistic ability to pay—that is, to pay without shrinking the economy. Through their media and think tanks, they have convinced populations that the way to get rich most rapidly is to borrow money to buy real estate, stocks and bonds rising in price—being inflated by bank credit—and to reverse the past century's progressive taxation of wealth.

To put matters bluntly, the result has been junk economics. Its aim is to disable public checks and balances, shifting planning power into the hands of high finance on the claim that this is more efficient than public regulation. Government planning and taxation is accused of being "the road to serfdom," as if "free markets" controlled by bankers given leeway to act recklessly is not planned by special interests in ways that are oligarchic, not democratic. Governments are told to pay bailout debts taken on not to defend countries in military warfare as in times past, but to benefit the wealthiest layer of the population by shifting its losses onto taxpayers.

The failure to take the wishes of voters into consideration leaves the resulting national debts on shaky ground politically and even legally. Debts imposed by fiat, by governments or foreign financial agencies in the face of strong popular opposition may be as tenuous as those of the Habsburgs and other despots in past epochs. Lacking popular validation, they may die with the regime that contracted them. New governments may act democratically to subordinate the banking and financial sector to serve the economy, not the other way around.

At the very least, they may seek to pay by reintroducing progressive taxation of wealth and income, shifting the fiscal burden onto rentier wealth and property. Re-regulation of banking and providing a public option for credit and banking services would renew the social democratic program that seemed well underway a century ago.

Iceland and Argentina are most recent examples, but one may look back to the moratorium on Inter-Ally arms debts and German reparations in 1931. A basic mathematical as well as political principle is at work: Debts that can't be paid, won't be.

A credit card is given the chop at a Move Your Money action in the UK. Across the globe, people are leaving big banks to join credit unions, removing their cash from the global casino.

Speculative financial transactions add up each day to $1.3 trillion, fifty times more than the sum of all commercial exchanges.

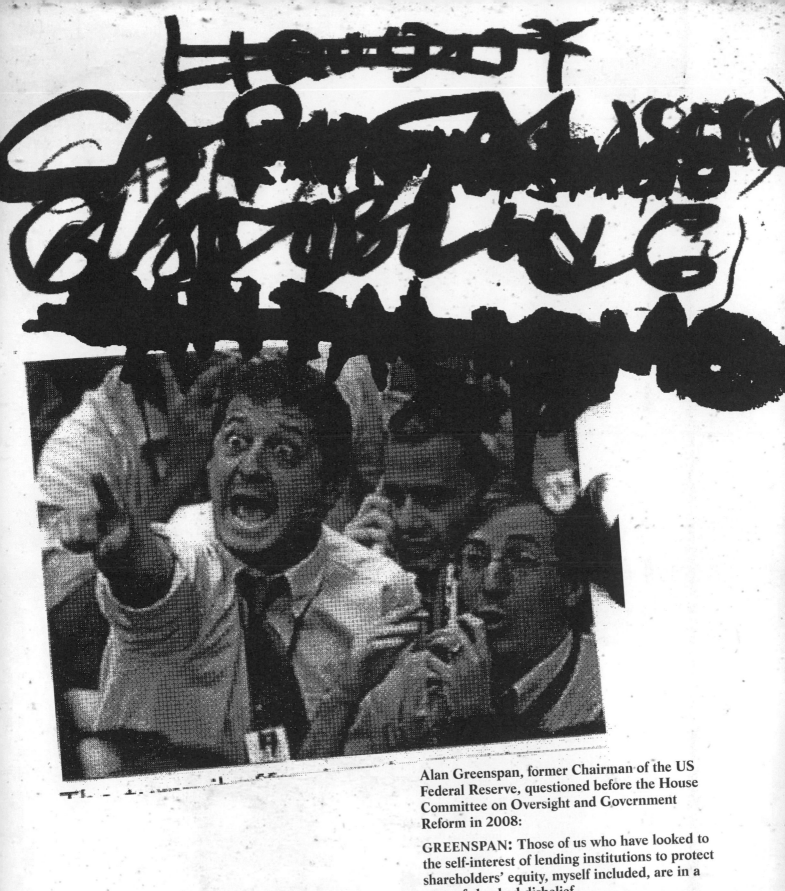

Alan Greenspan, former Chairman of the US Federal Reserve, questioned before the House Committee on Oversight and Government Reform in 2008:

GREENSPAN: Those of us who have looked to the self-interest of lending institutions to protect shareholders' equity, myself included, are in a state of shocked disbelief.

CHAIRMAN: Do you feel that your ideology pushed you to make decisions that you wish you had not made?

GREENSPAN: Yes, I've found a flaw. I don't know how significant or permanent it is. But I've been very distressed by that fact.

**DARK**      **POOLS OF**
**MONEY** roam the
financial ecosystem looking
for quick kills. Using sophisticated
computer algorithms, traders place
thousands of orders per second, only
to reverse them a few moments later.
Sometimes these forays are not designed to
actually buy shares, but only to test the market
and glean information about rivals. Traders scramble to gain
the advantage by moving their computers next to the stock
exchange's own servers, thus cutting transaction times down to
millionths of a second. More than 70 percent of equity trading
in America is of this hyper variety, with other nations quickly
catching on. High Frequency Trading (HFT) escalates the
obsessive impulses of capitalism to an entirely new level
of abstraction. Today HFT stands as one of the most
ingenious schemes yet devised for getting money to
beget money

to beget money

to beget money

to beget money

to beget money

to beget money

to beget money

to beget money

to beget money

to beget money

to beget money

to beget money

**WITHOUT** $ **END.**

At the peak of the 2008 meltdown the international financial system was trading derivatives valued at one quadrillion dollars per year. This is ten times the total worth of all products made by the world's manufacturing industries over the last century.

Looking out upon the withered American Dream, many of us feel a deep sense of betrayal. Unemployment, financial insecurity and lifelong enslavement to debt are just the tip of the iceberg. We don't want to merely fix the growth machine and bring profit and product to every corner of the earth. We want to fundamentally change the course of civilization. The American Dream betrayed even those who achieved it, lonely in their overtime careers and their McMansions, narcotized to the ongoing ruination of nature and culture, unconsciously aching because of it, endlessly consuming and accumulating to quell the insistent voice: "I wasn't put here on Earth to sell a product. I wasn't put here on Earth to increase market share. I wasn't put here on Earth to make numbers grow."

No one deserves to live in a world built upon the degradation of human beings, forests, waters and the rest of our living planet. Speaking to our brethren on Wall Street, no one deserves to spend their lives playing with numbers while the world burns. Ultimately, we are protesting not only on behalf of the 99% left behind, but on behalf of the 1% as well. We have no enemies. We want everyone to wake up to the beauty of what we can create.

Charles Eisenstein

# A NEW WAY

High school students protest education cuts in Santiago, Chile, March 2012.

# OF BEING

...

# HEY
## MR. ECONOMICS PROFESSOR,

How come the financial meltdown of
2008 caught almost all of you academics,
policy makers and think tanks flat-
footed, shaking your heads in disbelief?
How is it possible that not even one in a
hundred of you saw the crisis coming?

**THE NEW YORK TIMES MAGAZINE** HOW DID ECONOMISTS GET IT SO WRONG?

**BUSINESS WEEK** WHAT GOOD ARE ECONOMISTS ANYWAY?

**THE FINANCIAL TIMES** SWEEP ECONOMISTS OFF THEIR THRONE!

**ATLANTIC MAGAZINE** WILL ECONOMISTS ESCAPE A WHIPPING?

**MONEY MAGAZINE** HOW TO REBUILD A SHAMED SUBJECT*

No scientific discipline has ever suffered such
a devastating blow to its credibility ... so Mr.
Professor, how come nothing has changed?
Why are we still being taught the same old
stuff? Shouldn't a basic reassessment of the
curriculum be happening at our university?

* Courtesy of Ed Fullbrook, How to Bring Economics into the 3rd Millennium by 2020.

# II. PARADI

## Hey you lost souls and latte sippers out there,

Back in 1989, when we started *Adbusters*, there was
something profound about the idea that the Earth
was alive, that it was *Gaia* … that the rivers were
her veins, the forests her hair, the oceans her lungs
… that this planet was a living breathing entity. This
meme captured the imagination of a generation

# GM LOST

The dawning realization that we were killing nature … clear-cutting forests, poking holes in the ozone layer, expanding deserts and turning rain into acid kept us awake at night … we felt a compelling call to action.

When the world got together at the Rio Conference in 1992, we all thought it was the beginning of a global mind shift. For once, the world united and set things right.

But in the two decades since then the situation has only deteriorated. Pollution has become boring. Catastrophic weather has become routine. Environmental scars are now as commonplace as TV ads for starving children—none of it shocks us anymore. Fatigue has set in. And while we slept, species extinction, resource depletion, biodiversity loss—all the vital health curves of the planet—started heading exponentially out of control.

Today we live in a world where the oceans are rising and acidifying, the Arctic permafrost is starting to bubble with its deadly stores of methane and the climate is steaming like never before. All seven billion of us are suddenly filled with an uneasy feeling in our gut each time we look up at the sky. We gaze into the future and it is no longer a place of hope. Even as we go about our daily lives, care-free,

sipping lattes and zooming around in our automobiles, we are racing toward the end of the world with no plan of escape. We, the people running this experiment of ours on Planet Earth, have lost control of our own destiny … but it is considered impolite to acknowledge that fact in public.

The next few years will see flooded coastal megacities, resource wars, massive human migrations and sudden stock market collapses. As this happens, the demonic industries and squid-like megacorporations will continue to expand … and our leaders will implore us not to worry, to carry on as usual, to believe that the solution is just around the technological corner.

For those of us who feel that we have reached a special tipping point moment in human history, one that holds the future of Earth in the balance, how do we then approach our studies? Do we now see ourselves as planetary household managers ready to embark on an Earth crisis offensive? Are we ready to wage an all-out meme war for Planet Earth? Or do we sip away the foam on our lattes?

ASK YOUR PROFESSOR:

**How does climate change factor into our study of economics?**

# THE KONDRATIEFF WAVE

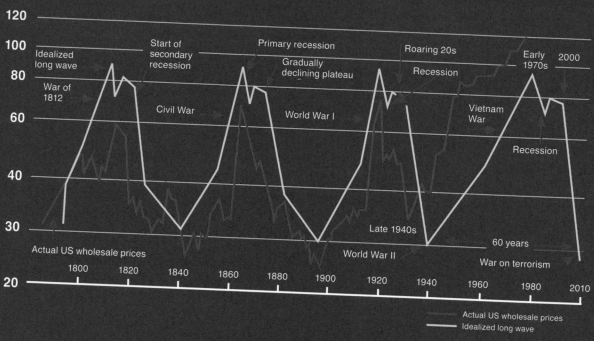

Idealized long wave

War of 1812

Start of secondary recession

Civil War

Primary recession

Gradually declining plateau

World War I

Roaring 20s

Recession

Vietnam War

Early 1970s

2000

Recession

Late 1940s

World War II

60 years

War on terrorism

Actual US wholesale prices

1800 1820 1840 1860 1880 1900 1920 1940 1960 1980 2010

120 100 80 60 40 30 20

Actual US wholesale prices
Idealized long wave

The Kondratieff Wave is a cyclical trend in long-term market behavior. Cycles last roughly fifty years and are broken into four seasons: winter, spring, summer and fall. Capitalist economies appear to follow distinct patterns of growth and recession, often regardless of economic policy over the duration of the wave. Athough the Kondratieff Wave (Super Cycle) has correlated strongly with the ebb and flow of economies for two centuries, neoclassical economists deny its validity. Soviet economist Nikolai Kondratieff first documented the cycle in 1925. He was imprisoned and executed for his findings.

# France tries to save its wildflowers

Poppies survive ... fields near Touraine

**By ELLEN BROWN**

Across France, wildflowers are disappearing from the landscape. Traditional favorites like the pheasant's eye, cornflower, corncockle and Venus's looking glass could soon vanish entirely. Seven of the nation's 102 wildflowers are already extinct with 52 others facing a similar future. "All over Europe the situation is the same, with these species in serious decline," says Amélie Coantic from the Environment Ministry. The plants are closely tied to the annual harvest cycles and the cause and consequences of their disappearance is yet unknown.

# BILL REES

## "LET'S ADMIT THAT OUR BELIEFS ARE KILLING US"

Bill Rees is a global leader in ecology and professor emeritus at the University of British Columbia, Canada. His book, *Our Ecological Footprint: Reducing Human Impact on Earth*, revolutionized the field of urban planning.

Famed Canadian ecologist Bill Rees spends most of his time these days making the links between ecology and neuroscience. After hundreds of papers documenting the declining health of Earth's biosphere and years spent in the field as an urban planning expert, he's searching for the optimal motivational curve between human limits and human action.

Unlike the majority of ecological scientists who tail off the end of a catastrophe speech with a plea to the never-ending resilience of the human spirit, Rees encourages people to focus on social psychology for clues on how to convince humanity about the hard choices necessary to steer civilization from collapse. So far he fears that only a catastrophe can re-set the neuropathways responsible for the social myths that govern our most destructive actions.

"We don't respond to the data ... what is it about the human mind that is so easily fooled into doing something that is self destructive when all the evidence is clear that [exhaustion] is the case?"

In a recent paper titled "The Ecological Crisis and Self-Delusion: Implications for the Building Sector," Rees argues that mainstream solutions like hybrid cars, green buildings, smart growth and urban density not only ignore the fundamental concept of ecological overshoot but could end up doing more harm than good in convincing people that consumption is a solution.

As a researcher he is no stranger to the often-limited impact scientific findings have on human behavior. He is the man who coined one of the most recognizable terms in environmental science today—Ecological Footprint. In 1996, Rees along with graduate student Mathis Wackernagel, published *Our Ecological Footprint: Reducing Human Impact on the Earth*, providing a mathematical model to determine sustainable levels of consumption for cities and civilizations. The model is a staple of sustainability planning in the world. The degree to which its valuations are actually heeded, however, remains to be seen.

"In spite of all the rhetoric, all of the political bafflegab around sustainability, absolutely nothing has been put into place. [There are] no policies in the international arena that have had any detectable impact on the general direction of the human ecological footprint."

The premise of Ecological Footprint (EF) is that human beings depend on nature. While this ought to be a given, it is almost universally absent from mainstream economic models and philosophies. EF is a measure of carrying capacity, the amount of resources and waste sink volume it takes to sustain a single human's consumption. It treats the global system as a whole rather than examining communities in isolation. Five categories of consumption—food, housing, transportation, consumer goods and services—are measured and their corresponding resource draw subtracted from surrounding and global eco-systems. In

1996 the average North American used 4.5 hectares of the Earth to meet their needs with the average European not that far behind. At the time, Rees and Wackernagel calculated that the planet was already in overshoot–one and a half Earths were needed to maintain 1996 levels of global consumption, and three Earths needed if the entire globe was brought to the level of an American. Fifteen years on, and after much publicity and political coverage, the global footprint of the Earth has increased to 2.7 hectares per person, the majority of it treaded in the developed world. This is already significantly higher than the 2.1 hectares per person they originally estimated for sustainable consumption. Now, according to the Global Footprint Network, the average American footprint is 8 hectares; Canadian 7.1; Australian 6.84; German 5.08; South Korean 4.87; Mexican 3.0; Iranian 2.68; Chinese 2.21; Kenyan 1.1; Angolan 1.0; Pakistani 0.77; Malawian 0.73.

Today we live in a world of ecological surplus nations and ecological deficit nations. All industrialized states in Europe, the Americas and much of East Asia are in ecological debt. If they were cut off from global trade they would immediately collapse, their resource bases far below what is necessary for their populations to survive. The remaining ecological surplus societies are in the poorest corners of the world, primarily Sub-Saharan Africa. It is from these impoverished surplus ecosystems that deficit states increasingly draw their life support systems.

"Let's admit that our beliefs are killing us," Rees says as he describes the faith-based system of economics today. He points out a maxim by one of the earliest thinkers in economics and sustainability, W. Stanley Jevons, as an example of how our larger cultural myth ignores scientific analysis. "It is a confusion of ideas to suppose that the economical use of fuel [or any other resource] is equivalent to diminished consumption. The very contrary is the truth," Jevons wrote in 1865.

Rees asserts that the Jevons paradox, the idea that greater efficiency leads to greater consumption, not less, has been wholeheartedly ignored by economists. Instead, permanent substitution, or factor productivity, first articulated by neoclassical economics Nobel laureate Robert Solow, is the standard ideal– we'll eat jellyfish when the tuna is dead; sea worms when the jellyfish are dead; bottom feeders when the worms are dead and so on and so forth. What we'll eat when the bottom feeders are dead nobody knows.

Once a quiet researcher, Rees believes scientists have a duty to speak out in a world where government, ideologies and private industry actively work to discredit sound science. Early on in his career he was told that his life as a professor at the University of British Columbia would be "nasty, brutish and short" if he continued waxing on about Earth's carrying capacity. Inspired with a fire that only threat can produce, Rees not only carried on with his study but eventually broke the sacred fourth wall of scientific objectivity, calling on researchers and scientists like himself not to just throw their data into the political spin machine, but to interpret it as well.

"It has been a gradual realization that not only is society not receptive to the data and information but that society will organize to explicitly frustrate and deny the science in order to maintain the status quo."

It will take a new cultural myth, Rees says, like the one that "uncooled" smoking tobacco, to turn the tables towards a sustainable future. Excessive consumption and growth need to become symbols of shame not status. According to the evolutionary psychology he's immersed himself in of late, only collective social pressure can rearrange the destructive neuropathways reinforcing our worst habits. The evolutionary advantage of optimism helped us to become one of the most successful species on Earth, but now our hopeful-thinking hardwiring, our belief that tomorrow will always be miraculously better than today, is working against us. We need a dose of realism, Rees says, to save ourselves.

Darren Fleet

**ASK YOUR PROFESSOR:**

Are the self-organizing principles of markets that have emerged in human cultures over the past 300 years in conflict with the self-organizing principles of ecosystems that have evolved over the past billion years?

# MANFRED MAX-NEEF

Manfred Max-Neef is a Chilean-born economist and environmentalist. He is a recipient of the Right Livelihood Award, the alternative to the Nobel Prize. Max-Neef ran for the Chilean presidency in 1993. This excerpt is from *Economics Unmasked: From Power and Greed to Compassion and the Common Good*, co-authored by Philip B. Smith.

## "WE ARE LIVING IN A FOOL'S PARADISE"

The world's present industrial civilization is handicapped by the coexistence of two universal, overlapping and incompatible intellectual systems: The accumulated knowledge of the past four centuries of the properties and interrelationships of matter and energy, and the associated monetary culture which has evolved from folkways of prehistoric origin.

The first of these two systems has been responsible for the spectacular rise, principally during the last two centuries, of the present industrial system and is essential for its continuance. The second, an inheritance from the pre-scientific past, operates by rules of its own, having little in common with those of the matter-energy system. Nevertheless, the monetary system, by means of a loose coupling, exercises a general control over the matter-energy system upon which it is superimposed.

Despite their inherent incompatibilities, these two systems during the last two centuries have had one fundamental characteristic in common, namely exponential growth, which has made a reasonably stable coexistence possible. But, for various reasons, it is impossible for the matter-energy system to sustain exponential growth for more than a few tens of doublings, and this phase is by now almost over. The monetary system has no such constraints, and, according to one of its most fundamental rules, it must continue to grow by compound interest.

Looked at in this way, growth is forced on us, willy-nilly, by the custom of measuring wealth in terms of money. This brings about the appearance of spontaneous increase of wealth by compound interest, a sort of abiogenesis impossible with real wealth. It is clear that without an external source of energy, in this case fossil fuels, the growth syndrome would not have become so important.

The monetary system—in short, the idea that all wealth, all value, can be expressed in terms of so much money—is embedded in our whole culture. It is embedded so deeply that when a group of (mostly) exact scientists was called upon by the United Nations Development Programme (UNDP), the United Nations Department of Economic and Social Affairs (UNDESA) and the World Energy Council (WEC) to make an assessment of the world's energy use and availability, the assessment (WEA) was carried out entirely in monetary units, which are quite meaningless in the assessment of energy use and energy carriers. A meaningful assessment can only be made in energy units (joules). We return to the question of assessment of energy sources shortly.

## COMPOUND INTEREST AND WEALTH

Other writers have spelled out in detail the unavoidable negative consequences for human well-being and social stability of, and the religious nature of the belief in, growth as the great panacea. But there seems to be little awareness that the monetary intellectual system is an integral part of modern society's worldview, and how it forces the economy to grow (or else wither). Frederick Soddy, a Nobel Prize-winning natural scientist who understood economy better than most economists, exposed the error in reasoning that has led practically everyone to accept the widespread misconception that compound interest creates wealth. It does not create wealth at all, but rather debt. It diverts a continually increasing part of the stream of wealth created by the production sector of the population and transfers it to the creditors, frequently leaving the wealth-producer holding the (empty) bag.

But first, what is wealth? A reasonable definition of wealth is that proposed by Soddy, and recently summarized by Herman Daly.

For Soddy the basic economic question was "How does man live?" and the answer was "By sunshine." The rules that man must obey in living on sunshine, whether current or palaeozoic, are the first and second laws of thermodynamics. This in a nutshell is "the bearing of physical science upon state stewardship." Wealth is for Soddy "the humanly useful forms of matter and energy." Wealth has both a physical dimension, matter-energy subject to the laws of inanimate mechanism, and a teleological dimension of usefulness, subject to the purposes imposed by mind and will. Soddy's concept of wealth reflects his fundamental dualism and his belief that the middle world of life and wealth is concerned with the interaction of the two end worlds of physics and mind in their commonest everyday aspects. That Soddy concentrated on the physical dimension in order to repair the consequences of its past neglect should not be allowed to lead one to suppose that he proposed a monistic physical theory of wealth.

What should be clear from this exposition is that debts are not wealth. Wealth has an irreducible physical dimension and debt is a purely mathematical, or imaginary quantity. An essential property of wealth is that it is a stream, practically all of which is produced on a daily basis and expended within a short time. Some forms of wealth have a certain permanency, though. It is not necessary to try to evaluate how much wealth can actually be stored, or for how long, in order to get an overall picture. Even that part of wealth that can be stored is slowly reduced to zero by depreciation and rot. What is important is that wealth is real and debt is not. As Daly puts it, "the positive physical quantity, two pigs, represents wealth and can be seen and touched. But minus two pigs, debt, is an imaginary magnitude with no physical dimension." This is far from an unimportant difference, as Soddy explains.

Debts are subject to the laws of mathematics rather than physics. Unlike wealth, which is subject to the laws of thermodynamics, debts do not rot with old age and are not consumed in the process of living. On the contrary, they grow at so much percent per annum, by the well-known mathematical laws of simple and compound interest … The process of compound interest is physically impossible, though the process of compound decrement is physically common enough. Because the former leads with passage of time ever more and more rapidly to infinity, which, like minus one, is not a physical but a mathematical quantity, whereas the latter leads always more slowly towards zero … the lower limit of physical quantities.

The source, or raw material, from which wealth is produced, was, during much of the longest part of humankind's history, only sunlight acting upon living and dead matter, organized through human effort. Hydrocarbons laid aside by life processes, long before humans came into being, have recently been added to the source of wealth production. These are now, since a few hundred years ago, in the process of being used (up), thereby making a larger stream of wealth temporarily possible. These hydrocarbons are exceedingly important for the functioning of our present industrial society. Without them the whole concept of compound interest would not have become as important as it is.

The following quotation from Daly, drawing on publications of Soddy, again concurs with Hubbert's thesis that real wealth can grow for a time only, but debt (not being real) can grow to infinity:

Although debt can follow the law of compound interest, the real energy revenue from future sunshine, the real future income against which the debt is a lien, cannot grow at compound interest for long. When converted into debt, however, real wealth "discards its corruptible body to take on an incorruptible." In so doing, it appears "to afford a means of dodging nature," of evading the second law of thermodynamics, the law of random, ravage, rust and rot. The idea that people can live off the interest of their mutual indebtedness is just another perpetual motion scheme—a vulgar delusion on a grand scale … Debt grows at compound interest and as a purely mathematical quantity encounters no limits to slow it down. Wealth grows for a while at compound interest, but, having a physical dimension, its growth sooner or later encounters limits. Debt can endure forever; wealth cannot, because its physical dimension is subject to the destructive force of entropy. Since wealth cannot continually grow as fast as debt, the one-to-one relation between the two will at some point be broken—i.e., there must be some repudiation or cancelation of debt.

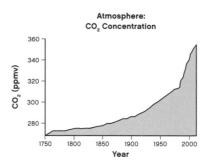

## REAL DEBTS AND THE ENERGY COSTS OF ENERGY

Although, as explained above, monetary debts are not real, real debts can exist. Knowing the dollar cost of extracting an energy carrier from the crust of the Earth can be useful for a businessman looking for profit, but the real cost can be given only in matter energy units; in this case the total energy cost of (1) extraction, purification and removal from the biosphere of polluting products of the carrier and of the waste produced by the purification and extraction, and (2) the energy used in construction and later decommissioning of the plant that converts the energy carrier into useful energy, plus operating costs (expressed in energy units). The energy value of the carrier is the total useful energy delivered minus the sum of these costs.

To take an example: Consider that we haven't the faintest idea how much net energy humankind has extracted from the fossil fuels burned in the last two centuries. This is because the energy cost of removing the pollutants from the biosphere, particularly the $CO_2$ (to at least a level that would guarantee that life on Earth, as we now know it, will not be threatened), is completely unknown, simply because this removal has not even been seriously contemplated. Burning fossil fuels without considering this cost indicates an *après nous le déluge* attitude—an attitude that we in the rich countries are all guilty of, to a greater or lesser degree. If the production of $CO_2$ and other pollutants were to be drastically reduced, the interlocking, symbiotic living systems of the biosphere would finally *pay* the debt for humankind in the course of centuries. If, on the contrary, the $CO_2$ emissions stay the same as today or increase further, they will finally wreak havoc on all that lives, empowering the resilience of the life-supporting capacity of the biosphere.

Or consider the disposal of the radioactive pollution left behind by the fission reaction in nuclear (power and weapons-materials) reactors. These pollutants constitute a real debt that humankind will have to pay. The biosphere has no defense against radioactivity, although, through radioactive decay, nature will eventually pay the debts herself, but only in a time frame of hundreds of thousands of years. That such a time frame is of no relevance for humankind should give pause for thought.

In this and most other cases of physical debt it is only meaningful to express this debt in energy units (joules), which are not only real, but conserved. The egregious financial custom of discounting the (monetary) value of resources is

therefore not applicable to energy sources, although it is erroneously used in financial calculations and policy. In the monetary system where value is expressed in nonphysical terms (money), a debt that cannot be paid can be wiped off the ledger as a "bad debt"—it is not a conserved quantity. But in the real world of matter and energy, debts are anything but arbitrary, and will be paid, if not in energy and matter then in the suffering of the living systems of the biosphere.

That such real energy debts are piling up, unpaid, means that we are living in a fool's paradise. Public awareness of this is systematically discouraged by business organizations only interested in the quarterly bottom line, and their spiritual confrères, the mainstream economists.

Not all debts that humankind has built up through bad housekeeping can be expressed in energy terms. Worth mentioning are the persistent organochlorides, poisonous to all life, that have been produced by the chemical industry are present in easily measurable quantities in mothers' milk all over the globe. Other units would have to be used to express this debt, but as far as we know we have no means of repaying it, while the production continues, in most cases, unabated.

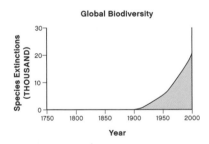

COMPOUND INTEREST, PEAK OIL AND THE END OF GROWTH

What compound interest does for the creator is quite different from what it does to the debtor. If a debt was just a debt until paid back, with or without a certain percentage added to it, then it would not bring about a long-term increase in the division of the wealth stream from the debtor to

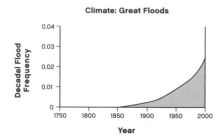

**Climate: Great Floods**

the creditor. But with compound interest in the game a steadily increasing stream of wealth is diverted from the debtor to the creditor, long after the original diversion, presumably for useful purposes, has ceased.

When money is borrowed by wealth producers, a steadily growing fraction of the wealth created by their productive work is thereafter diverted to the creditor from the total stream of produced wealth. In order for the system to maintain itself without progressively impoverishing the productive sector there must be a steadily increasing stream of wealth produced. The essence of Hubbert's argument is that as long as there is a continuously growing use of fossil fuels, added to the constant input from sunlight, the two systems, matter and energy on the one hand, and money on the other, can coexist. As long as this condition persists, it appears, superficially, that it is "natural" that the use of energy and matter from the Earth's crust grows continuously.

It is, in fact, quite unnatural; and in the long period before the steadily growing use of fossil fuels made it possible, it didn't happen—and people did not think that growth was a normal thing. Over the course of millennia, improvements in agriculture progressively raised the yield of solar energy and made larger populations viable, but these were gradual changes that did not seem to change people's way of thinking. The exceptionally abrupt but, above all, quantitatively enormous increase

brought about by the use of fossil fuels did, however, so that today most people believe that growth is normal and can continue indefinitely. When the time comes that the growth in the use of fossil fuels ceases, the coexistence of the two systems will become impossible, and the extremely painful adjustment to non-growth will take place.

There will be many crises when oil begins to get scarce. The following is only one, though perhaps the most ghastly. The highly productive grains developed in the so-called "Green Revolution," which both led to and made possible the greatest explosion of population in humankind's history, can be grown thanks only to large inputs of artificial fertilizers and pesticides. These are industrial products, the manufacture of which depends directly on the readily available energy in oil. This translates into several billions of people being alive at this moment because of the temporary extra energy input (beyond that of sunlight) of petroleum. When this is depleted there will be no way to feed the entire population of Earth and mass starvation will be inevitable. Optimists see the present decrease of the growth in oil discovery and production as an aberration, and assume that the tempo of discovery will soon rise again. This may happen, but even so such a rise will certainly not last more than another decade. Continuous growth within a physically finite system is then certain to stop.

**ASK YOUR PROFESSOR:**

Why is it easier to imagine a total catastrophe which ends all life on Earth than it is to imagine a real change in capitalist relations?

# A HISTORY

We exhaust the richest and most accessible of the Earth's mineral deposits; clear the old-growth forests; fish the oceans to exhaustion. Potable water becomes a costly commodity. We go deeper and deeper into the earth's crust to get oil. Our lives are threatened by the very methods and technologies we invented to enrich them.

For thousands of generations, humans are nature—subject to its laws, its sunrises, moon cycles, tides, feasts and famines. Then we begin to modify our surroundings: Damming and channeling rivers, breeding cereal grasses, draining swamps, domesticating animals. Humans diverge from nature. Our barely perceptible footprint grows deeper, larger, more clearly delineated: Like a field instead of a meadow, a road instead of a path.

Agriculture spreads, and coal fuels the Industrial Revolution. Nature remains abundant, but railroads, cities, freeways, airports and industrial parks carve a kind of landscape the earth has never known.

1800

1900

# OF PROGRESS

We find ourselves in the age of diminishing returns. Environmental cleanups—expensive industrial scrubbers and waste treatment plants ... long-term storage for dangerous, indestructible wastes—all become essential to sustain a growing economy. Competition for resources becomes fevered, spawning discord and conflict. Medical costs bloat as quality of life shrivels. We have been issued the warnings: Collapsed fisheries, erratic weather, cancer epidemics. The planet, and all living things, are in cataclysmic distress.

We abandon everything we thought we knew about progress. We completely reimagine industry, nutrition, communication, transportation and housing. We rehabilitate consumer culture, and create a level and holistic playing field for living and future generations. Humanity, and the world it depends on, are sustained.

We continue down the road of unrestrained growth until it is too late. Global ecosystems erode beyond any chance of repair or renewal. The Earth's capacity is reached and exceeded; economic growth starts to yield negative returns. The crash begins. No austerity measure—no matter how radical—can halt the descent.

**2000**

**2100**

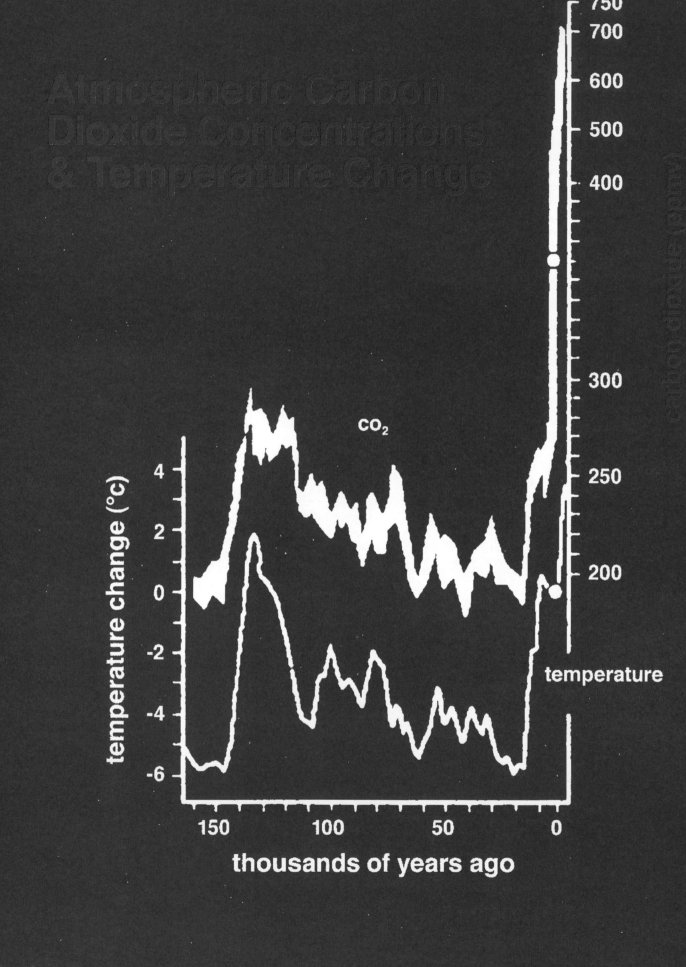

you are
the perfect
crime

You blame China.
You blame India.
You blame America.
You blame the CEOs,
the oil companies,
the vague and incoherent "system,"
the international regulatory regimes,
the hypocrisy of the left,
the righteousness of the right,
the educators,
the economy,
your parents,
your childhood,
your job,
your bank account,
your mental health,
your government,
everyone and everything
but yourself.

Wake up!
This is no joke.
This is actually happening and your five-
planet lifestyle is the primary cause of it.

# GLOBAL ECONOMY

Once the body has used up all its fat reserves, the muscles are broken down in order to obtain energy. The small intestine atrophies and it becomes increasingly difficult for the victim to absorb nutrients from what little food he or she is able to obtain. As a defense mechanism the body reduces the activity of the vital organs such as the heart and liver and the victim suffers not only from the muscular debility but from a more general and overpowering fatigue ... the skin becomes stretched, shiny and hypersensitive. Blood pressure drops and the victim is plagued by keratitis (redness and soreness of the cornea), sore gums, headaches, pains in the legs, neuralgic pains, tremors and ataxia (a loss of control over the limbs). Just before death the victim veers wildly from depression to irritation and then a profound torpor ... the heart atrophies ... organ failure is the final cause of death.

Lizzie Collingham, *The Taste of War*

# WHAT DOES IT MEAN TO BE FREE?

Should the right to emit greenhouse gases be shared equally by all people on Earth? This universal one-standard-for-all idea is called the "per capita principle" and it could be the only fair way to drastically reduce $CO_2$ emissions and avoid irreversible climate catastrophe. Applying this principle would allow each of the planet's seven billion people an annual emissions quota of 2.8 tons of $CO_2$. That's harsh news for North Americans and Australians who emit 20 tons of $CO_2$ per person each year. Citizens of the United Kingdom, Japan and Spain won't be happy either: They pump out 9 tons annually. Yet all of Central America, South America, India and Africa are comfortably below the 2.8 ton quota. We in the West bear the moral culpability for the ecological crisis because it is our disproportionate emissions that are driving climate change. Will we have the self-discipline and spiritual fortitude to accept responsibility, live differently and shrink our ecological footprints … or will we continue to take the freedom to consume to apocalyptic proportions?

Carbon dioxide hits record high

CALVIN KLEIN AD, *VOGUE*, MARCH 2011

# China to be hotbed of luxury

**By Georgina Rehman**

Dirty alleyways, rusty bikes, torn trousers, thrifty peasants and financial prudence are quickly becoming a thing of the past in China. With more than a million millionaires, nearly a third of them reaching the club in the past year alone, China is now the second largest luxury goods market in the world, exceeded only by Japan. Spurred on by two decades of unprecedented economic growth, luxury retailers are lining up in droves for their slice of the Chinese pie. Gucci sales rose 39 percent in the first half of 2011. Bottega Veneta: 80 percent. The Giorgio Armani Group has three hundred stores with plans for at least thirty more to be opened per year. Louis Vuitton, Versace, Cartier and Hermes are also expanding. And high-end automobile makers—Ferrari, Porsche, Buggatti—are reporting their highest sales ever in Asia.

YOUR ECONOMY NEEDS YOU TO KEEP CONSUMING

kickitover.org

# PSYCH 283 DISSOCIATIVE SURVIVAL COGNITION

## INTERDISCIPLINARY STUDIES   CRN # 1789   CREDIT TO ALL MAJORS

Climate change and economic uncertainty are constantly in the news. Population pressures are pushing arable lands to exhaustion while rising foods costs threaten to suck millions of people back into abject poverty. In the natural world, twenty-seven unique organisms go extinct per day, planetary biorhythms are slipping from alignment and invasive species are aggressively spreading across all bio kingdoms.

At the same time, the United States is run by a corrupt corporatocracy bent on maximizing profits, spends more on its vast military machine than the next ten nations combined, churns out more $CO_2$ per capita than any nation on Earth and keeps its population pacified with endless streams of entertainment, misleading political directives and positive projections for the future.

We will examine the psychological roots of those struck with concern over this apparent dissonance and highlight contemporary strategies to combat arguments suggesting a need for paradigmatic, societal, economic or personal change. Grounds for the erosion of context will be explained, empathy for others will be problematized and the psychological benefits of conspicuous consumption will be detailed in full.

Can America reinvigorate its enlightenment ideals and lead the way toward a truly free, just and sustainable world? More importantly, why care? Psych 283 Dissociative Survival Cognition will provide you with the rationalization skills necessary to navigate the ethical stresses of comfortable, mindless affluence.

Required texts:
*Principles of Economics (1890 edition)*. Alfred Marshall
*The Road to Serfdom*. Friedrich von Hayek
*A Shore Thing*. Nicole "Snooki" Polizzi
*Garfield: A Collected Works*. Jim Davis

**Mon–Fri, 9am–5pm**          **5 Credits**          **Professor TBA**

## PEAK EVERYTHING

## PEAK OIL

## PEAK NATURE

In just the past 100 years (mostly the last five decades) human numbers have quadrupled to seven billion, energy use has increased sixteenfold, fish catches grew by an unsustainable factor of thirty-five and industrial production is up more than fortyfold. To produce food and goods for people, industrial processes now fix more atmospheric nitrogen and inject it into terrestrial systems than do all natural terrestrial processes combined. Various forms of pollution, including greenhouse gases, have reached dangerous levels. Meanwhile, half of the land area of Earth has been directly transformed by human action, more than half of the planet's accessible fresh water is already being used by people and climate change hangs like a dark cloud over global civilization.

**Bill Rees**

In Saudi Arabia, which was wheat self-sufficient for more than twenty years, the wheat harvest is collapsing and will likely disappear entirely within a year or so as the country's fossil (nonreplenishable) aquifer is depleted. In Syria and Iraq, grain harvests are slowly shrinking as irrigation wells dry up. Yemen is a hydrological basket case, where water tables are falling throughout the country and wells are going dry. These bursting food bubbles make the Arab Middle East the first geographic region where aquifer depletion is shrinking the grain harvest. While these Middle East declines are dramatic, the largest water-based food bubbles are in India and China. A World Bank study indicates that 175 million people in India are being fed with grain produced by overpumping. In China, overpumping is feeding 130 million people. Spreading water shortages in both of these population giants are making it more difficult to expand their food supplies.

**Lester Brown**

Between 2010 and 2050 it is estimated that in the US there will be a 164 percent increase in cases of diabetes, with the largest increase in type 2 diabetes. And as if that were not enough, over the next five years, 60 percent of diabetes sufferers across developed economies will have more than one long-term condition, including (but not limited to) chronic heart disease, chest maladies, muscular ailments, vascular problems or neurological complications. The US Alzheimer's Association estimates that over the same period, the associated costs of Alzheimer's could top $1 trillion (roughly 7 percent of the country's annual GDP in today's terms for just that one disease). So, against this backdrop, how can the US win?

**Dambisa Moyo**

CAPITALISM

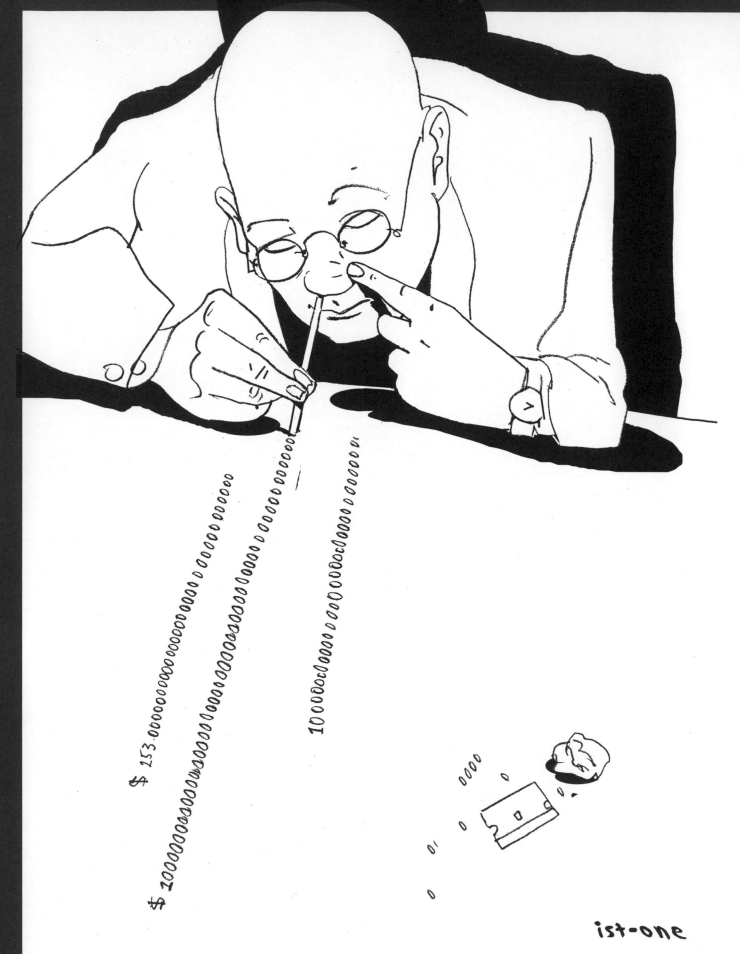

$ 153.00000000000000000000000

$ 10000000000000000000000000000

10000000000000000000000000000

ist-one

# II.2 LOGIC FREAKS

## Hey you dilettantes, feinschmeckers, keeners,

Modern economics is sick. Economics has increasingly become an intellectual game played for its own sake and not for its practical consequences for understanding the economic world. Economists have converted the subject into a sort of social mathematics in which analytical rigor is everything and practical relevance is nothing.

At least three Nobel laureates have expressed their concerns. At a very early stage Wassily Leontief in 1982 objected that models had become more important than data:

> *Page after page of professional economic journals are filled with mathematical formulas . . . . Year after year, economic theorists continue to produce scores of mathematical models and to explore in great detail their formal properties; and the econometricians fit algebraic functions of all possible shapes to essentially the same sets of data.*

Ronald Coase in 1997 complained: "Existing economics is a theoretical system which floats in the air and

which bears little relation to what happens in the real world." Near the end of his life, Milton Friedman observed: "Economics has become increasingly an arcane branch of mathematics rather than dealing with real economic problems."

What happened after these prestigious complaints? David Colander lamented in 2009 that none of these prominent warnings "had any effect on US graduate economic education." As Mark Blaug wrote pessimistically in 1998: "We have created a monster that is very difficult to stop."

The problem is not necessarily mathematics per se, but the obsession with technique over substance. Arguably there is a proper place for some limited use of useful heuristics or data-rich models within economics. But what should determine their adoption is not their technical aesthetics, but their usefulness for helping to explain the real world.

Geoffrey Hodgson

**Q:**

# HOW TO THINK?

Man and his relationship to God...

Man and his relationship to Nature...

The difference between right and wrong, good and evil...

The distinction between subject and object, cause and effect, mind and matter, heaven and earth

The Western Mind thinks and rethinks formulates and re-formulates, tests and retests ideas, feelings, aims and standards

It is this mind that laid the foundations of the scientific method ...

And it is this mind that for two thousand years has tried to prove the existence of God by using the laws of logic.

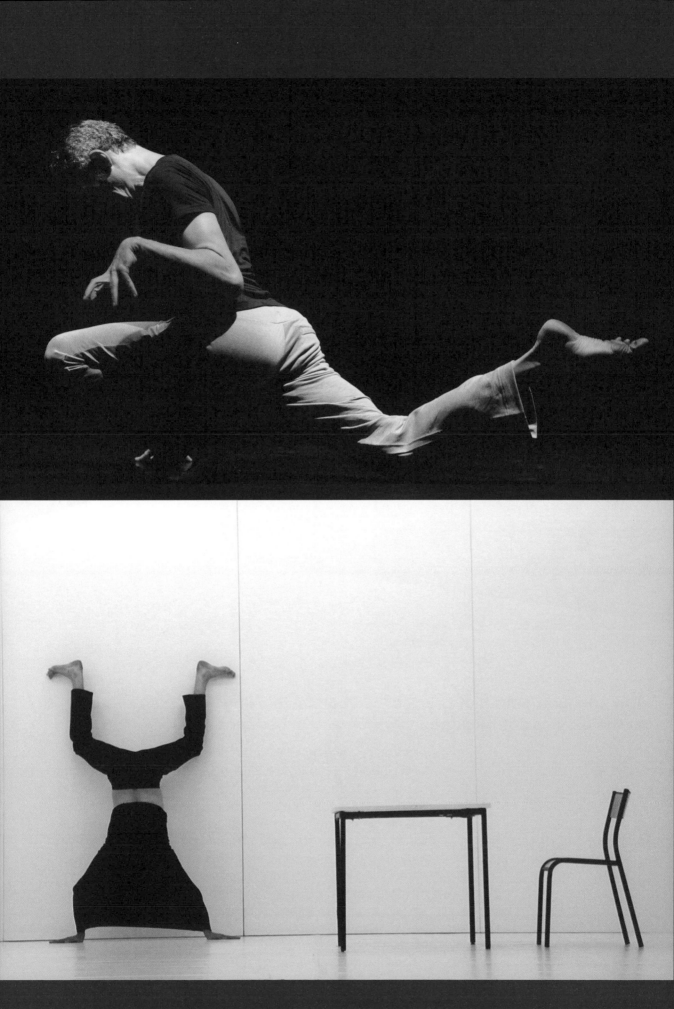

## The encouragement of precise, categorical thinking at the expense of background vision and experience

—an encouragement which from Plato's time on has flourished to such impressive effect in Western thought—has now reached a point where it is seriously distorting both our lives and our thought. Our whole idea of what counts as scientific or professional has shifted towards literal precision—towards elevating quantity over quality and theory over experience—in a way that would have astonished even the seventeenth century founders of modern science. We see everything natural now as an object, inert, senseless and detached from us.

Iain McGilchrist, *The Master and his Emissary*

Piet Mondrian,
*The Red Tree,*
1908-10

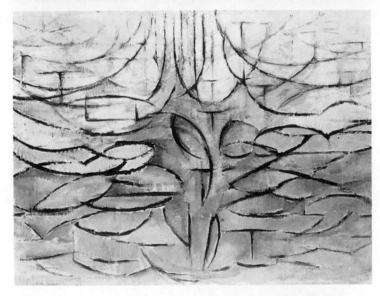

*The Gray Tree,* 1911

*Apple Tree In Bloom,* 1912

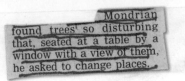

Mondrian found trees so disturbing that, seated at a table by a window with a view of them, he asked to change places.

my concern is
with the rythms
of nature
— POLLOCK

PROGRESS
PROGRESS
PROGRESS
PROGRESS
PROGRESS
PROGRESS
PROGRESS
THE END

# rational
# utility
# maximizer

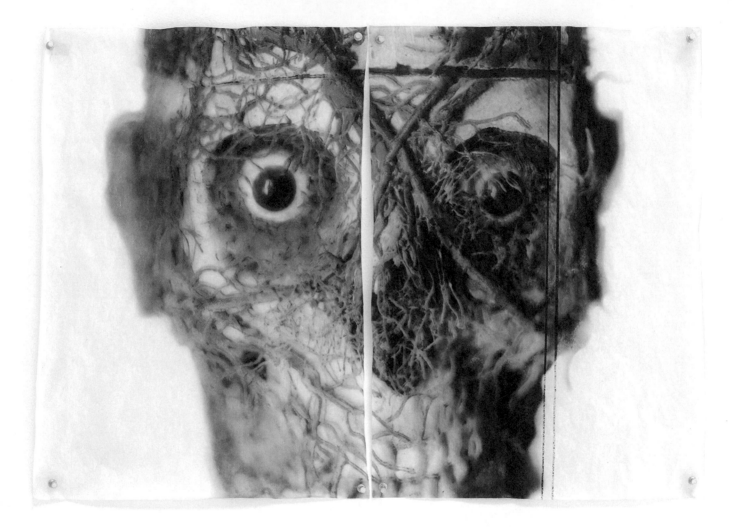

*Communism doesn't work because we're too selfish; socialism doesn't work because people cheat the system; welfare doesn't work because people won't work unless they have to; environmentalism is doomed because there's no financial incentive to care ... and yet, people routinely pull over to the side of the road to help a stranger in need; soldiers volunteer to die in wars for abstract ideals; activists willingly get arrested for a higher cause; parents instinctively sacrifice their own well-being, their dreams, everything, for their children.*

# perfectly competitive markets

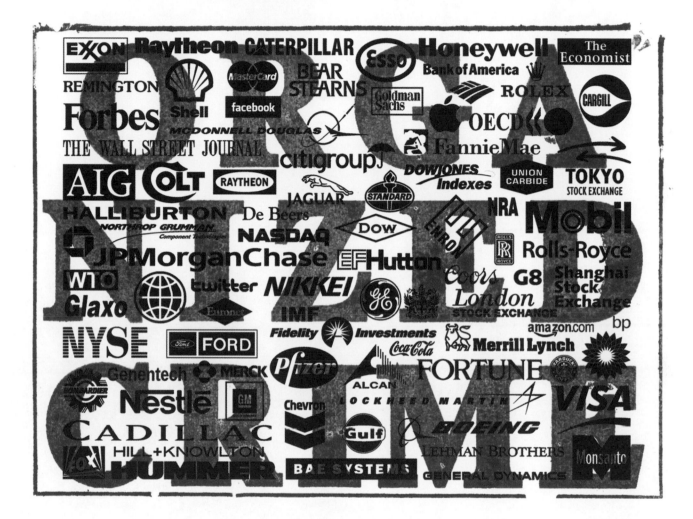

Whether it's the sneakers we run around in, the music we listen to, the car we drive, the smartphones we tweet with, the books we love, our favorite salad dressing or that big bottle of bubbly sugar water we grab from the soft drink aisle of our supermarket ... just about every intimate corner of our lives is dominated by two or three megacorporations who control the lion's share of the market. Add it all up across the board and the top one hundred of them pretty well run the show.

AND THEN
IT HIT ME...

Instrumental rationality—the calculation of the most efficient options for achieving a given desire—has overwhelmed Western thinking over the past three hundred years, generating a cold, empirical, calculating mindset.

# THE FOUNTAIN OF PROSPERITY

Designed by New Zealand economist Bill Phillips in 1949, the Moniac is a long-forgotten hydro-mechanical computer. Standing seven feet high and five feet wide. It uses water, valves, tubes, pumps and plastic tanks to demonstrate the macro workings of the economy. The water, representing money, is dyed blood red so observers can follow its movement through the machine. Once initiated, the red money flows down from the large treasury tank into various smaller containers and pathways, including healthcare, education, imports and interest rates. Operators of the Moniac can limit or add red money and watch to see what will happen. When one chamber draws more than another, or the treasury flow is restricted, reservoirs like taxation, savings, liquidity and income feel the effects. Soon after its invention, business departments at leading universities like Harvard, Cambridge and Oxford bought copies of the machine to use as teaching tools. So too did the Ford Motor Company and the Central Bank of Guatemala. In total, fifteen copies were made. The name "Moniac" is sometimes said to be a combination of money, mania and computation.

# THE NEOCLASSICAL LOBBY

It should be noted that although the fabrication of the neoclassical economists was successful, and accepted as legitimate by the academic communities, it coexisted with other visions, such as the institutional economics as proposed by Veblen and others. During the 1930s, without disappearing, it was displaced by Keynesianism, yet continued to coexist with it as well as with other approaches, such as those proposed by the Marxians. Other schools, such as the Post-Keynesianist, Austrian, Behaviorist and Feminist, added their own contributions up to the late 1960s. Up to then, students such as myself (Manfred) had the option of multiple perspectives when analysing economic problems, and courses such as Economic History and History of Economic Thought—now completely vanished from the curricula—were fundamental in every department of economics.

The extraordinary thing about nineteenth-century neoclassical economics is that it has achieved its final success in the late twentieth century. This is amazing indeed. We no longer have a physics of the nineteenth century, nor a nineteenth-century biology or astronomy or geology or engineering. All sciences have shown a permanent evolution. Economics is the only discipline where problems of the twenty-first century are supposed to be interpreted, analysed and understood using nineteenth-century theories. In a necrological impulse, "mainstream" economists of today look for guidance and inspiration in a cemetery of 150 years ago, as if nothing had happened since. This is preposterous to say the least, and the fact that universities go along with it is, as we see it, is an epistemological scandal of immense proportions.

The opportunity for neoclassical economics to slowly push other economic visions out of the way was dramatically enhanced during the late 1960s when the RAND Corporation and the United States Air Force (institutions backed by the Pentagon) launched a lavish program to fund research in mathematical economics. The reason was that military experts believed that game theory and other mathematical tools could be important for national defence. Most of the money went to the Big Eight universities—California, Harvard, Princeton, Columbia, Stanford, Chicago, Yale and M.I.T.—which happily adapted the orientation of their economics departments so as to guarantee the continuous flux of those massive financial resources. Given the weight and the international prestige of the Big Eight, the fact that they consecrated neoclassical economics as the definitive economic doctrine inevitably induced other universities of the Western world to follow suit. Furthermore, over one thousand economists—the great majority—employed since the late 1960s by the International Monetary Fund and the World Bank have gone through the indoctrination of the Big Eight. It should therefore be no surprise that during the last three decades of the twentieth century and the beginning of the new millennium, neoliberalism, as an economic doctrine, has managed to dominate the entire world.

Manfred Max-Neef and Philip B. Smith, *Economics Unmasked*

# ALAN WOLFE

# "I WAS HEARTENED BY THE FIRST SUSTAINED ATTACKS ON NEOCLASSICAL ECONOMICS"

Alan Wolfe is a professor of political science and director of the Boisi Center for Religion and American Public Life at Boston University. He has authored more than twenty books and frequently contributes to *The New York Times* and *The Washington Post*.

When I first began hearing about what Bruno S. Frey, professor of economics at the University of Zurich, calls the "revolution" in his discipline, my reaction was one of delight. As far as I was concerned, it could not happen fast enough. Neoclassical economists had insisted upon the primacy of self-interest only in order to model human behavior, but the way rational choice theory developed (at the University of Chicago in particular) suggested that self-interest was not just a fact for these thinkers, but also an ideal: Not just how people do act but also how they should act. Their relentless advocacy of market-based public policies was finally ideological—and, by my lights, ideologically wrong. Also the jargon grew impenetrable, and the mathematics ostentatious and obnoxious. When Chicago-style economists started to apply their methods to other social science disciplines, and then to virtually all the perplexities of human life, the charge of academic imperialism could be added. Friedrich August von Hayek and Milton Friedman had always seemed to me to be marginal and somewhat bizarre thinkers, especially when compared to such intellectual titans as John Maynard Keynes and Joseph Schumpeter. The rapid spread of their ideas throughout so much of academia did not bode well for the future.

And so I was heartened by the first sustained attacks on neoclassical economics. For one thing, the thinkers who launched them—Daniel Kahneman and Amos Tversky—seemed to be geniuses of some sort. Both had good reason to become fascinated with how human beings make decisions. Kahneman was born in Tel Aviv in 1934 and raised in Paris; his family decided to remain in France after the Nazis took over the country, and then to rely on business connections to spring his father from the death camps, and then to move to Palestine before the creation of the state of Israel. Tversky was born in Haifa in 1937. At the age of nineteen, he earned Israel's highest military decoration for rescuing a fellow soldier from an exploding device (injuring himself in the process). These men grew up under conditions that might have led them to divide the world into black and white, good and evil, but this did not happen. Instead they developed an appreciation of human complexity, even a love for it. "Some people were better than others," Kahneman described what he learned from his parents, "but the best were far from perfect and no one was simply bad."

The collaboration of Kahneman and Tversky produced one of the major intellectual accomplishments of the late twentieth century: A series of ingeniously designed experiments that raised uncomfortable questions about "utility maximization," which was the major assumption of microeconomics. To wit: It makes no difference in theory whether you lose a ticket to a play or lose the $10 that the ticket cost, but when people lose the ticket they are far less likely to buy another one than when they lose the money. Kahneman and Tversky's explanation is that we create a mental account such that it makes sense to us to pay $10 to see a play but not $20, even though the utility sacrificed by losing the ticket and the money is identical.

Tversky died of cancer in 1996. Kahneman won the Nobel Prize in economics in 2002, and is an emeritus professor at Princeton. Between them, they rattled the role of reason in the pantheon of human motives. They made clear that even if we think we know what is in our own best interest, we frequently make decisions based on misinformation, myopia, and plain quirkiness. The picture of human nature that they developed was—in contrast to the world of homo economicus—ironic, skeptical, almost wickedly complex.

No single figure did more to bring the insights of these two economic psychologists (or psychological economists) to economics than Richard H. Thaler of the University of Chicago. "When I read this paper," he wrote of Kahneman and Tversky's classic article "Judgment Under Uncertainty," which appeared in 1974, "I could hardly contain myself." Although trained in neoclassical economics, Thaler developed something of a furtive addiction to what his immersion in psychology had revealed to him. In the 1970s he spent considerable time with Kahneman and Tversky, after which he published a series of papers applying their insights to a wide range of economic activity, especially those involving finance. *Quasi Rational Economics*, published by the Russell Sage Foundation in 1991, collected those early papers and made them influential. The title of the volume suggested that we are not always rational and we are not always irrational. Yes, people deviate from the models of human behavior associated with neoclassical economics, but usually "in well-defined situations under careful laboratory controls," as well as "in natural settings such as the stock market." The theme of Thaler's book was that traditional economic assumptions about human behavior needed to be altered, not replaced.

What Kahneman and Tversky began and Thaler solidified is now frequently called behavioral economics. Its leading figures continue to sparkle. Steven D. Levitt, the co-author of *Freakonomics*, writes decent prose—or at least is willing to work with a journalist who does; and he, too, teaches at Chicago. The topics that behavioral economists address range far and wide, and often have little to do with the realm of getting and spending. They are interesting, intriguing, and sometimes too cute: Raising children, deterring crime, gambling, choosing names. The public-policy implications associated with this way of thinking are anything but predictably right-wing, and in the person of Austan Goolsbee, another economist at Chicago who served as Barack Obama's chief economic adviser until 2011, they now figure prominently in American politics.

Thaler has recently collaborated with his former legal colleague Cass R. Sunstein on a book called *Nudge: Improving Decisions About Health, Wealth, and Happiness*, which introduces a concept that the authors call "libertarian paternalism." This provocative oxymoron seeks a middle way between laissez-faire and the heavy hand of governmental regulation: Public policy, by providing "choice architecture," can push people toward decisions that make the most overall sense, as opposed to coercing them or being indifferent to their preferences. Only time will tell whether "libertarian paternalism" offers a new way of thinking about public policy that can lead to major legislative accomplishment, or instead represents the kind of bland centrist politics that a decidedly non-Chicago economist, Paul Krugman, denounces as hopelessly naïve. But there is no denying that just as Levitt brought behavioral economics to the bestseller lists, Thaler and Sunstein are bringing it to the think tanks and maybe even to the West Wing.

# Mobil Mart

**News**

**ASK YOUR PROFESSOR:**

## Is economics an exact science?

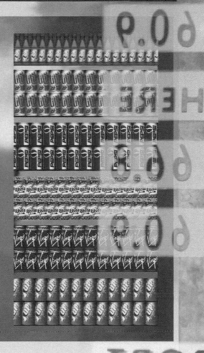

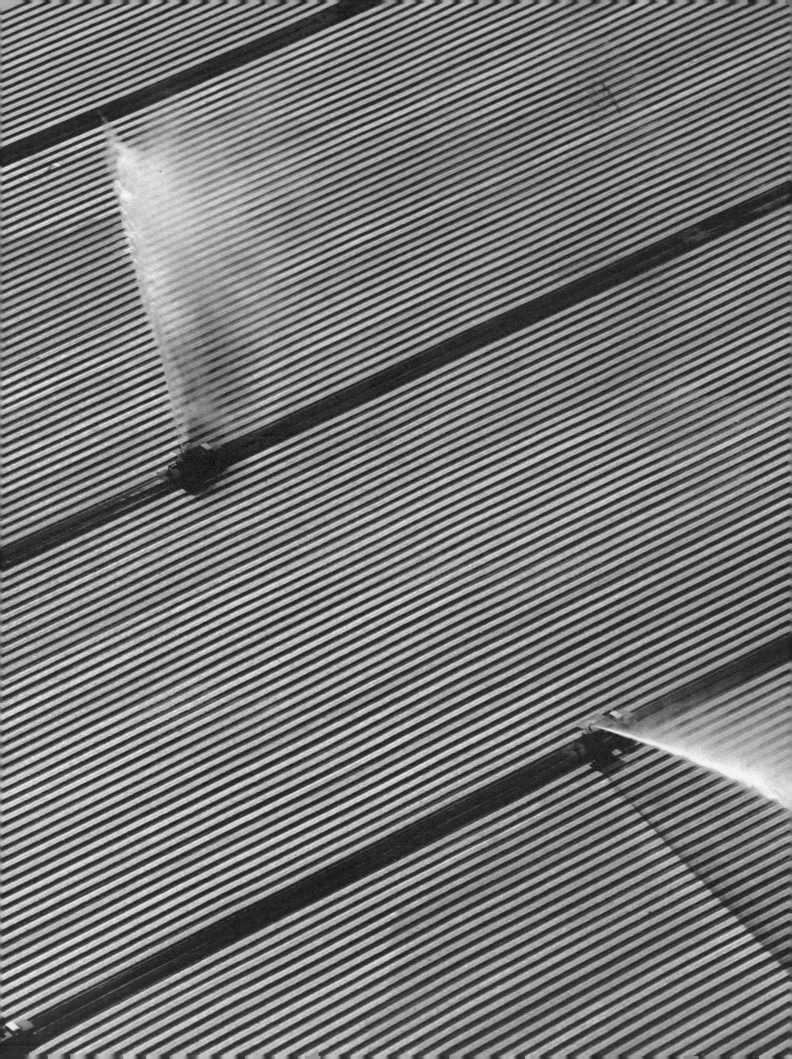

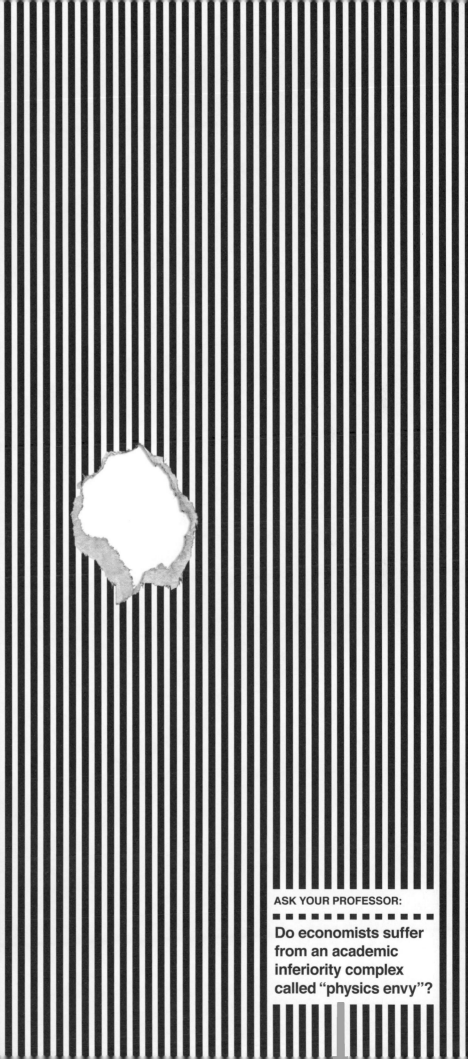

ASK YOUR PROFESSOR:

Do economists suffer from an academic inferiority complex called "physics envy"?

$$\frac{\partial V}{\partial t} + \frac{1}{2}\sigma^2 S^2 \frac{\partial^2 V}{\partial S^2} + rS\frac{\partial V}{\partial S} - rV = 0.$$

Risk. Profit. Hedging. Mathematics. Bets. Options. Derivatives. It started as a worthy idea, the quest to quantify risk and create a more predictable bond economy. Conceived by economists Fischer Black and Myron Scholes in 1973, and joined with the research of former Harvard economist Robert C. Merton, the Black-Scholes model had gained large-scale influence on Wall Street by the 1990s. In 1997 the originators of the proof won the Nobel Prize.

The formula works by attempting to accurately determine an asset's value over time, using a handful of abstracted market indicators like interest rate, portfolio value, strike price, volatility and original stock cost. The sum of the equation produces a risk indicator and allows investors to hedge accordingly and to trade ever-expanding complex packages of economic bets and diced-up financial goods. Think of it like this: What the IBM chess computer Deep Blue (with its 200 million calculations per second) did to world chess champion Garry Kasparov, the Black-Scholes proof and its formulaic heirs have done to traders.

The arrival of complex mathematical functions on Wall Street meant that the days of tossing a coin over when to buy and sell, or basing a deal on a hunch, were over. The human impulse at the heart of trading, with all of its emotional faults, memory lapses and superstitious whims, became obsolete. CEOs of the globe's biggest firms were suddenly able to take tremendous financial risks with seeming confidence, assured in the scientific safety of financial reason. The simple equation, never meant to be more than an indicator, morphed into the greatest irrational belief in rationality of our time. By 2008 hundreds of complicated abstractions and applications of the original proof were the talisman in every investor's pocket, doing to numbers what alchemists once claimed to do to bars of lead—turn them into gold.

How it all ended—crash—none of the subsequent algorithms and numerical riddles had a clue. Unphased, the humans holding the burst bubble, long removed from any intuitive financial feeling, have continued more than ever to put their faith into logic freak algebra rather than common sense.

Darren Fleet

**Hey all you** 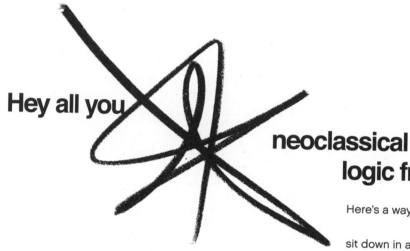 **neoclassical
logic freaks out there,**

Here's a way to put a bit of jazz into your life:

sit down in a quiet spot

half-close your eyes

breathe slowly, rhythmically

calm yourself right down

empty your mind

put a halt to all those spurious thoughts that keep bubbling up ...

try to live 30 seconds of your life without thinking a single thought.

Can you do it?

Keep trying ... with a bit of practice
you'll soon be able to last 30 seconds
and then more and more ... you'll
soon be able to tame that incessant
chatter in your busy, busy mind.

Q: WHO GROWS UP HAPPIER ...

THE SUBURBAN KIDS IN NORTH AMERICA

OR THE KIDS IN THE SLUMS OF DHAKA?

*Invisible hand;*
*Mother of inflated hope.*
*Mistress of despair!*
Etheridge Knight

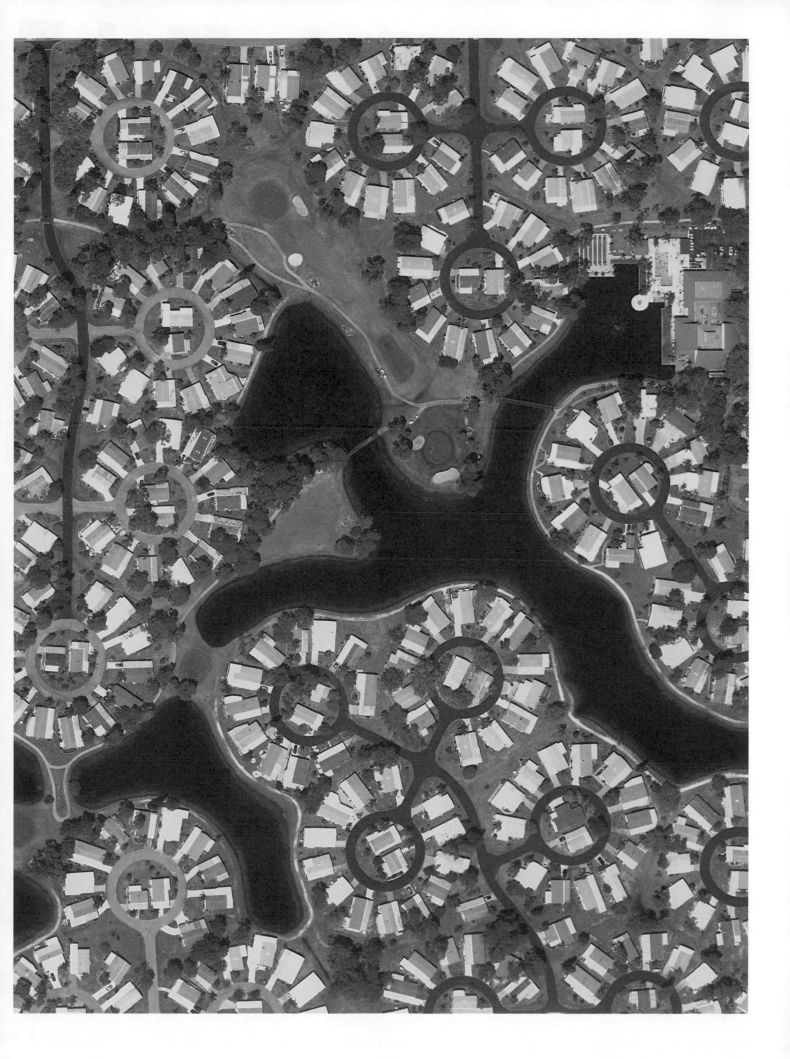

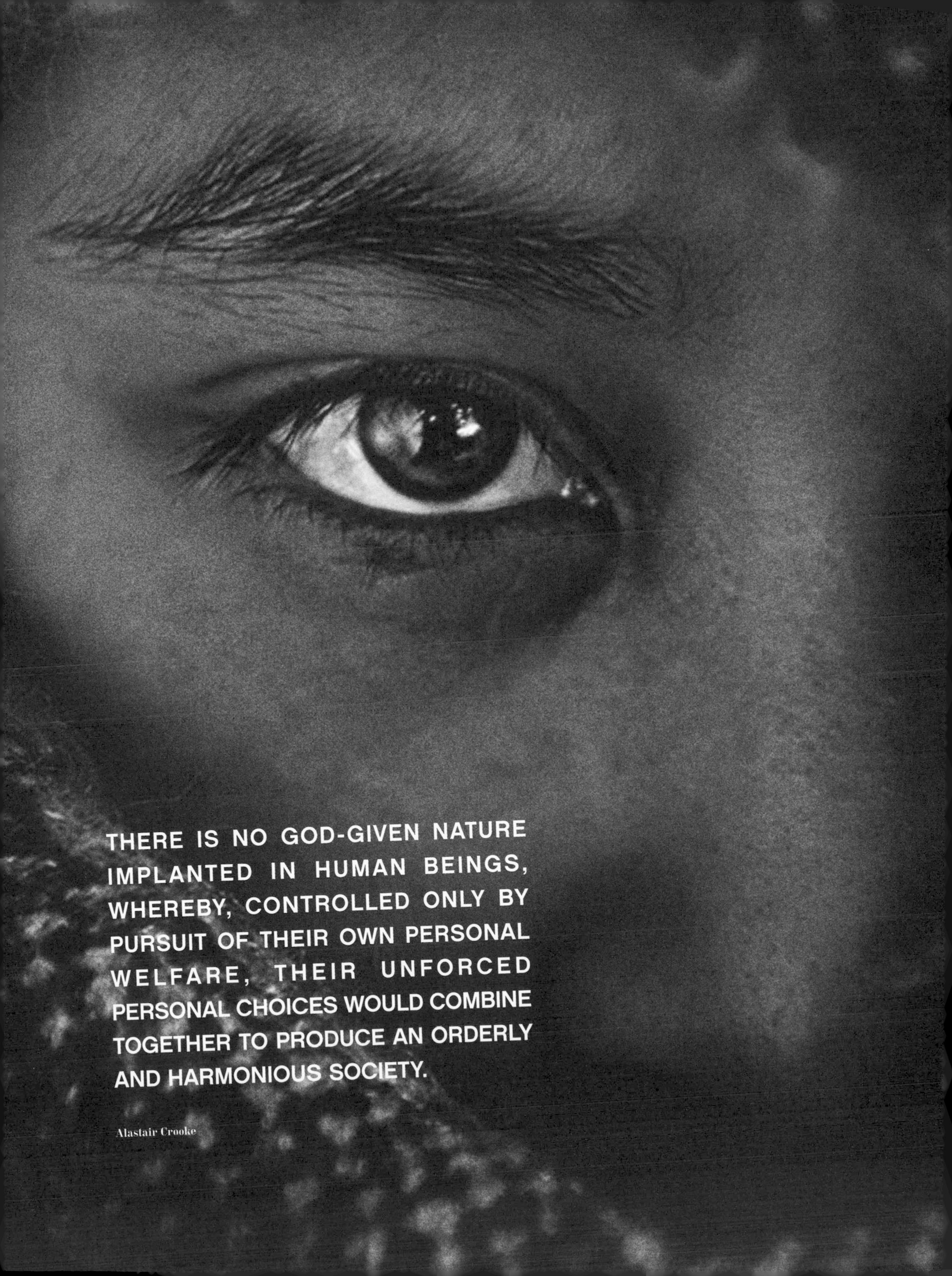

THERE IS NO GOD-GIVEN NATURE
IMPLANTED IN HUMAN BEINGS,
WHEREBY, CONTROLLED ONLY BY
PURSUIT OF THEIR OWN PERSONAL
WELFARE, THEIR UNFORCED
PERSONAL CHOICES WOULD COMBINE
TOGETHER TO PRODUCE AN ORDERLY
AND HARMONIOUS SOCIETY.

Alastair Crooke

R.I.P
NEOCLASSICAL
ECONOMICS

*post in corridor*

kickitover.org

**IV. THE**

This process of creative destruction is the essential fact about capitalism.

Joseph A. Schumpeter

# MEET MAVERICKS

## Hey meme warriors,

For the last few generations, things have been pretty quiet on campus. Voices of dissent bayed in the distant wilderness while the neoclassicists held court, pontificating on cable news and sowing seeds of delusion with rosy predictions in the business pages of newspapers. For twenty years—until just before the 2008 meltdown—Alan Greenspan sat on high as the chairman of the US Federal Reserve, dispensing arcane economic wisdom like an all-knowing god. For half a century, the neoclassical worldview ruled as the underlying economic framework and political ideology of our time.

But now things are starting to heave.

The dire warnings of Nobel Prize winning scientists about the possibility of a catastrophic climate tipping point has sent ripples of fear through the public imagination. Is nature really dying? Could global warming really do us in? Are "externalities" really as insignificant as economists say?

The financial train wreck of 2008 caught all but a handful of the neoclassicists off-guard, signaling loud and clear that they were living in an imaginary world almost totally disconnected from reality. At think tanks, in front of their Econ 101 classes and at meetings of the American Economic Association, the neoclassicists still keep up a brave front. But students are feeling uneasy, comedians are having a field day, and the internet is buzzing with swarms of apostate websites. Last November, in a grand iconic gesture, students of Gregory Mankiw's class at Harvard University walked out in protest at the kind of economics they were being taught.

The old certitudes are crumbling. The memesters are readying their stencils, masks and manifestos. The old school practitioners are in retreat, forced finally to admit that their understanding of nonlinear, real-world systems is frail at best and that their mathematical models have very limited value. Everything, from banking, financial regulation and credit, right down to the bedrock fundamentals of economics— growth, progress, happiness, freedom—are all now being rethought. The profession is entering an almost Nietzschean period of creative destruction.

# JOSEPH STIGLITZ

# "ECONOMICS — IT'S SORT OF LIKE A CLUB"

Joseph Stiglitz has served as both vice president and chief economist for the World
Bank. Stiglitz also chairs at the Brooks World Poverty Institute and is a member of the
Pontifical Academy of Social Sciences. Stiglitz, along with George Akerlof and Michael
Spence, won the Nobel Prize in Economics in 2001. His latest book is *Freefall: America,
Free Markets, and the Sinking of the World Economy*. Ecological economist Tom Green
talked to Stiglitz about the shortcomings of contemporary economics.

## On fashion trends in economics

Everybody likes to have their articles approved by others in the profession. If you stand outside the mainstream, you're not going to get the accolades you get when you're in the mainstream. It's sort of like a club—it's a lot easier being a member of the club than not being a member of the club. Part of the difficulty is that the club is trying to focus on the issues of the day: In one period the issue is inflation, in another period it's unemployment. With that shortsighted focus, there is quite often a failure to see the broader picture. The economics establishment has particular views on "orthodox theory," and at various times it shifts from one thing to another. Monetarism was the orthodoxy for a while, even though there was no scientific basis for monetarism. It was a big fad; almost everyone was a monetarist. And then, almost as fast as monetarism came in, people discovered it wasn't working and they abandoned it. When inflation became the big problem in the 1970s, people forgot about the big lessons of Keynesian economics. The lessons hadn't disappeared, but the world was focusing on inflation. Now, we're in another episode where the economy is going through a serious downturn and people are thinking about why economies go into downturns. It turns out that the theories most people have been talking about for the past fifteen to twenty years aren't very helpful in addressing current issues.

## On why introductory textbooks continue to teach the old models

I think there are two reasons for that. First, it's easier. Demand and supply are easier to explain than theories of imperfect information, or at least some people think they are. Second, there is a bit of a political agenda. It's not a surprise that Mankiw [author of *Principles of Economics*] was on the Council of Economic Advisors under President Bush and they tried to push forward a particular ideological view that markets work perfectly. I don't think most people think the economy is functioning perfectly. Financial markets are dealing with information and risk, and those are topics books like Mankiw's—the old-fashioned textbooks—simply don't deal with adequately. And that's the real danger: if people learn outdated economics and they wind up trying to make a decision about regulation—or another aspect of economic policy—they are simply not equipped to deal with the problem.

## On the invisible hand

A simple way to explain why the invisible hand doesn't work is to ask: Did the top executives' pursuit of self-interest in the case of Enron lead to global economic efficiency? Did the managers of the big banks—Citibank, Merrill Lynch, all the ones dealing in subprime mortgages—lead to economic efficiency for the American economy? I think it's pretty clear it didn't, and one can see why it didn't. These managers were pursuing their own bonuses, but maximizing their income was not consistent with maximizing societal welfare. Adam Smith said that maximizing self-interest and social interest were coincident, and I think that sort of dramatic illustration shows that they are not.

## On sustainability

I think what we've realized is the world cannot afford an extension of our lifestyle to the rest of the world. The problem is that India and China are on the way to trying to imitate our lifestyle. These are two countries with 2.4 billion people. Growth in China has been unbelievable, growing close to ten percent for thirty years. China is already the second largest producer of automobiles, and if it continues on that path, the planet is really at risk. But we say, "Oh you can't do this. It's alright for us to have this profligate lifestyle, but you can't because you might damage the planet." What we have to say is we are changing our lifestyle and there has to be a global compact, a social compact, that we all have to have a lifestyle that treats the planet with the respect that it needs.
A healthy economy involves using our time efficiently and getting enjoyment out of our time. Spending two hours commuting is not a good use of anybody's time. There are many ways in which we are very inefficient. We have not thought through efficient land management. I was in a meeting in France where they were talking about how to redesign a whole city to make it more environmentally efficient, to make sure there is less waste, that the energy that is put out is captured and used and reused. There are lots of things we can do to increase our overall efficiency.

# 02

# LOURDES BENERÍA

# "THERE IS NO EMOTION OR LOVE INVOLVED IN DECISIONS BASED ON ECONOMIC RATIONALITY"

## ON WHY ECONOMICS IS SO RESISTANT TO CHANGE

Economics is a very hegemonic discipline, even though there are so many heterodox economists that protest this arrogance and this unwillingness to discuss criticisms. Compared to other social sciences that have integrated gender much more easily, conventional economics has been one of the most impenetrable disciplines. It has been difficult, if not impossible, for orthodox economics to incorporate feminist issues.

Part of the resistance is because economists think of themselves as developing scientific tools of analysis, and some of the issues raised by feminists seem too remote to this culture: Economists think that they are more "scientific" than other social scientists. The salaries of economists are higher than those of other social scientists—even in universities, let alone in the business world. Economics is called the queen of the social sciences because it mimics physics and uses math.

Mathematics gives the impression that economics is scientific and so you cannot question it. But you have to dig into the assumptions. For example, look at the area known as "household economics." The neoclassical assumptions used to set up these models imply that men and women are free and equal individuals negotiating rationally what's best for the household. Some models assume that decisions are made by a "benevolent patriarch" who understands what's best for the household and each member. There is no emotion or love involved in decisions based on economic rationality.

But the fact is—as feminists have pointed out—within a household, men and women can be very unequal subjects, and decisions are not merely rational. Men have often had better educational opportunities—they may own land, they may control the money, they typically have more power. The picture of reality portrayed by these models is very androcentric or male-biased. Policies based on these models can underestimate how they affect men and women differently.

The problem is that to deal with gender relations you have to incorporate power into the analysis. Neoclassical economics does not deal with power relations; it tends to focus on purely economic issues. In contrast, the so-called "bargaining models" can focus more directly on power and asymmetric relations within the household.

Occupiers embrace in Times Square. New York. October 2011.

Lourdes Benería is a professor of gender and economic development at Cornell University and the author of *Gender, Development and Globalization: Economics as if People Mattered.* Her research centers on feminist economics, labor markets, women's work and globalization, with a special focus on Latin America. She spoke with ecological economist Tom Green.

## ON THE PERILS OF MAXIMIZATION

Economics is the big maximizing discipline: We want to maximize utility, maximize growth, maximize income and maximize production—given some constraints of course. We assume that the capitalist maximizes profits. For years and years the discipline has not taken into consideration the economic costs generated by all this maximization without any checks, and we are now seeing the consequences. The earth is in danger of not being able to support all this unregulated economic activity, and we now have a very serious ecological crisis. We cannot think only about maximizing anymore. At the very least we have to think about maximizing subject to some conditions. Our discipline is totally in need of rethinking. Economists talk about sustainable development with a very weak notion of what sustainability means. Scientists are telling us that it is impossible to even sustain what we have been taking for granted so far—especially in the high-income countries. We have to start reducing consumption, which means reducing the production that is causing so many problems to the earth. What the ecological crisis means is that economists have to start almost at zero in terms of rethinking the discipline.

# 03

# JULIE MATTHAEI

## "ONCE TENURED, I COULD RELAX A BIT AND TAKE MORE RISKS WITH MY TEACHING"

Julie Matthaei is an economics professor at Wellesley College and a cofounder and board member of the US Solidarity Economy Network (www.ussen.org). She coedited *Solidarity Economy: Building Alternatives for People and Planet*, available at www.lulu.com/changemaker.

Wellesley hired me in 1978 as the college's first and only radical economist. I was hired in response to student pressure: While doing their junior year studies abroad, students had been exposed to theories other than mainstream American neoclassical economics and they wanted these views represented at school. The department posted a job for someone to teach what they called "competing paradigms of economics." I was a PhD candidate in economics at Yale, where I studied with David Levine (Yale's one Marxist economist … he didn't get tenure). I applied and was hired.

All Wellesley economics faculty were required to teach two of the required "core" courses. I was assigned to introductory and intermediate microeconomics and given the mainstream textbook, but I refused to teach mainstream economics straight. Instead, I presented the material in the textbook, critiqued it and taught the outlines of the alternative, radical view. I remember feeling that by criticizing the economics bible I was engaging in a deeply subversive activity. I used to imagine that a huge arm would reach into the classroom, pick me up and carry me off. Luckily nothing of the sort happened. Instead, based on my popularity with students and the success of my first book, *An Economic History of Women in America*, I received a permanent, tenured position.

Once tenured, I could relax a bit and take more risks with my teaching. I began to realize that my critiques of mainstream economic theory and advanced capitalist economy seemed to be backfiring. From the very first time I presented the supply and demand framework to my intro econ students, for example, I pointed out that supply and demand curves only determine prices in perfectly competitive markets … which don't exist. I considered this key to my students' education, especially since mainstream economists apply the framework inappropriately so often, yet many of them continued to forget this key fact on their tests.

Teaching about market equilibrium, a situation in which there is neither shortage nor surplus of a product, presented another particularly bothersome failure. I always took care to explore the fact that equilibrium—where the supply and demand curves cross, and quantity supplied equals quantity demanded—does not mean that everyone is happy, or that basic needs are met. Many people could, in fact, be starving because they are too poor to be able to "demand" what they need. Even when no lines or shortages exist, people can still be dying from starvation. Despite my lessons, many of my students were unable to point out the falseness of the statement "everybody is happy in equilibrium" on their tests. They left my class accepting the free market/neoliberal line that government policies which intervene in markets—such as minimum wages or rent control—are inherently bad because they prevent markets from getting to equilibrium. I wanted to pull my hair out. It seemed the more I critiqued mainstream economics, the more I strengthened its hold on most of my students.

At first I tried to heighten my criticism of mainstream economic theory, and to begin it earlier in the course. I would criticize supply and demand curves and marginal utility curves before I even drew them. As I taught the theories, I would interlace critique in virtually every sentence. This approach, however, frustrated my students: Why was I teaching it to them if it was wrong? How could they learn the material if I didn't present it to them completely before attacking it? While some of my students—usually those who were radical themselves—understood and appreciated my criticism, many of them found it confusing, alienating and discouraging.

A similar problem emerged with my radical critique of advanced capitalism. My classes on radical economics presented the neo-Marxist view that large corporations dominated the economic landscape: Oppressing workers, brainwashing consumers through advertising to keep them enslaved by the work/spend cycle and manipulating the government to do their bidding through campaign financing and bribes. I juxtaposed this view with that of our mainstream text, which obscured corporate power by focusing on small, helpless firms controlled by sovereign consumers who—when market failures made it necessary—use their votes to get the government to intervene on their behalf. I was amused—and dismayed—to find that many of my students' exams showed they actually thought I had been teaching them about two different countries!

Even as I adjusted my teaching to make sure my students understood that these were two views of the US economy, however, I realized another problem. The students who believed in the radical view were also convinced that large corporations were so powerful that nothing could be done about them. Instead of inspiring my students to radical activism, I had taught them to be cynical and resigned about the prevailing economic dysfunction and injustice. If they couldn't do anything about it, they figured, why not at least get rich by becoming an investment banker?

Then I learned about the spiritual principle of nonreaction. When you react to someone, you are letting him determine your behavior rather than choosing it yourself. My teaching was largely reactive: By centering on a critique of the text I was continually "reacting" to the book rather than achieving my goal of demolishing mainstream economics—in my students' heads and in the world. My radical critiques of large corporations were also a reaction, and only emphasized corporate power to such a degree that it made my students feel helpless.

I began to evolve a new way of teaching that focuses less on mainstream economic theory and powerful, profit-motivated corporations. Now we begin the term identifying both pressing economic problems and the global warming crisis. I point out the problems associated with consumers, workers and firms acting in self-interested and materialistic ways. I present, discuss and give examples of the emerging "solidarity economy," which is based on socially responsible or "high road" economic values, practices and institutions: Ethical consumption, fair trade, socially responsible corporations. This puts materialistic competitive consumerism and traditional profit-motivated corporations on the defensive. From this point of view one wonders why anyone ever believed that a solely profit-motivated corporation, dedicated to serving its owners (the stockholders), would be able to do right by its other stakeholders: Consumers, workers, suppliers, government and the environment.

Or why anyone would imagine that buying more and more material things would bring true fulfillment.

One of my most successful assignments in recent terms was based on the PBS documentary *Affluenza and Me*, which analyzes contemporary consumer culture in the US as an illness. The symptoms of this "affluenza" are overwork, time shortage, debt, breakdown of family relationships, ecological destruction, etc. We also read and discussed an excerpt from P. A. Payutto's book *Buddhist Economics*, which presents enlightened consumption as building well-being through resistance to advertising and cravings, knowledge of one's true needs and service to the whole.

I no longer teach the core aspects of mainstream microeconomics as some superpower theory. I now present microeconomics as a theory that understands some aspects of the economy but misses others. It's a theory whose models can only be used if their limitations are acknowledged, and if they are supplemented by other concepts and understandings. The supply and demand curve framework, for example, can be very helpful in elucidating problems in contemporary labor markets—such as below-subsistence level wages caused by an excess of labor.

I no longer teach my students about corporate power as an overpowering monolithic force but as something which has to be continually constructed through the collaboration of consumers, workers, managers, government officials and laws. I show them that it is something that needs to be radically reconstructed through socially responsible behavior.

I teach my students how to make their microeconomic decisions—as consumers, workers, entrepreneurs, parents and citizens—in ways that create well-being for themselves and their loved ones. I teach them how to use their economic power to express and actualize their deepest values—to repudiate the false god of money and the prevailing economic religion of the market. I teach them that enlightened self-interest involves behaving in a socially responsible manner, since we all depend on each other … and on the whole. We all have to do our part to save both the planet and ourselves—there is plenty that we can do by aligning our economic decisions with our true values.

# MANFRED MAX-NEEF

"I worked for about ten years in areas of extreme poverty in the Sierras, in the jungle and urban areas of Latin America. And one day at the beginning of that period I found myself in an Indian village in the Sierra in Peru. It was an ugly day. It had been raining non-stop. And I was standing in the slum. And across from me, a guy was standing in the mud—not in the slum, in the mud.

in the mud. He was a short guy … thin, hungry, jobless, five kids, a wife and a grandmother. And I was the fine economist from Berkeley. As we looked at each other, I suddenly realized that I had nothing coherent to say to that man in those circumstances, that my whole language as an economist was absolutely useless. Should I tell him that he should be happy because the GDP had grown 5 percent or something? Everything felt absurd. Economists study and analyze poverty in their nice offices, they have all the statistics, they make all the models and are convinced they know everything. But they don't understand poverty."

# GEORGE **AKERLOF**

# "ECONOMISTS HAVE TO START ADDING NORMS AND MOTIVATIONS BACK INTO THEIR MODELS"

Although economics has progressed in the last fifty years, important aspects of human motivation are still missing from it. I am trying to effect a return to a more sensible and pragmatic economics. Until recently, simplistic assumptions about human behavior have misled theory and misguided policy. We need to once again base our models on, as Keynes put it, "our knowledge of human nature and ... the detailed facts of experience." We now know that people often do not behave rationally. What we need to include in economic models are the norms and motivations that guide human behavior. People have very firm notions about how they and other people should behave, although they often don't know exactly where these notions come from. Economics has eschewed this kind of motivation and, as a result, it's more solemn than it should be, and it's also a lot less fun. There are many issues in which economics could offer more powerful analysis, and there are many issues in which it gets the wrong answer. It claims that it has insights, but these insights are wrong.

If you go back forty or so years, norms and motivations would have been part of economists' analyses. Then an intellectual movement which said we should be much more scientific and derive everything from principles of maximization arose. For some reason or other, the notion that people actually care about how we should or shouldn't behave got left out of the methodology. Economists tried to make their models very simple and, as a result, we have a less good economics than we would have had otherwise.

Models that are restricted to economic motivations make it very difficult to explain such important phenomena as inflation. It's also very difficult to explain why the monetary authority has an effect on the level of employment and output and to explain the trade-off between inflation and unemployment. The same type of problem applies to many different areas of microeconomics. We lose a lot of the explanation of how organizations work, we lose a great deal of the economics of gender, we lose a lot of the economics of minority poverty—especially why minorities tend to have high levels of poverty.

Part of the problem arose back in 1953, when Milton Friedman urged his fellow economists to rely on parsimonious models, simple models, that explain the world with a minimum of variables. Parsimony was erroneously defined as making models dependent on what we consider to be economic arguments—how individuals seek to maximize their utility and what gives them utility—is narrowly defined and mainly focused on consumption. The interpretation of parsimony shouldn't include the idea that norms don't matter, because in fact norms really do matter.

Economists have to start adding norms and motivations back into their models. People have some kind of view as to how they should be behaving. What makes us happy is largely whether we feel we live up to that view. The way economics is sometimes taught suggests the path to well-being is maximizing consumption opportunities, creating opportunities for the economy to grow so consumers can consume more. But this model has shortcomings. Economists have contributed to the shortcomings by missing the inclusion of norms and motivations. Once you've met some basic needs, what makes you happy is having a view of what you should be doing ... and doing it.

George Akerlof is a professor at the University of California, Berkeley. He won the 2001 Nobel Prize in Economics (shared with Michael Spence and Joseph E. Stiglitz) for his paper "The Market for Lemons: Quality Uncertainty and the Market Mechanism." Akerlof has worked to incorporate human psychology into economic models since 1970. His recent publications include *Animal Spirits: How Human Psychology Drives the Economy, and Why It Matters for Global Capitalism, Explorations in Pragmatic Economics* and *Thoughts on Global Warming*. He spoke with ecological economist Tom Green about what's missing from mainstream economics.

# 06

# STEVE KEEN

Steve Keen is associate professor of economics and finance at the University of Western Sydney and the author of *Debunking Economics*. Check out his blogs at debunkingeconomics.com and debtdeflation.com/blogs.

# "NEOCLASSICAL ECONOMICS IS NOT MERELY WRONG, BUT DANGEROUS"

**The most important thing that global financial crisis has done for economic theory is to show that neoclassical economics is not merely wrong, but dangerous.**

Neoclassical economics contributed directly to this crisis by promoting a faith in the innate stability of a market economy, in a manner which in fact increased the tendency toward instability of the financial system. With its false belief that all instability in the system can be traced to interventions in the market, rather than the market itself, it championed the deregulation of finance and a dramatic increase in income inequality. Its equilibrium vision of the functioning of finance markets led to the development of the very financial products that are now threatening the continued existence of capitalism itself.

Simultaneously it distracted economists from the obvious signs of an impending crisis—the asset market bubbles, and above all the rising private debt that was financing them. Paradoxically, as capitalism's "perfect storm" approached, neoclassical macroeconomists were absorbed in smug self-congratulation over their apparent success in taming inflation and the trade cycle, in what

they termed "The Great Moderation." Ben Bernanke's contribution to this is worth quoting at length:

… the low-inflation era of the past two decades has seen not only significant improvements in economic growth and productivity but also a marked reduction in economic volatility… a phenomenon that has been dubbed "the Great Moderation". Recessions have become less frequent and milder, and … volatility in output and employment has declined significantly…. The sources of the Great Moderation remain somewhat controversial, but … there is evidence for the view that improved control of inflation has contributed in important measure to this welcome change in the economy …

It is all very well to have economic theory dominated by a school of thought with an innate faith in the stability of markets when those markets are forever gaining—whether by growth in the physical economy, or via rising prices in the asset markets. In those circumstances, academic economists aligned to *Post Autistic Economics* (*Real World Economics Review*) can rail about the logical inconsistencies in mainstream economics all they want: They will be, and were, ignored by government, the business community, and most of the public, because their concerns don't appear to matter.

They can even be put down as critics of capitalism—worse still, as proponents of socialism—because it seems to those outside academia, and to neoclassical economists as well, that what they are attacking is not economic theory, but capitalism itself: "You think markets are unstable? Shame on you!"

The story is entirely different when asset markets crash beneath a mountain of debt, and the ensuing fallout threatens to take the physical economy with it. Now it should be possible to have the critics of neoclassical economics appreciated for what we really are: Critics of a fundamentally false theory of the operations of a market economy, and tentative developers of a new, realistic analysis of the nature of capitalism, warts and all.

## CHANGING PEDAGOGY

Given how severe this crisis has already proven to be, the reform of economic theory and education should be an easy and urgent task. But that is not how things will pan out. Though the "irresistible force" of the Global Financial Crisis is indeed immense, so to is the inertia of the "immovable object" of economic belief.

Despite the severity of the crisis in the real world, academic neoclassical economists will continue to teach from the same textbooks that they used in 2008 and earlier (laziness will be as influential a factor here as ideological commitment). Rebel economists will be emboldened to proclaim "I told you so" in their non-core subjects, but in the core micro, macro and finance units, it will be business as usual virtually everywhere. Many undergraduate economics students in the coming years will sit gobsmacked as their lecturers recite textbook theory as if there is nothing extraordinarily different taking place in the real economy.

The same will happen in the academic journals. The editors of the *American Economic Review* and the *Economic Journal* are unlikely to convert to Post-Keynesian or Evolutionary Economics or Econophysics any time soon—let alone to be replaced by editors who are already practitioners of nonorthodox thought. The battle against neoclassical economic orthodoxy within universities will be long and hard, even though its failure will be apparent to those in the nonacademic world.

Much of this will be because neoclassical economists are genuinely naïve about their role in causing this crisis. From their perspective, they will interpret the crisis as due to poor regulation, and to government intervention in areas that should have been left to the market. Aspects of the crisis that cannot be solely attributed to those causes will be covered by appealing to embellishments to basic neoclassical

theory. Thus, for example, the Subprimes Scam will be portrayed as something easily explained by the theory of asymmetric information.

They will seriously believe that the crisis calls not for the abolition of neoclassical economics, but for its teachings to be more widely known. The very thought that this financial crisis should require any change in what they do, let alone necessitate the rejection of neoclassical theory completely, will strike them as incredible.

In this sense, they are like the Maxwellian physicists about whom Max Planck remarked that "a new scientific truth does not triumph by convincing its opponents and making them see the light, but rather because its opponents eventually die, and a new generation grows up that is familiar with it."

But physics is charmed in comparison to economics, since it is inherently an empirical discipline, and quantum mechanics gave the only explanation to the empirically quantifiable black body problem. Planck's confidence that a new generation would take the place of the old was therefore well-founded. But in economics, not only will the neoclassical old guard resist change, they could, if economic circumstances stabilize, give rise to a new generation that accepts their interpretation of the crisis. The is how the success of the Keynesian counter-revolution came about, and it is why we have entered this crisis with an even more rabid neoclassicism than confronted Keynes in the 1930s.

The first thing that the global financial crisis should therefore do to economics is to galvanize student protest about the lack of debate within academic economics itself, because dissident academic economists will be unable to shift the study of economics themselves without massive pressure from the student body.

I speak from my own experience, when I was one of many students who agitated against neoclassical economics in the early 1970s at Sydney University, and campaigned for the establishment of a Political Economy Department. Were it not for the protests by the students against what we then rightly saw as a deluded approach to economics, the non-neoclassical staff at Sydney University would have been unable to affect change themselves.

Though we won that battle at Sydney University, we lost the war. The economic downturn of the mid-1970s allowed for the defeat of what Joan Robinson aptly called the Bastard Keynesianism of that era, and its replacement by Friedman's "monetarism." Our protests were also wrongly characterized as being essentially anticapitalist. Though there were indeed many who were anti-capitalist within the Political Economy movement, the real target of student protest was a poor theory of how capitalism operates, and not capitalism itself.

Similar observations can be made about the PAECON (Post Autistic Economics) movement today, where student dissatisfaction with neoclassical economics in France spilled over into a worldwide movement. Though the initial impact of the movement was substantial, neoclassical dominance of economic pedagogy continued unabated. The movement persisted, but its relevance to the real economy was not appreciated because that economy appeared to be booming. Now that the global economy is in crisis, student pressure is needed once more to ensure that, this time, real change to economic pedagogy occurs.

Business pressure is also essential. Business groups to some degree naïvely believed that those who proclaimed the virtues of the market system, and who argued on their side in disputes over income distribution, were their allies in the academy, while critics of the market were their enemies. I hope that this financial catastrophe will convince the business community that its true friends in the academy are those who understand the market system, whether they criticize or praise it. As much as we need students to revolt over the teaching of economics, we need business to bring pressure on academic economics departments to revise their curricula because of the financial crisis.

## CHANGING ECONOMICS

The pedagogic pressure from students and the wider community has to be matched by the accelerated development of alternatives to neoclassical economics. Though we know much more today about the innate flaws in neoclassical thought than was known at the time of the Great Depression, the development of a full-fledged alternative to it is still a long way off. There are multiple alternative schools of thought extant—from Post Keynesian to Evolutionary and Behavioral Economics, and Econophysics—but these are not developed enough to provide a fully fledged alternative to neoclassical economics.

This should not dissuade us from dispensing completely with the neoclassical approach. For some substantial period, and especially while the actual economy remains in turmoil, we have to accept a period of turmoil in the teaching of and research into economics. Hanging on to parts of a failed paradigm simply because it has components that other schools lack would be a tragic mistake because it is from precisely such relics that a neoclassical vision could once again become dominant when—or rather if— the market economy emerges from this crisis.

Key here should be a rejection of neoclassical microeconomics in its entirety. This was the missing component of Keynes's revolution. While he tried to overthrow macroeconomics shibboleths like Say's Law, (the principle that business owners are inherently rational and will not hoard money) he continued to accept not merely the microeconomic concepts such as perfect competition, but also their unjustified projection into macroeconomic areas—as with his belief that the marginal productivity theory of income distribution, which is fundamentally a micro concept, applied at the macro level of wage determination.

From this failure to expunge the microeconomic foundations of neoclassical economics from post–Great Depression economics arose the "microfoundations of macroeconomics" debate that led ultimately to rational expectations representative agent macroeconomics, in which the economy is modeled as a single utility maximizing individual who is blessed with perfect knowledge of the future.

Fortunately, behavioral economics provides the beginnings of an alternative vision as to how individuals operate in a market environment, while multi-agent modeling and network theory give us foundations for understanding group dynamics in a complex society. They explicitly emphasize what neoclassical economics has evaded: That aggregation of heterogeneous individuals results in emergent properties of the group which cannot be reduced to the behavior of any "representative individual" amongst them. These approaches should replace neoclassical microeconomics completely.

The changes to economic theory beyond the micro level involve a complete recanting of the neoclassical vision. The vital first step here is to abandon the obsession with equilibrium.

The fallacy that dynamic processes must be modeled as if the system is in continuous equilibrium through time is probably the most important reason for the intellectual failure of neoclassical economics. Mathematics, sciences and engineering long ago developed tools to model out of equilibrium processes, and this dynamic approach to thinking about the economy should become second nature to economists.

An essential pedagogic step here is to hand the teaching of mathematical methods in economics over to mathematics departments. Any mathematical training in economics, if it occurs at all, should come after students have done at least basic calculus, algebra and differential equations—the last area being one about which most economists of all persuasions are woefully ignorant. This simultaneously explains why neoclassical economists obsess too much about proofs, and why non-neoclassical economists like those in the Circuit School have had such difficulties in translating excellent verbal ideas about credit creation into coherent dynamic models of a monetary production economy, as Graziani has noted.

Neoclassical economics has effectively insulated itself from the great advances made in these genuine sciences and engineering in the last forty years, so that while its concepts appear difficult, they are quaint in comparison to the sophistication evident today in mathematics, engineering, computing, evolutionary biology and physics. This isolation must end, and for a substantial while economics must eat humble pie and learn from these disciplines that it has for so long studiously ignored. Some researchers from those fields have called for the wholesale replacement of standard economics curricula with at least the building blocks of modern thought in these disciplines, and in the light of the catastrophe economists have visited upon the real world, their arguments carry substantial weight.

For example, in response to a paper critical of trends in econophysics, the physicist Joe McCauley responded that, though some of the objections were valid, the problems in economics proper were far worse. He therefore suggested that:

> *The economists revise their curriculum and require that the following topics be taught: calculus through the advanced level, ordinary differential equations (including advanced), partial differential equations (including Green functions), classical mechanics through modern nonlinear dynamics, statistical physics, stochastic processes (including solving Smoluchowski-Fokker-Planck equations), computer programming and, for complexity, cell biology. Time for such classes can be obtained in part by eliminating micro and macroeconomics classes from the curriculum. The students will then face a much harder curriculum, and those who survive will come out ahead. So might society as a whole.*

The economic theory that should eventually emerge from the rejection of neoclassical economics and the basic adoption of dynamic methods will come much closer than neoclassical economics could ever do to meeting Marshall's dictum that "the Mecca of the economist lies in economic biology rather than in economic dynamics." As Thorstein Veblen correctly surmised over a century ago, the failure of economics to become an evolutionary science is the product of the optimizing framework of the underlying paradigm, which is inherently antithetical to the process of evolutionary change. This reason, above all others, is why the neoclassical mantra that the economy must be perceived as the outcome of the decisions of utility maximizing individuals must be rejected.

Economics also has to become fundamentally a monetary discipline, right from the consideration of how individuals make market decisions through to our understanding of macroeconomics. The myth of "the money illusion" (which can only be true in a world without debt) has to be dispelled from day one, while our macroeconomics has to be that of a monetary economy in which nominal magnitudes matter— precisely because they are the link between the value of current output and the financing of accumulated debt. The dangers of excessive debt and deflation simply cannot be comprehended from a neoclassical perspective, which—along with the inability to reason outside the confines of equilibrium—explains the profession's failure to assimilate Fisher's prescient warnings; few people realize that Friedman's preferred rate of inflation in his "Optimum Quantity of Money" paper was "a decline in prices at the rate of at least 5 percent per year, and perhaps decidedly more."

The discipline must also become fundamentally empirical, in contrast to the faux empiricism of econometrics. By this I mean basing itself on economic and financial data first and foremost—the collection and interpretation of which has been the hallmark of contributions by econophysicists—and by respecting economic history, a topic that has been expunged from economics departments around the world. It, along with a non-Whig approach to the history of economic thought, should be restored to the economics curriculum. Names that currently are absent from modern economics courses (Marx, Veblen, Keynes, Fisher, Kalecki, Schumpeter, Minsky, Sraffa, Goodwin, to name a few) should abound in such courses.

Ironically, one of the best calls for a focus on the empirical data sans a preceding economic model came from two of the most committed neoclassical authors, 2004 Nobel Prize winners Finn Kydland and Edward Prescott, when they noted that "the reporting of facts—without assuming the data are generated by some probability model—is an important scientific activity. We see no reason for economics to be an exception." The failure of these authors to live up to their own standards should not be replicated in post-neoclassical economics.

# HERMAN DALY

# "IT IS BLIND ARROGANCE TO CONTINUE PREACHING AGGREGATE GROWTH AS THE SOLUTION TO OUR PROBLEMS"

Herman Daly is a former World Bank economist and professor at the University of Maryland's School of Public Policy. He co-founded the heterodox journal *Ecological Economics*. He received the Right Livelihood Award in 1996, the alternative to the Nobel Prize.

The Earth as a whole is approximately in a steady state. Neither the surface nor the mass of the earth is growing or shrinking; the inflow of radiant energy to the Earth is equal to the outflow (the greenhouse effect has slowed the outflow, but the resulting temperature increase will force it back up); and material imports from space are roughly equal to exports (both negligible). None of this means that the earth is static—a great deal of qualitative change can happen inside a steady state, and certainly has happened on Earth.

The most important change in recent times has been the enormous growth of one subsystem of the earth, namely the economy, relative to the total system, the ecosphere. This huge shift from an "empty" to a "full" world is truly "something new under the sun," as historian J. R. McNeil calls it in his book of that title. The closer the economy approaches the scale of the whole Earth, the more it will have to conform to the physical behavior mode of the Earth. That behavior mode is a steady state—a system that permits qualitative development but not aggregate quantitative growth. Growth is more of the same stuff; development is the same amount of better stuff (or at least different stuff). The remaining natural world is no longer able to provide the sources and sinks for the metabolic throughput necessary to sustain the existing oversized economy—much less a growing one. Economists have focused too much on the economy's circulatory system and have neglected to study its digestive tract. Throughput growth means pushing more of the same food through an ever larger digestive tract; development means eating better food and digesting it more thoroughly. Clearly the economy must conform to the rules of a steady state—seek qualitative development, but stop aggregate quantitative growth. GDP increase conflates these two very different things.

We have lived for two hundred years in a growth economy. That makes it hard to imagine what a steady-state economy (SSE) would be like, even though for most of our history mankind has lived in an economy in which annual growth has been negligible. Some think an SSE would mean freezing in the dark under communist tyranny. Some say that huge improvements in technology (energy efficiency, recycling) are so easy that it will make the adjustment both profitable and fun.

Regardless of whether it will be hard or easy, we have to attempt an SSE because we cannot continue growing, and in fact so-called "economic" growth already has become uneconomic. The growth economy is failing. In other words, the quantitative expansion of the economic subsystem increases environmental and social costs faster than production benefits, making us poorer not richer, at least in high-consumption countries. Given the laws of diminishing marginal utility and increasing marginal costs, this should not have been unexpected. And even new technology sometimes makes it worse. For example, tetraethyl lead provided the benefit of reducing engine knock, but at the cost of spreading a toxic heavy metal into the biosphere; chlorofluorocarbons gave us the benefit of a nontoxic propellant and refrigerant, but at the cost of creating a hole in the ozone layer and a resulting increase in ultraviolet radiation. It is hard to know for sure that growth now increases costs faster than benefits since we do not bother to separate costs from benefits in our national accounts. Instead we lump them together as "activity" in the calculation of GDP.

Ecological economists have offered empirical evidence that growth is already uneconomic in high-consumption countries. Since neoclassical economists are unable to demonstrate that growth, either in throughput or GDP, is currently making us better off rather than worse off, it is blind arrogance on their part to continue preaching aggregate growth as the solution to our problems. Yes, most of our problems (poverty, unemployment, environmental degradation) would be easier to solve if we were richer—that is not the issue. The issue is: Does growth in GDP any longer really make us richer? Or is it now making us poorer?

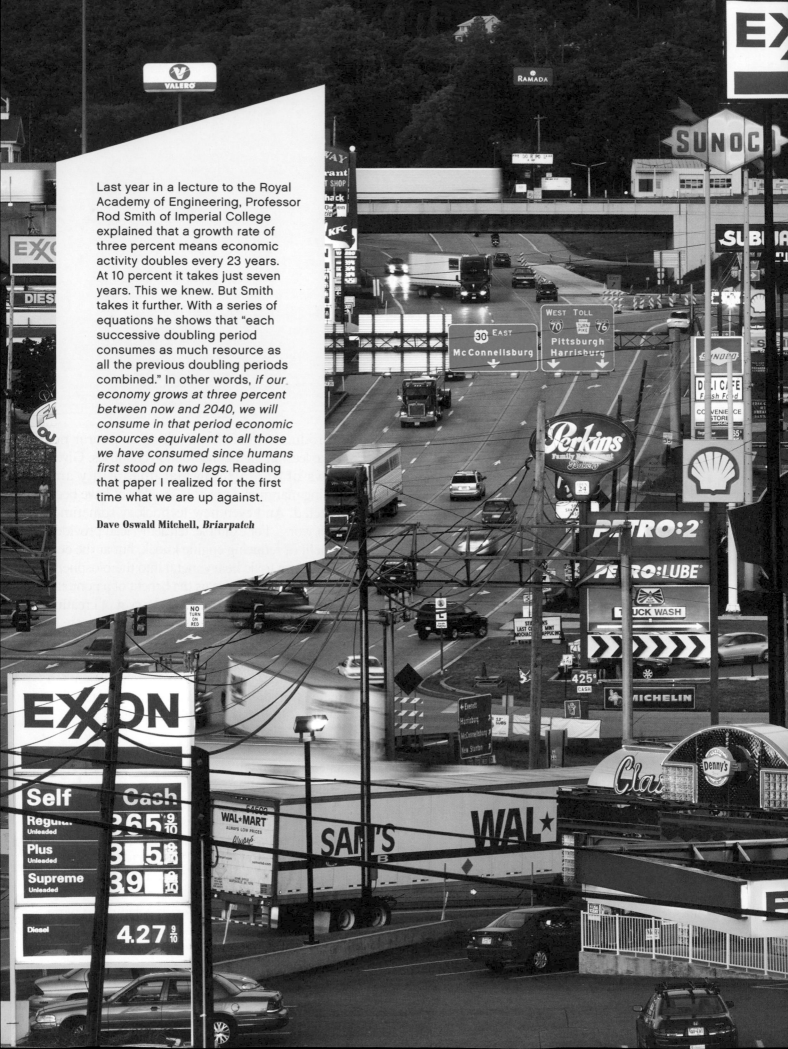

Last year in a lecture to the Royal Academy of Engineering, Professor Rod Smith of Imperial College explained that a growth rate of three percent means economic activity doubles every 23 years. At 10 percent it takes just seven years. This we knew. But Smith takes it further. With a series of equations he shows that "each successive doubling period consumes as much resource as all the previous doubling periods combined." In other words, *if our economy grows at three percent between now and 2040, we will consume in that period economic resources equivalent to all those we have consumed since humans first stood on two legs.* Reading that paper I realized for the first time what we are up against.

**Dave Oswald Mitchell,** *Briarpatch*

ASK YOUR PROFESSOR:

What do you think of Herman Daly's idea of a steady state economy?

# 08

# TED TRAINER

# "ZERO GROWTH HAS PROFOUNDLY RADICAL IMPLICATIONS"

Ted Trainer is a lecturer at the University of New South Wales in the faculty of social work.

The growth problem is not just that the economy has grown to be too big, now depleting resources and damaging and eventually destroying ecosystems. The more central problem is that growth is integral to the system. Most of the system's basic structures and mechanisms are driven by growth and cannot operate without it. Growth cannot be removed leaving the rest of the economy more or less as it is. Unfortunately people in the current "De-growth" movement tend to think growth is like a faulty air conditioning unit in a house, which can be taken away and the rest of the house will function more or less as it did before.

— If you do away with growth then there can be no interest payments. If more has to be paid back than was lent or invested, then the total amount of capital to invest will inevitably grow over time. The present economy literally runs on interest payments of one form or another; an economy without interest payments would have to have totally different mechanisms for carrying out many processes. Therefore almost the entire finance industry has to be scrapped, and replaced by arrangements whereby money is made available, lent, invested etc., without increasing the wealth of the lender. That is incomprehensible to most current economists, politicians and ordinary people.

— The present economy is driven by the quest to get richer; this motive is what ensures energetic search for options, taking of risks, construction and development, etc. The most obvious alternative is for these actions to be motivated by a collective effort to work out what society needs, and organize to produce and develop those things. This involves an utterly different world view and driving mechanism. Such a society would have to find another way to ensure innovation, entrepreneurial initiative and risk taking.

— The market is about maximizing, about producing, selling, and investing in order to make as much money as possible from the deal, and then seeking to invest, produce and sell more, in order to again make as much money as possible. In other words there is an inseparable relation between growth, the market system and the accumulation imperative that defines capitalism. If we must cease growth we must scrap the market system.

— The above changes cannot be made unless there is also a profound cultural change, involving nothing less than the abandonment of the desire to gain. For more than two hundred years our Western society has been focused on the quest to get richer, to accumulate wealth and property. This is what drives all economic activity, such as the innovative and development behavior of firms and the behavior of individuals and firms in the market, and it is at the core of national policy. People work to get as much money as possible. Firms strive to make as much profit as possible and to get as big as possible. People trade in order to end up richer than they were. Nations strive to become richer all the time.

The cultural transition to zero-growth economy requires an enormous change in the current mentality which has been the driving force in Western culture for several hundred years.

# 09

# BERNARD STIEGLER

# "THE CONSUMERIST MODEL HAS REACHED ITS LIMITS"

Bernard Stiegler taught himself philosophy while imprisoned for armed robbery between 1978 and 1983. He has since become a leading French philosopher of technology. This article was adapted from his recent book, *For a New Critique of Political Economy.*

Those who advocate stimulating consumption as the path to economic recovery want neither to hear nor speak about the end of consumerism. Yet, those who advocate stimulating investment are no more willing to call the consumerist industrial model into question. The French version of "stimulating investment" argues that the best way to save consumption is through investment, that is, by restoring "profitability," which will in turn restore an entrepreneurial dynamism itself founded upon consumerism and its counterpart, market-driven productivism.

In other words, this "investment" produces no long-term view capable of drawing any lessons from the collapse of an industrial model based on the automobile, on oil, and on the construction of highway networks, as well as on the Hertzian networks of the culture industries. This ensemble has until recently formed the basis for consumerism, yet today it is obsolete, a fact which became clear during the autumn of 2008. Frankly speaking, this "investment" is not an investment: It is on the contrary a disinvestment, an abdication which consists in doing no more than burying one's head in the sand.

This "investment policy," which has no goal other than the reconstitution of the consumerist model, is the translation of a moribund ideology. It is a desperate attempt to prolong the life of a model which has become self-destructive by denying and concealing for as long as possible the fact that the consumerist model is now massively toxic (a toxicity extending far beyond the question of "toxic assets") because it has reached its limits. This denial is a matter of trying, for as long as possible, to maintain the colossal profits that can be accrued by those capable of exploiting the toxicity of consumerism.

The consumerist model has reached its limits because it has become systemically short-termist, because it has given rise to a systemic stupidity that structurally prevents the reconstitution of a long-term horizon. This "investment" is not an investment according to any terms other than those of pure accounting: It is a pure and simple reestablishment of the state of things, trying to rebuild the industrial landscape without at all changing its structure, still less its axioms, all in the hope of protecting income levels that had hitherto been achievable.

Such may be the hope, but these are the false hopes of those with buried heads. The genuine object of debate raised by the crisis ought to be how to overcome the short-termism to which we have been led by a consumerism intrinsically destructive of all genuine investment, that is, of investment in the future, a short-termism which has systemically, and not accidentally, been translated into the decomposition of investment into speculation.

Whether we must, in order to avoid a major economic catastrophe, and to attenuate the social injustice caused by the crisis, stimulate consumption and the economic machine such as it still is, is a question as urgent as it is legitimate so long as such a policy does not simply aggravate the situation at the cost of millions and billions of euros or dollars while at the same time masking the true query, which is how to produce a vision and a political will capable of progressively moving away from the economico-political complex of consumption so as to enter into the complex of a new type of investment. This new kind of investment must be a social and political investment or, in other words, an investment in a common desire, what Aristotle called philia, and which would then form the basis of a new type of economic investment.

Between the absolute urgency which obviously imposes the imperative of salvaging the present situation and of avoiding the passage from a global economic crisis to a global political crisis that might yet unleash military conflicts of global dimensions and the absolute necessity that consists in producing a potential future in the form of a political and social will capable of making a break with the present situation there is clearly a contradiction. Such a contradiction is characteristic of what happens to a dynamic system (in this case, the industrial system and the global capitalist system) once it has begun to mutate.

Economic growth is mistakenly seen as synonymous with well-being. The faster we cut down forests and haul in fish stocks to extinction, the more GDP grows. Even crime, war, sickness and natural disasters make GDP grow, simply because these ills cause money to be spent … We need to rethink our entire growth-based economy so that we can thrive more effectively on our own resources in harmony with nature. We do not need to accept as inevitable a world of impending climate chaos and financial collapse.

Bhutan Prime Minister Jigme Thinley

**Hey you unrepentants out there,**

Questioning growth used to be heretical. Not anymore. What economist out there today can honestly claim that never-ending growth can be sustained on a finite planet? The time has come to proclaim the opposite truth: The God of growth is dead. We're now at the beginning of a monumental mind shift that will do to economics what Luther did to Christianity, what Bacon did to science, what Nietzsche did to philosophy. Our boldest minds are embarking on a new quest: How to manage our planetary household—how seven, and soon ten billion of us and the future generations ahead can survive and find a modicum of happiness—without crashing *Gaia*.

# 10

# BRIAN DAVEY

# "PERHAPS WE CAN CREATE A SOCIETY IN WHICH A GOOD LIFE IS POSSIBLE"

Brian Davey is a freelance ecological economist who lives in Nottingham, UK.

When I booked two weeks in advance for the Beyond Growth Conference in Berlin this past year it was easy to get a seat—they only expected 1,000 participants. However, at the closing session, to everyone's collective surprise, organizers said nearly 2,500 had participated in the event, an unusual outpouring for supposed radical ideas.

By the numbers it's now clear that post-growth thinking has arrived in Germany and it's difficult to believe that it won't soon be a major political force. More than fifty organizations were supporting, funding and promoting the event—including several prominent think tanks and foundations. It was a major convergence.

The host, ATTAC, (the Association for the Taxation of Financial Transactions to Aid Citizens), is growing throughout Europe. For a number of years, academics developing social justice and ecological critiques of globalization have been joining. Many different strands of political opinion from hard left to post-growth green can be found in ATTAC's ranks. They have succeeded in engaging European trade unions, many of which were fully involved in the discussions. A few years ago there was difficulty bridging the division between the ecological and environmental politics of the greens and the social and other focuses taken up by the left and trade unions. But ATTAC, who embrace broad diversity, have been able to lift partisan actors above the fray. While there are still divisions, they're handled non-acrimoniously and, as a major union there said, it's clear there is now an explicit consensus that social and ecological problems must be worked on together.

## THE WEALTH OF DEGROWTH
Vandana Shiva opened the congress and made a major statement about how Indian growth is rooted in a host of destructive practices and processes. Her main point was that growth is only a measure of financial activity, not well-being. When you look at what is growing in India you find that the pains of development are damaging to the least powerful, and are effectively polarizing wealth. Growth, she said, is not the answer. What is needed is a different development model—one that is socially just and ecologically sane. What this alternative development model can be or should be in the global south was a major theme. Particularly influential were

voices and ideas from Ecuador and Bolivia. In the search for overarching visions and goals for a post-growth economy, activists in Germany have picked up on the voices of indigenous communities in South America, especially the idea of Buen Vivir—Gutes Leben in German—Good Life. The starting point for this idea of Good Life is the cosmology, philosophy, culture and political economic ideas of a diversity of indigenous communities and tribes in the Andean region. The culture and thinking of these communities are reemerging after centuries of colonialism, Catholicism and the impact of having their economies subordinated to resource extraction.

## BUEN VIVIR: A VISION FOR THE FUTURE?
The indigenous communities of the Andes already have the alternative to growth. It is their traditional notion of Sumak Kawsay, a Quecha word that is translated into Spanish as Buen Vivir. Sumak Kawsay puts the relationships of humans and communities to nature as their central point. It is an idea that existed prior to colonialism and the corresponding development of the extraction industries and plantation monocultures. The fact that these alternatives are coming forward now and are influencing the politics and constitutions of Ecuador and Bolivia is incredibly important. It not only gives rise to states that explicitly reject growth and "development" as their goals, but reflects a neo-emancipation process. The indigenous people in the Andes have for centuries been repressed and marginalized but now are able to put their own ideas into the political process. (In Bolivia 55 percent of the population are indigenous peoples, from thirty-six different ethnic groups. European people are a mere 15 percent. In Ecuador the indigenous population is 35 percent of the total population.) It seems obvious to say that common ways of thinking about growth and development among the population of the industrial countries assumes that people in poor countries would want to develop along a similar path to that followed in the industrial world—this is the direction of "progress" and reason. That is, after all, why they are called developing countries. However, for indigenous peoples development and growth has actually been a long history of colonial exploitation, suffering, racism and oppression of women, not to mention the destruction of Mother Earth. It is by no means the case that all of these people see development as a desirable future. On the contrary many indigenous

peoples have reason to counterpose the current state of things and celebrate their traditional lifestyles as having an important contribution to prevent an economically suicidal path for the planet.

## IS CONSUMERISM REALLY A PART OF HUMAN NATURE?

I recall an email exchange with a *Financial Times* journalist who was certain that poor people everywhere wanted to have electrical household appliances, a car, and all other sorts of modern stuff. This assumption that consumerism is a natural and inevitable feature of human nature is not something that one can assume of Buen Vivir. For example, Elisa Vega from Bolivia, who leads the department for de-patriachalization at the Ministry for Decolonialization, was sure about the quality of life associated with traditional ways of living when she spoke at the conference. Her grandfather lived to 110 years and was active to the last day. He did not save money but saved up plentiful reserves of nonperishable foodstuffs. Vega said that indigenous peoples were not consumption oriented. There was no point in having more than was necessary. If you saw her again, she said, she would be wearing the same traditional dress and the same jewelry as the day you first met her, the jewelry being centuries old. Things must be protected and made to last. What was important to indigenous peoples were family and community relationships—and the relationship to Mother Nature, Pachamama. In this respect Buen Vivir is very different from any kind of individualistic idea of Good Life. It is only conceivable in the social context in which people live. It involves striving for harmony and balance rather than dominance. This is important because the concept is rooted in plurality and a coexistence based on respect—both of human communities and of nature. Thus decolonization in the Andean region is not tending to the creation of a new monolithic point of view but is seen as needing to be built on a diversity of cultures. Nor is it about a simple return to ancestral and traditional thinking. Buen Vivir not only allows differences but actively seeks them out. Thinkers from the Andes communicate with other cultures as well as with dissident Western thinkers and make reference to philosophers like Bloch and Benjamin, as well as Aristotle and the philosophers of deep ecology. So what does this Buen Vivir consist of? The general principles can be summarized as follows:

Harmony and balance of all and with all. Complementarity, solidarity and equality. Collective well-being and the satisfaction of the basic needs of all in harmony with Mother Earth. Respect for the rights of Mother Earth and for human rights. Recognition of people for what they are and not for what they own. Removal of all forms of colonialism, imperialism and interventionism. Peace between people and with Mother Earth.

This is the very antithesis of the idea of consumerist well-being—which is largely focused on material possessions so that people can organize themselves within a status hierarchy over and above others. One is reminded of the book by Wilkinson and Pickett, *The Spirit Level,* which shows clearly that well-being and health is directly correlated with the degree of equality in a society. Social harmony is important to Good Life, and is enhanced by greater connection with nature.

## THE RIGHTS OF THE EARTH

Let us now turn to the rights of Mother Earth, or Pachamama. It was on the basis of the rights of Mother Earth that the Bolivian government rejected the Copenhagen compromise and then went on to organize their own conference in Cochabamba where they put forward and agreed a Charter for the Rights of Mother Earth in 2010. To understand Pachamama properly one has to understand "Pacha" as a key concept for cultures in the Andes. It is an ambiguous concept that refers to the totality of being. It includes not only space and time but also forms of life that transcend space and time. "Pacha is not only time and space, it is the ability to have an active participation in the universe, to immerse in it, to be in it. Manqhapacha is the telluric (earth related) dimension of the Pacha, it relates to the inner earth as the origin," Thomas Fatheuer writes. Indigenous people not only do *not* see the earth as a resource store that belongs to them—they see themselves as part of the earth, they are walking and living pieces of the earth. They do not have an anthropocentric world view with humans as the peak of creation and its owner—their view is nature-centric with humans as participants and parts in this world. According to the Cochabamba Convention of April 22, 2010, the following rights of Mother Earth were suggested:

The right to life and to existence. The right to be respected. The right to continue its cycles and life processes free from damage caused by humans. The right to protection of its identity and integrity as a diverse, self directed and interrelated being. The right to water as the source of life. The right to clean air. The right to all around health. The right to freedom from contamination and pollution by toxic and radioactive wastes. The right not to be impaired by genetic modification or having its structure modified, which would threaten its life and health functions. The right to speedy and complete rescission of human activities which breach the principles of the declaration.

This is not sustainable development, nor can it even be described as designing and arguing for a green economy. Neither is it the same as putting decarbonizing the economy into focus as a central aim. It puts into question all our European concepts of modernity in which nature is "out there" as an external store of resources and a sink available for human use. This is a different voice, coming from a different cultural viewpoint outside the Western tradition. This civilization paradigm, with its assumed superiority, is now challenged.

## RESISTING THE PRESSURE TO EXPLOIT
But what of the practice? Ecuador and Bolivia have been making their own path in South America but they have not been able to completely sever themselves from the processes of capitalist development. Both Alberto Acosta and Elisa Vega explained how hard it was in practice to oppose the priorities and pressure of global economic forces. Global economic stresses are experienced in their countries as a drive to open up to exploitation for mining and energy interests they said. And as Thomas Fatheuer argues, it is an irony of history that it turns out to be Bolivia of all places that has the world's greatest reserves of lithium, a strategic resource of the future—necessary for batteries for mobile phones and electric cars. The temptation to mine is overwhelming. When the Bolivian government negotiates with Japanese interests for a strategic economic partnership it is reproducing another form of what was repeatedly called "extractionist economics" in the Beyond Growth congress. It remains to be seen how this will work itself out. There are dangers of Buen Vivir being

pressured into a compromise of Buen Vivir Lite. There are also some economic models to discourage the easy-money pressure of resource extraction in developing countries, but they would involve richer nations taking an economic hit. An example in tune with Buen Vivir principles is whether to open up exploitation of oil reserves in the Yasuni area of Ecuador, which is part of the rainforest and has a high level of biodiversity. Alberto Acosta has suggested that Ecuador leave the oil in the ground and be compensated by rich countries for doing that—however at a price much under the world price for oil. So far no developed nations have shown a willingness to take up the offer. What I took from this discussion was the need to stop assuming that development is either necessary or that it is what everyone naturally wants—including people in poor communities. Perhaps especially in many poor communities. I recall a description of how in Ireland the people living on the west coast adjacent to the Corrib gas field rejected onshore development even though they were offered a lot of money. The truth is, and this was also expressed by Vandana Shiva, most development leads to the expropriation of poor people, poisoning of their living environment, immense suffering and precarious alternative forms of employment—with the benefits going to a smaller group and the corporate elite.

## ECOLOGY AND SOCIALISM UNITE
For many of the left-wingers who attended the Beyond Growth Conference, the problem of growth is a problem of capitalism in so far as capital is driven by competition and profit maximization to continually increase monetary valuations for the owners of the economy. As a simplification one might even say: Of course the left would be against growth because growth means more capitalism, with all its effects. But this then raises the issue of what a valid alternative might look like. I did not notice anyone here arguing for the ideas that were in circulation a few decades ago—a centrally planned economy, whether led by a party hierarchy or under some form of worker control. If Buen Vivir was part of a discussion about the alternative vision for society beyond growth (a vision clearly needing adaption to conditions in the industrial countries) what are the alternative means of delivery for a post-growth and therefore, for the left, a postcapitalist economy? For many here the buzz term was Solidarity Economy.

## ENDGAME OPTIMISM

But what of the state? What chance is there for meaningful top-down change? What can be gained from political engagement and activity? There was much talk of the need for democratization to facilitate the post growth economy and to support its new and emerging arrangements. However there was also great skepticism for how much can be achieved at this time. The grip of big corporate lobby interests over politics at national and European level is simply too great. This is important to consider when evaluating green growth. Of course green growth is a corporate agenda. Its assumption is that state policies to promote clean technologies, improving the efficiency with which natural resources are used, can achieve a drastic decoupling whereby the consumption of natural resources and energy is reduced, even as the growth process continues. This was doubted because the state was simply not strong enough against corporate interests. As Tim Jackson from the UK said in this workshop, there is no doubt that relative decoupling can take place (reduction in resource use per unit of production) but absolute decoupling (a real reduction in resource use) requires falling production, and that requires a system change. Indeed most of the presenters here agreed that the problems we face are systemic—sometimes seeing systemic in Marxist terms, sometimes not. Whatever. There is no doubt that the state is part of the system too—bound in by the interests of big corporate groups—and in current conditions absolute decoupling is not going to happen. The state is a weak instrument for the kind of change that has to happen. It is a little better in the more democratic societies perhaps. But too weak nonetheless. In these circumstances where are we to see the possibilities for real change occurring? How do we get the necessary top-down to support the bottom up? My own view, expressed in the decoupling workshop, was to argue that systemic change from one system to another is a much more far-reaching process than the simple adoption of a policy. One way of looking at it is to compare it with the reconfiguration of a computer which must be switched off—and then on again—if reconfiguration is to take place. Perhaps the nearest that we will come to this will be the chaos caused by peak oil. I pointed out that a few months ago a department in the German army had produced a document that foresaw chaos because of peak oil—particularly the possibility that it would lead to a financial system collapse. I suggested the need to think about what program would be needed to prepare for the surviving of a switching off and on again—what political economic ecological program would help us start again in a very different direction toward a solidarity economy?

In the concluding session of the conference an ATTAC spokesman said he felt the discussion at this Beyond Growth congress had been much more positive than other events he had been to where there had been gloomy or alarming predictions of collapse. Collapse prophecies can put people off (though, at the beginning of the conference Niko Paech argued that we have to prepare people for what is to come). Perhaps we can and must combine both perspectives. A contraction is coming whether we like it or not. But by preparing we can shape what is to come, rather than being passive victims.

Perhaps we might even find that we are able to create a society in which Good Life is possible.

COLORGUARD
cheer

**Antidepressants Surge**

By BEN BEADON

Antidepressant use in America rose by nearly 400 percent over the past two decades, according to the US Center for Disease Control. From 1988 to 2008 the number of Americans on Selective Serotonin Reuptake Inhibitors (SSRIs) like Paxil, Prozac and Zoloft increased sharply, with one in ten Americans now taking the pills. Today, these drugs are the most widely prescribed class of medication to Americans between the ages of 18 and 44.

A Tunisian protestor mocks state police in 2011.

**THE HIGHEST FORM OF JIHAD IS TO SPEAK THE TRUTH IN THE FACE OF AN UNJUST RULER.**

—Saying of Prophet Muhammad

# 11

# TAREK EL DIWANY

# "MY CONVERSION TO ISLAMIC ECONOMICS"

Tarek El Diwany is a London-based financial
advisor and founder of Zest Advisory, LLP.
This story originally appeared in *People First
Economics*, published by New Internationalist.

I first applied for work in the City of London as a derivatives dealer in the late 1980s. Over casual chats I was informed that the City demanded a rare combination of intellect, eloquence and sharpness. Those in possession of this skill set would be rewarded handsomely, for the City was a place where talent was recognized, irrespective of age. So I was told, and it occurred to me that if I could succeed in this environment, then I would have proven my worth to the many doubting Thomases around me. A new Porsche 911 said so much more than mere words could.

Thus I acquiesced to the notion that success is measured by the amount of money that one earns. In the City I met many people who were fully committed to that notion, and who implemented it on a grand scale. Money was the sole measure of success. Make money, and you would be promoted. Fail to make money, and you would be sacked. Or moved to the training department. Financial products were invented and marketed not because they met a client need, but because they made an enormous profit for the bank or finance company. Research "stories" were told in order to sell financial securities that insiders wouldn't touch with a barge pole. Massive gambles were taken with billions worth of depositors' finds, while in the public the language of "prudent-banking" was dished out in solemn tones. Investment decisions were frequently made by people whose technical knowledge was shockingly poor, and sometimes for the flimsiest of reasons. "Shares were up ten after a good lunch," joked one of my bosses, and what a lunch it was!

I found that I was rather good at making money, although few of the financial theories that I had learned at university seemed to apply in my work. For example, the simplest of laws of supply and demand didn't seem to work with regard to City salaries. If there were one hundred applicants for each City job, why did the pay rates remain so obstinately high? If African countries were being told that good economic management meant running a balanced budget, why was it that the US and Britain, two of the most prosperous nations on earth, almost never ran a balanced budget? Even the cardinal rule of monetarism, that inflation could be reduced by raising the rate of interest, didn't make sense to me. The available data showed that a rise in interest rates actually had the opposite effect, by increasing the cost of mortgage repayments.

Despite my nagging doubts about the financial system, what eventually changed my perspective on the City were the attitudes and values that I encountered along the way. These undoubtedly rubbed off on me, but there comes a time when one is forced to make a choice between two ways of life. Clients were being treated as prey, when I wanted to treat them as human beings. Money had become a God, but I wanted to find out:

"Who is God? What does He expect of me?" This kind of talk was like death on the trading desk. It caused colleagues to go silent. Worse, it caused colleagues to stop ringing us.

Resigning one's post while at the top of the tree is almost unheard of in the City, but to do so in exchange for a career in Islamic finance was something that my colleagues found almost laughable. To me it offered the combination of ethics and profit that I had been looking for. For others, it represented an unacceptable interference by religion in the science of finance. Orthodox economists in particular liked to make that point. Religion was loaded with value judgments, they said, while economists dealt impartially with facts on the ground.

But such arguments overlooked the possibility that modern finance had itself become a religion. Here, the purpose of commercial activity was to maximize shareholder value, and the unit of measure was almost exclusively a monetary one. Stress, pollution, divorce and crime, all of these could be conveniently ignored when measuring Gross Domestic Product. In this manner, a monetarily rich but unhappy society was seen as better off than a monetarily poor but happy one. Was this not a massive value judgment for modern finance to make?

As a newly practicing Muslim I discovered that the purpose of life is to worship the Creator, and that life is merely a test to determine whether we can fulfill this purpose. Wealth is a means for worshiping the Creator, not an end in its own right. To make the accumulation of wealth an objective of life is to worship wealth instead of the Creator, and this is one of the most fundamental errors that a human being can make. However, as in any test, we have the freedom to make that error. We can follow the commands of the Creator or ignore them and go our own way.

The responsibilities that the Creator requires us to fulfill include many that are understood by both religious and secular minds. If people are free to murder or steal from one another, if the one who has wealth does not pay the wealth tax, if the one who has power does not dispense it with justice, then the whole of society suffers. For any individual to enjoy a right, she or he must shoulder a corresponding responsibility, and the surest way to destroy human rights is for individuals to shirk their human responsibilities.

Among the responsibilities required of mankind, one above all has been relegated in the modern age. This is the prohibition of usury and it is common to the three Abrahamic faiths. However, unlike murder or theft, the destructive impact of usury is not always obvious and this has sustained much debate on the topic over many centuries in both East and West. For the Islamic jurist, usury encompasses a variety of commercial practices of which the fee charged by a moneylender is but one. Deuteronomy prohibits usury among the Jews, and the Gospel of Luke advises Christians to "lend hoping for nothing thereby." Indeed, the only violent act of Jesus' ministry was to expel the usurers from the temple, and as recently as five hundred years ago those who profited from the act of lending money were committing a crime under English law.

Today, everything has changed. The one who was despised in centuries past is now our financial overlord, inhabiting the plushest of city boardrooms. This remarkable transformation could not have been achieved without a heavy dose of legal semantics. In Rome during the early thirteenth century, Hispanus termed "inter esse," that which "in between is." By the middle of the sixteenth century, Henry VIII permitted the charging of interest up to a rate of 10 percent. Thus began the fall of the Christian prohibition of usury. Henceforth, only the practice of charging "excessive" interest was to be proscribed.

The ability to practice usury was in olden times limited by the amount of gold or silver coins available to the moneylender. In the seventeenth century, a critical development in England largely removed this limiting factor. Here, early bankers took deposits of gold coins and in return issued paper receipts promising repayment on demand. In due course, merchants began to use the bankers' receipts in payment for goods and services. It was easier to hand over a paper receipt to a seller than to travel to the bank in order to withdraw coins first. This behavior allowed the bankers to dramatically enlarge their business as moneylenders because, from now on, when the public came to borrow money, the banker could lend them freshly printed paper receipts. This policy had one great advantage. Unlike gold, paper receipts could be manufactured at little or no cost. "The Bank hath benefit of interest on all moneys which it creates out of nothing," was how William Paterson, first Director of the Bank of England, put it in 1694. The more paper receipts bankers printed, the more loans they could make and the more interest they could earn. It was therefore 'in their interest' to create as much money as possible. But this policy had dire consequences for the rest of society. The more money that was issued into circulation, the more prices began to rise throughout the economy. And because every unit of paper money was issued under a loan contract. The indebtedness of society grew remorselessly over time. If a banker called in the paper loans, a vicious recession could easily result. The political power that this gave to the banks was not lost on President Andrew Jackson. In his farewell address of 1837, he accused the Bank of the United States of having done exactly this in an attempt to defeat his program on banking reform:

> The distress and alarm which pervaded and agitated the whole country when the Bank of the United States waged war upon the people in order to compel them to submit to its demands cannot be yet forgotten. The ruthless and unsparing temper with which whole cities and communities were oppressed, individuals impoverished and ruined, and a scene of cheerful prosperity suddenly changed into one of gloom and despondency to be indelibly impressed on the memory of the people of the United States. If such was its power in time of peace, what would it have been in a season of war, with an enemy at your doors? No nation but the free men [sic] of the United States could have come out victorious from such a contest; yet, if you had not conquered, the government would have passed from the hands of the many to the few, and this organized money power, from its secret conclave, would have dictated the choice of your highest officials and compelled you to make peace of war, as best suited their own wishes.

If the banking classes favored men of similar inclinations with their loans of newly created money, a small group of individuals could quickly and quietly amass great influence over the commercial and political life of the nation. Today, this is a reality that extends into media and academia with devastating consequences at the intellectual level. Financial newspapers hesitate to publish material that is hostile to their largest source of advertising revenue, and the huge volumes of research and commentary that pour forth from researchers in the banking sector are similarly slanted by financial pressures. From cradle to grave, the issues of money creation and usury therefore tend to remain in the background, disguised by a terminology that is impenetrable to the lay person. As John Kenneth Galbraith wrote in *Money Whence it Came, Where it Went*: "The study of money, above all other fields in economics, is the one in which complexity is used to disguise the truth or to evade the truth, not to reveal it."

Nations across the world have thereby come to accept that interest-based debt is a normal fact of economic life. For most in the paradoxically labeled "rich world," there is nothing dangerous or shameful in perpetual indebtedness. Our parents' advice to save for things that we want in life is now mocked as an old-fashioned delusion. Why save, when the desire to consume can be satisfied now? Materialist ideologies reinforce such attitudes substantially. If there is no afterlife, then surely we must try to enjoy this life as much as possible?

Yet the inexorable rise of debt makes the enjoyment of life a distant dream for much of humanity. In the poorer countries, the objective becomes mere survival, if necessary by dint of politically spiked loan agreements. In 1997, the United Nations Development Programme estimated that up to five million children die in Africa every year because of the pressures that debt service places upon national budgets. Tanzania and Uganda were among many whose debt service payments exceeded the entire national budget for healthcare. The consequences of developing country indebtedness are ecological in nature too. For example, the fastest deforesting countries in the world are among its most indebted, as rainforests are sacrificed in order to earn the foreign exchange that will pay off creditors in the rich countries.

The model of borrowing funds at interest in order to invest and generate profit has now accumulated a long track record of failure in dealing with such problems. A glance at IMF figures on developing country debt tells a story of ever-climbing debt levels over five decades.

Occupiers interrupt a JPMorgan Chase recruiting session at Yale University, Spring 2012.

As for aid, the entire package of assistance given by the developed countries to the developing world is typically less than a quarter of the debt service payments that flow in the opposite direction. The widely trumpeted Heavily Indebted Poor Countries (HIPC) program of debt relief promoted by the IMF and the World Bank in 1996 required widespread austerity budgets of the kind rarely implemented in the West, yet after more than a decade in operation only one nation out of forty-two had been removed from the list of HIPC countries.

Underlying all of these problems is the practice of usury. In Islam, it is seen as fundamentally wrong for a financier to make a profit from a client even when that client's business is failing. Instead, the financier must share both the profits and the losses of those finances, much like modern equity investors do. This simple requirement ties together the interests of financier and clients in a way that interest-based lending never can. When a financier can only make a profit if the client makes a profit, then financiers are much more careful about whom they finance. In interest-based finance, those who wish to obtain loan finance are often those who have the most collateral to offer, not those who have the best projects. Poor people with good business ideas therefore tend to stay poor under the interest-based system, precisely because they lack collateral and cannot therefore attract finance for their businesses.

The possibility of life without interest-based finance or money creation by a privileged elite is amply demonstrated by the history of Islamic empire. Here, profit-sharing, usury-free trade credit, charitable donation and zakat combined to fulfill the entire spectrum of society's needs. All of this was built upon the foundations of a commodity money system that held its purchasing power across centuries, where today's money cannot even hold its value across a single decade. Many of the great universities and hospitals of the Muslim world were funded by endowments, and

much of its transport infrastructure from zakat funds. The modern private finance initiative cannot compete with these method of financing. Interest charges typically devour at least a third of a project costing, with the result that today's infrastructure is a shadow of our former achievements. Just compare the flimsy modern extension to London's St. Pancras railway station with the beautiful original that John Betjeman helped save for the nation.

The fact that an alternative economic paradigm was once achieved in the Muslim world is a vital lesson for our time. It is therefore rather sad that instead of re-establishing that paradigm, modern Islamic financiers have rushed to adopt the institutional structures and product range of the interest-based world. Gone for now are the dreams of Islamic economists in the 1960s, who argued for a banking system that shared risk and reward with its clients. In its place we find an industry that camouflages interest-based loans with Islamic terminology and excuses its lack of vision by reference to the overarching realities of modern banking and finance.

The clients of banks, Islamic or otherwise, are not entirely passive actors in this tale of woe, for most of them adopted interest-based leverage as the basis of their business activities. Why would an entrepreneur who makes a 20 percent profit on funds invested want to share that profit with investors, if he can finance himself using a loan at 5 percent interest? And if borrowing $100 at 5 percent interest allows a company to make $20 profit, then why not borrow $100 million and make $20 million in profit?

The inevitable commercial consequence of this mentality is that firms borrow as much as possible. In doing so, they can swallow up much of the competition and dominate their sector of the market. Interest-based leverage largely explains the tendency towards large-scale business operations throughout much of the Western world today. Five supermarkets now control more than

75 percent of the British grocery trade, where fifty years ago thousands of independent retailers could be found competing with one another. In the fashion sector, although Dorothy Perkins, Burtons, BHS, Miss Selfridge, Top Man, Top Shop and Wallis compete for customers on many British high streets, this isn't quite the idyll of free market capitalism that first greets the eye. All of these shops are controlled by one retail tycoon, Philip Green, who lives his tax-free life in Monaco. In the construction sector the consequences of interest-based leverage are even more obvious. The beautiful towns and villages of yesteryear are being replaced with the anonymous housing estates that emanate from the drawing boards of massive corporations and bank mortgage departments. Housing has become a means not for building a community, but for extracting wealth from it. Thus, the financial resources that used to go towards making our buildings beautiful, now go to paying the interest charges and dividends of a few large corporations.

As independent owner-managed businesses decline in importance, the number of employees at or near the minimum wage is increasing dramatically. This feature alone has devastating consequences in terms of customer service and job satisfaction, for the one who owns her or his business tends to care much more for it than the one who works on a low wage and shares none of its success. Conveniently for those who proclaim the victory of modern finance capitalism, the resulting decline of morale among millions of British workers appears nowhere in our headline statistics on economic performance.

The above are just some of the features of life under the interest-based financial system. We should not have to live like this, but one small example from my own professional experience helps to demonstrate why we do. Some years ago our firm helped to develop and launch a radical new home-purchase scheme in Britain. It is based on a partnership arrangement in which a prospective home-buyer and financier together purchase a property as partners.

The home-buyer may then occupy the property as a tenant, but can instead elect to rent the property to a third party. Both partners share any rental income and any capital gains or losses on the property price, in line with their partnership ratios, and the home-buyer may from time to time buy portions of the property from the financier at market value. In this scheme, the home-buyer is never in debt for she or he has not borrowed money nor is required to buy the financier's share of the property. "Negative equity," repossession and sleepless nights are a thing of the past under this approach to home finance. When we launched our product in London during 2005, we did so in the hope that it could be part of a wider solution for the reduction of household debt. Alas, we were met by a wall of silence from British financial institutions. Bankers, lawyers, consultants, brokers and property dealers, all were dipping their snouts in the trough of easy credit and were in no mood to adopt an alternative model of home finance. In this business, profits came from debt expansion, not debt reduction. This is precisely why those who have helped create the credit crisis should not be charged with finding a solution. To do so is to place the fox in charge of the chicken run.

As of late March 2009, trillions of newly created money have been fed to the banking industry in just a few months. It may prove hard to withdraw this money from circulation at a later date, in which case a historic hyperinflation is likely to ensue. This in turn will place the Western world but a few steps from dictatorship and war. It would be a brave person who bets against a financial establishment with a three hundred-year track record of survival, but if the interest-based monetary system is sustained it will be the cause of still greater crises and suffering in generations to come. Replacing it is therefore the critical struggle of our time.

It is not a system we can reform.

We must simply defeat it, because if we don't, it will defeat us.

Goldman ~~Sachs~~ *Viagra*

# Asset Management

You never stop growing.™

ASK YOUR PROFESSOR:

Retiring well means different t
Which is why millions of mutua
help their dreams come true. T

**Should we slow down
fast money with a
Robin Hood Tax?**

but
r stra
sor a

HARVARD BUSINESS REVIEW, JAN/FEB 2011

Indian laborers nap during a lunch
break at a workshop in Mumbai, India.

ASK YOUR PROFESSOR:

**Why is there nothing about Islamic economics in our curriculum?**

WE ARE HERE

V.

BIRTH       OF

BI

# CHAPTER FIVE

# A NEW SCIENCE
# NOMICS

## Hey you outliers & world changers out there,

Five hundred years ago astronomers following Ptolemy's geocentric model of the universe were tearing their hair out trying to make sense of all their calculations of the sun, moon and stars moving around above us in the night sky. It was only when Copernicus pointed out that we are not the center of the universe—the sun does not revolve around the Earth but rather the other way around—that all their convoluted calculations fell magically into place.

Today something eerily similar is happening in the science of economics: Economists and lay people alike are realizing that our human money economy is a subset of the Earth's larger bioeconomy and not the other way around.

This shift in perspective changes everything … it invites us to see the world with new eyes … to value things differently … to rethink growth … to redefine progress and how it is measured. Above all, it opens the door to a whole new mix of exciting economic policy alternatives for nations, businesses and individuals to pursue.

## NEOCLASSICAL PARADIGM

Earth as a subsystem of the human economy

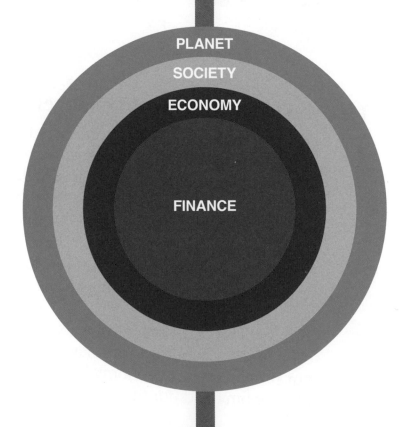

PLANET

SOCIETY

ECONOMY

FINANCE

## ECOLOGICAL PARADIGM

Human economy as a subset of the Earth's bioeconomy

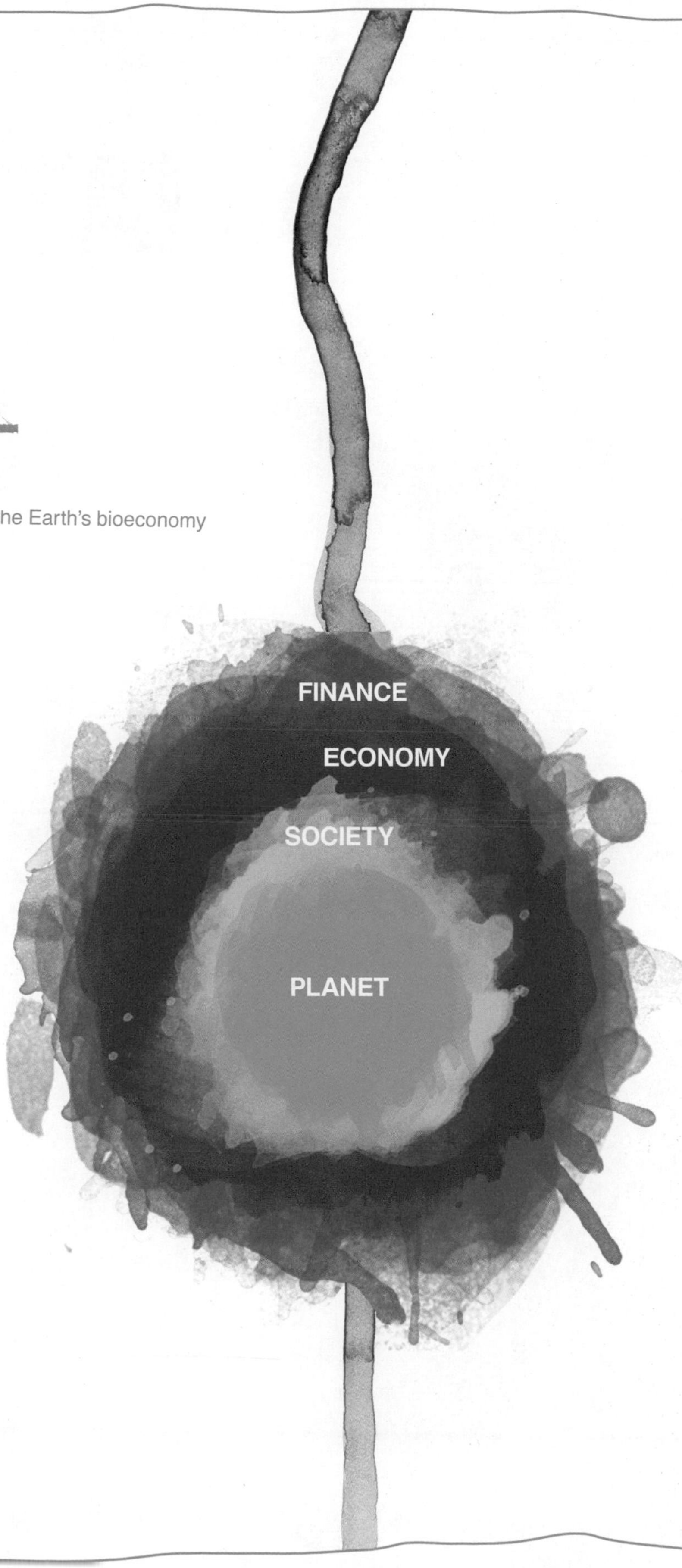

FINANCE

ECONOMY

SOCIETY

PLANET

NATURAL

# CAPITAL

After eons spent at the mercy of plagues, famines, storms and other savage acts of nature, a growing sense of human prowess—along with a seemingly inexhaustible endowment of resources—strengthened the conviction that humanity's story could now be written largely independent of the natural world.

Economics has embraced this radical worldview with gusto. When spikes in population and technological power raised concerns about resource scarcity, economists confidently predicted that free markets would prompt more efficient production and consumption. Nature, they assured us, would not be a roadblock to human progress. In the 1970s, Nobel economist Robert Solow made the claim (since recanted) that "the world can, in effect, get along without natural resources." Even today, most economics textbooks fail to take nature into account.

Economics can no longer pretend to operate independently of nature: Humanity's footprint now exceeds the Earth's ability to sustain it. The overshoot is especially high in wealthier countries. Industrial economies survive by dipping ever more deeply into reserves of forests, groundwater, atmospheric space and other natural resources—a practice that cannot be sustained.

In the same way that the Industrial Revolution saw factories, machines and other forms of manufactured capital replace land as the principle drivers of wealth production, "natural capital" is now vital to economic advance. Declines in oceanic fish yields, for example, are often caused by the growing scarcity of fish stocks (natural capital) rather than by a lack of fishing boats (manufactured capital). Modern fishing practices now overpower nature's ability to replenish the oceans.

Over the past twenty years the honeybee population has decreased by 30 percent. Though there is some element of mystery surrounding the precipitous decline, scientists are sure of one thing: Farmers' increased dependence on the use of toxic pesticides is threatening the survival of the very creature that pollinates their crops. Bees generate $19 billion a year through their work pollinating over ninety varieties of crops in North America alone, and scientists warn that there is no manufactured capital (technology) that can perform bees' vital function. If bee populations continue to decline, so will our ability to replenish the food supply.

If the planet as we know it is to survive and our story is to continue, we need to start taking natural capital into account. Indeed, in this moment of environmental crisis, we must subjugate our role to the momentous complexity and importance of the natural world.

Adapted from *State of the World 2008*, worldwatch.org.

Hand pollination of apple blossoms in Nepal. Bees in Maoxin County, at the border between China and Nepal, are now extinct, forcing people to pollinate apple trees by hand. It takes twenty to twenty-five people to pollinate one hundred trees, a task that can be performed by just two bee colonies.

**ASK YOUR PROFESSOR:**

Why are we selling off our planet's natural capital—the oil, fish, forests and minerals—and calling it income? Isn't this the most stupid of all mistakes that a planetary household manager can make?

# ECOSYSTEM SERVICES

If the bee disappeared off the surface of the globe then man would only have four years of life left. No more bees, no more pollination, no more plants, no more animals, no more man.

Albert Einstein

# ROBERT COSTANZA

## "THE ECONOMIES OF THE EARTH WOULD GRIND TO A HALT WITHOUT THE SERVICES OF ECOLOGICAL LIFE-SUPPORT SYSTEMS ..."

Dr. Robert Costanza is a professor at the Institute for Sustainable Solutions at Portland State University. Before PSU, he was the Gordon and Lulie Gund Professor of Ecological Economics and director of the Gund Institute for Ecological Economics at the University of Vermont.

What would the price tag on water be if every drop was engineered in a laboratory? Where would human waste go without the sinks the environment provides free of charge? Who would foot the bill for pollinating the millions of Earth's crops if bee populations suddenly disappeared? Until the 1990s questions like these were relegated to cultural studies, environmentalist propaganda and nature poems, not economics. The work of environmental economist Robert Costanza changed all that.

In 1997 Costanza and a team of researchers at the University of Vermont's Gund Institute released their landmark paper "The Value of the World's Ecosystem Services and Natural Capital" in the science journal *Nature*. In it they argued that Earth provides seventeen key ecosystems services—natural benefits to human welfare—at zero cost. Things like soil formation, climate regulation, water treatment, food production, waste treatment, nutrient cycling, raw materials, genetic resources, erosion control, recreation and human habitat would cost trillions if they had to come out of pocket.

"If ecosystem services were actually paid for, in terms of their value contribution to the global economy, the global price system would be very different from what it is today," Costanza says.

After scouring a global network of environmental data, Costanza and his colleagues estimated the value of Earth's services at 33 trillion US, twice the world GDP at the time. More importantly, their work highlighted that these line items are absent on the ledgers of the world economy. If Earth were a company, Costanza famously quipped, "we would definitely fire the CEO." In economical terms, the loss of these services would spark a financial meltdown unparalleled in modern history.

"Because ecosystem services are not fully 'captured' in commercial markets or adequately quantified in terms comparable with economic services and manufactured capital, they are often given little weight in policy decisions. This neglect may ultimately compromise the sustainability of humans in the biosphere," Costanza asserts.

Some environmentalists say there is a danger in quantifying nature because it could lead to further marketization of natural resources. Opponents in the neoclassical camp suggest that Earth's systems, though metaphysically valuable, remain valueless until mixed with human technology, and that equating environmental services to human services would cripple the economy. Despite opposition, this idea of ecosystem services is steadily gaining scientific and economic traction around the globe. It now figures prominently in UN Environment Programme reports and in international governmental debates about subsidizing developing nations to not exploit essential global ecological capital like rainforests and watersheds. This new way of valuing the Earth is a key concept in the emerging discipline of bioeconomics.

Darren Fleet

OVERSHOOT

In rich countries like Australia, consumption, resource use and ecological impact are so profoundly beyond sustainable levels that if our lifestyle were extended to all people, the Earth would tank in a single generation. Yet the supreme goal of almost every country is to increase material living standards, GDP, production, consumption, investment and trade as fast as possible; to mimic the model countries like mine established. There is no element in our suicidal condition that is more dangerous than this mindless obsession with accelerating the main factor causing our destruction.

The following points drive home the magnitude of our overshoot.

— If the nine billion people we will have on Earth within about fifty years were to use resources at the per capita rate of the rich countries, annual resource production would have to be about eight times as great as it is now.

— If nine billion people were to have a North American diet we would need about 4.5 billion hectares of cropland, but there are only 1.4 billion hectares of cropland on the planet.

— Water resources are scarce and dwindling. What will the situation be if nine billion people try to use water as we in rich countries do, while the greenhouse problem reduces water resources?

— The world's fisheries are in serious trouble now, most of them overfished and in decline. What will happen if nine billion people try to eat fish at the rate Australians do now?

— Several minerals and other resources are likely to be very scarce soon, including gallium, indium and helium; there are worries about copper, zinc, silver and phosphorous.

— Oil and gas are likely to be in decline soon, and largely unavailable in the second half of the century. If nine billion people were to consume oil at the Australian per capita rate, world demand would be about five times as great as it is now. The seriousness of this is extreme, given the heavy dependence of our society on liquid fuels.

— Recent "Footprint" analysis indicates that it takes 8 hectares of productive land to provide water, energy, settlement area and food for one person living in Australia according to the World Wildlife Fund. So if nine billion people were to live as we do, about seventy-two billion hectares of productive land would be needed. But that is about ten times all the available productive land on the planet.

— The most disturbing argument has to do with the greenhouse problem. It is very likely that in order to stop the carbon content of the atmosphere rising to dangerous levels, $CO_2$ emissions will have to be totally eliminated by 2050, (maybe as early as 2030). Geo-sequestration can't enable this, if only because it can only capture about 85 percent of the 50 percent of emissions that come from stationary sources like power stations.

These kinds of figures make it abundantly clear that rich world material "living standards" are grossly unsustainable. We are living in ways impossible for all to share. We are not just a little beyond sustainable levels of resource consumption—we have overshot by a factor of five to ten. Few seem to realize the magnitude of the overshoot, nor therefore about the enormous reductions that must be made, and the forced contractions ahead.

**Ted Trainer**

# IS ECONOMIC PROGRESS

## KILLING The PLANET

On March 18, 1968, early in his presidential campaign, Senator Robert Kennedy, the brother of assassinated president John F. Kennedy, stepped to the podium at the University of Kansas. His words seem as appropriate today as they were then, and they are worth quoting at length:

# REDEFINING PROGRESS

David Batker is chief economist and executive director of Earth Economics. He completed his postgraduate work under famed economist Herman Daly. He has taught in the training department of the World Bank and has worked with Greenpeace International.

John De Graaf is an independent documentary producer. He has won three Emmys and over one hundred national and international awards for filmmaking. He is co-author of *Affluenza: The All-Consuming Epidemic* and is national coordinator of Take Back Your Time, an organization that challenges overwork and time-poverty in North America.

This excerpt is from their recent book: *What's the Economy For, Anyway?: Why It's Time to Stop Chasing Growth and Start Pursuing Happiness.*

" For too long we seem to have surrendered personal excellence and community value in the mere accumulation of material things. Our Gross National Product now is over $800 billion dollars a year, but that Gross National Product counts air pollution, and cigarette advertising, and ambulances to clear our highways of carnage. It counts special locks for our doors and the jails for people who break them. It counts the destruction of the redwoods and the loss of our natural wonder in chaotic sprawl. It counts napalm, and it counts nuclear warheads, and armored cars for the police to fight the riots in our cities. It counts Whitman's rifle and Speck's knives and the television programs which glorify violence in order to sell toys to our children. Yet, the Gross National Product does not allow for the health of our children, the quality of their education, or the joy of their play. It does not include the beauty of our poetry or the strength of our marriages, the intelligence of our public debate or the integrity of our public officials. It measures neither our wit nor our courage, neither our wisdom nor our learning, neither our compassion nor our devotion to our country. It measures everything in short except that which makes life worthwhile. And it can tell us everything about America except why we are proud that we are Americans. "

Only ten weeks later, after winning the California Democratic presidential primary, Senator Robert Kennedy was found dead, felled by an assassin's bullet. In the four decades since, hardly a single political leader has gone where Kennedy did not fear to tread. He was far ahead of his time, but he had zeroed in precisely on the problems with GNP and GDP. It counts as positive a lot of things that make our lives worse, and it doesn't count at all so many things that make them better.

### What Counts in the GDP?

Here are some of the things that count positively toward the GDP:

Pollution. If groundwater is polluted, and we have to buy bottled water at a thousand times the price of tap water, the GDP rises. Because of enormous cleanup and legal costs, the oil belched by the BP *Deepwater Horizon* well in the Gulf of Mexico will contribute far more to the GDP than had that same oil actually made it to the refinery and been sold as gasoline, diesel, and other products. (The *Exxon Valdez* oil spill had a similar effect on the GNP two decades ago.) Cleaning oil off the beaches and wildlife can cost tens of thousands of dollars for every $100 barrel of oil cleaned up.

Crime. GDP increases as property loss claims arrive and people buy replacements for stolen goods. It increases as they install alarms and bars or hire guards. New prison construction, prison operating costs, and other crime costs all add to the GDP. We're actually better off with safe communities where such "defensive" expenditures are unnecessary. Crime requires defensive expenditures, which should be subtracted from the GDP. A recent Iowa State University analysis showed the social costs of a murder at $17.25 million.

Health Damage. Another "defensive" expenditure includes many health care costs. For example, over 350 billion cigarettes were sold in the United States in 2006, adding to the GDP. During the same year over $10 billion was spent treating lung cancer in the United States, which also added to the GDP. Instead of subtracting the cost of smoking-related cancer, the GDP treats it all as a positive benefit, the same as wheat production.

**ASK YOUR PROFESSOR:**

**How do you measure progress? How do you know if we're going forward or backward?**

Family breakdown. Divorce may not be good for families, but it is good for the GDP. A divorce can cost anywhere from $7,000 to $100,000. That total usually includes the lawyer's fees, the establishment of separate households and often the cost of therapy.

Debt, foreclosure and bankruptcy. When people or the government borrow too much and personal or national debt rises unsustainably, the GDP climbs. Even bankruptcies and foreclosures count positively in the GDP, since they incur legal costs, moving expenses, and replacement of lost housing or possessions. The average bankruptcy cost in 2010 was between $700 and $4,000, and with an estimated 1.5 million Americans declaring bankruptcy that year, it adds up.

Paper transfers and bursting bubbles. New "financial products," such as derivatives and credit default swaps, were at the heart of the 2008 financial crisis, driving worldwide recession. These "products" count highly positively in the GDP because they increase the incomes of insurance companies and investment banks. Yet their value can just as suddenly vanish, as happened in 2008 when packages of subprime loans suddenly had no buyers. The financial services account was the fastest growing part of the GDP, as income from the sales of bundled mortgages and derivatives ballooned. Such bubbles are seen as great economic successes when they should more properly be measured as harbingers of disaster. American International Group's (AIG) income from selling credit default swaps soared in 2006 to hundreds of millions of dollars adding to the GDP. By 2009 the company had lost over $61 billion due to the same credit default swaps. Even the Bureau of Economic Analysis (BEA) is considering changes.

Increasing scarcity. Depletion of natural resources is a cost to future generations. Yet scarcity is often reflected positively in the GDP. For example, as US and global oil reserves have been depleted, gas prices have risen, increasing the GDP even while raiding the wallet of anyone with a gas tank to fill. The GDP gives no clue as to whether the rise in the final market sales value is due to scarcity, productivity or market manipulation. Paying four dollars for a gallon of gasoline at the pump adds twice as much to the GDP as paying two dollars per gallon. Sure feels good adding more to the GDP.

Risk. The GDP does not take into account the risk of catastrophic costs. Retail electricity sold from nuclear power plants counts positively in the GDP. Expenditures attempting to minimize or clean up the Fukushima nuclear disaster also count positively. Due to the tremendous longevity of deadly nuclear isotopes, such as plutonium, the Environmental Protection Agency ruled that nuclear waste must be safely contained for one million years.

Now, consider a few important things that the GDP does not count:

Nature. Natural resources are the basis for many of our most productive economic assets. Seattle's drinking water, for example, is filtered by the forest of the upper Cedar River watershed. Its quality far exceeds drinkability standards. This saves the city $200 million in costs for a needless filtration plant. The valuable service of natural water filtration does not count in the GDP. But building a filtration plant and raising water prices to pay for it would count. Building a levee for New Orleans counts, but the greater value of hurricane protection provided by natural coastal wetlands does not. Buying a boat to catch fish counts. The habitat that produces the fish does not count. The obvious economic goods and services that nature provides every year to Americans do not count in the GDP.

Sustainability. The GDP says nothing about sustainability and does not discern whether activities contributing to the GDP are sustainable. The Atlantic cod fishery was the world's largest food fishery for over five hundred years. A few decades of overfishing caused the fishery to collapse. Overfishing counted more positively in the GDP in a single year than fishing at a lower sustainable rate. The GDP is incapable of distinguishing between the unsustainable demolition of a fishery and a sustainably managed fishery, such as the Alaskan salmon fishery.

Exercise. We all know it's good for our health, but it only counts if we pay to go to the gym or otherwise spend money. That daily walk we try to take may be good for our health, but it's a waste of time as far as the GDP is concerned.

Social connection. It's the most important thing we can do to be healthy and happy. But unless money is spent, friends and family are also a waste of time. The time Dave and John spend with their sons contributes nothing to the GDP. Unless they are buying the kids something. That counts.

Volunteering. It's the glue that holds communities together, and it will be increasingly important as budgets

for social services tighten. But if it's unpaid, it counts for nothing. It's just another GDP waste of time.

Housework. Domestic work isn't counted, as least not by the GDP. Hire a nanny; that counts. Hire a maid; that too. Hire a gardener or a carpenter; you're contributing to the GDP. Do it yourself, and you're slacking in your duties to our nation's preeminent measurement.

Price and quantity effects. The GDP does not separate between price effects and quantity effects. For example, if a company doubles the price of a car, it shows up in the GDP just as it would if the company built and sold two cars at the former price. This means the GDP is deeply flawed even as a measure of production, its original purpose.

Quality. One of the long-standing critiques of the GDP was the lack of quality adjustment. Without adjusting for quality improvements, the GDP overvalues lower quality higher priced goods and undervalues goods of higher quality and better performance. The dumber, slower, more expensive computer added more to the GDP than a smarter, faster, cheaper computer. Recently, the BEA implemented corrections for quality improvements for some goods including computers, software, and in 2011, communications equipment. This is done using a quality-adjusted price index calculated by the Federal Reserve Board. Yet for the vast majority of goods and services, quality improvements, which benefit both producers and consumers, still reduce GDP.

Just imagine you're stuck in a traffic jam, burning gas and choking on exhaust, requiring you to pull off and fill up the tank. The traffic jam has added to the GDP. If you got into a wreck, totaling your car and increasing the cost of your insurance while the wreck caused an even bigger traffic jam for everyone else, the GDP would rise even more. And if you were injured in the wreck and sent to the hospital for weeks of recovery, the GDP would rise still higher. And if you'd had an expensive divorce that morning, and your house burned down that evening, requiring legal fees, insurance claims and more new purchases, you would have had a completely stellar GDP day! Congratulations!

**FOLLOW-UP QUESTION:**

**If economists don't know how to measure progress, on what basis do they give policy advice to governments?**

Hey **you sleepwalkers out there,**

Man should fill his stomach with food one-third, water one-third, leaving the other one-third empty. *-Islamic saying*

What is the real cost of shipping a container load of toys from Hong Kong to Los Angeles? Or a case of apples grown in New Zealand to markets in North America? And what is the true cost of that fridge humming 24/7 in your kitchen ... that steak sizzling on your grill ... that car sitting in your garage?

Practically every one of the products we buy in the global marketplace is grossly undervalued. This is primarily because the environmental and corresponding social costs haven't been taken into account. Mass production drives per unit cost down well enough, but the cost of a sane and sustainable future is going up. Every one of the billions of purchases we make every day in the global marketplace pushes us a little deeper into the cosmic red.

**But what if we were to implement this simple idea: True cost?**

We calculate the hidden price associated with products—what the economists nonchalantly refer to as externalities—and incorporate them. We force the cost of every product in the global marketplace to tell the ecological truth.

We start with the little things: Plastic bags, coffee cups, paper napkins. Economists calculate these eco costs—say it's five cents per plastic bag, ten cents per cup and one cent per napkin—then we just tack that on. We're already doing that with the various eco-fees and eco-taxes included in the price of tires, cans of paint and other products. But now we abandon the concept of ancillary fees and taxes and implement straight true-cost pricing.

Over a ten-year period, we phase in true-cost eating. We raise the price of avocados from Mexico and shrimp from China to reflect the true cost of transporting them long distances. And we estimate and add on all the hidden costs of our industrial farming and food processing systems. That burger at McDonald's will cost you more—so will most meats, produce and processed foods. You can eat whatever you want, but you'll have to pay the true cost. Inevitably, your palate will submit to your wallet. Processed, mega-farmed and imported foods become more expensive as the cost of organic and locally produced food goes down. Bit by bit, purchase by purchase, the global food system heaves toward sustainability.

Then we phase in the true cost of driving. We add on the environmental cost of the carbon our cars emit, the cost of building and maintaining roads, the medical costs of accidents, the noise and the aesthetic degradation caused by urban sprawl and maybe even the military cost of protecting those crucial oil fields and oil tanker supply lines. Your private automobile will cost you around $100,000 and a tank of gas $250. You're still free to drive all you want, but instead of passing the costs on to future generations or innocent people halfway across the globe, you pay upfront. This is not a world where only the über-rich enjoy the spoils of elite products—quite the opposite. With such little demand for inefficient and polluting transport, we're forced to reinvent the way we get around. Demand for monorails, bullet trains, subways and streetcars would surge. We would demand more bike lanes and pedestrian paths and car-free urban centers. And gradually a paradigm shift in urban planning would transform urban life. Suddenly cities are built for people, not for automobiles. Parking lots disappear. Community gardens rise.

True-cost pricing is fraught with daunting, seemingly insurmountable problems. For conventional economists, it's a frightening, heretical concept that would slow growth, reduce the flow of world trade and curb consumption. It's so true that it must be false. It would force us to rethink just about every economic axiom we've taken for granted since the dawn of the industrial age. It could turn out to be one of the most traumatic economic/social/cultural projects that humanity has ever undertaken. And yet ... and yet ... the idea of a global marketplace in which the price of every product tells the ecological truth has a simple, almost magical ring to it. It makes sense, it feels right and it's totally nonpolitical. It's the one big idea that—if we are able to agree on it, implement it and muster the collective self-discipline to sustain it—could pull us out of the ecological tailspin we're in and nudge this failing experiment of ours on Planet Earth back onto the rails.

# WHAT IS THE TRUE COST OF
# A HALF-HOUR TRAFFIC JAM?

What is the ecological cost of clogging up a freeway system
for half an hour? Who foots the bill for the millions of autos
burning gas, diesel and kilowatts as they wait trapped in
traffic? You might say it's only the individuals watching their gas
tanks, but that would be wrong. The initial personal sacrifice
of time spent in gridlock is only a fraction of the cost. Untaxed
carbon emissions, environmental damage, respiratory illness,
deteriorating roads, extra emergency services hours, loss of
workplace production and business paralysis—these are a few
of the externalities left off the books. And then there are the
social costs. A recent Swedish study found that a daily commute
to work of forty-five minutes or longer increases an individual's
chance of divorce by 40 percent. Is your commute worth the

Print all entries • Use ballpoint pen • Press hard

# DEPARTMENT OF MOTOR VEHICLES

ES 00367930 4

# VIOLATION NOTICE

| DATE OF INFRACTION | TIME OF INFRACTION | LOCATION OF INFRACTION |
| VEHICLE MAKE | VEHICLE LICENSE NO. | METER NO. |
| STREET ADDRESS | CITY | PROV/STATE |

## VEHICLE INFRACTION

This form of transport incurs economic costs on the city which have not been included in the retail price. Your operation of this vehicle makes you personally liable for the following:

| Climate change | Conflict over oil |
| Depletion of non-renewable resources | Environmental clean up costs |
| Time wasted in gridlock | Hindering bicycle and pedestrian activities |
| Noise pollution | Smog-related health problems |

**THE FOLLOWING WAS USED TO CALCULATE YOUR FINE:**

| Average cost of an automobile if the social and environmental costs were added to the sticker price | $70,413 * |
| Average cost of a new automobile to consumer — | $28,050 |
| **YOUR FINE** = | **$42,363** |

**THIS CAN BE PAID IN THE FOLLOWING FORM:**
A) By switching to another mode of transport such as public transit or bicycle, you stop draining the municipality of much needed public funds; in this case, your fine will be waived.
B) By financially supporting organizations which attempt to redress the economic damages your form of transport incurs; in this case, your fine will be waived.

**IF YOU DISPUTE THIS FINE, THE TRIAL WILL BE HELD IN YOUR OWN CONSCIENCE**

NOTE: FAILURE TO CHANGE OUR TRANSPORTATION HABITS MAY SUBJECT US ALL TO A GRIM FUTURE

* Source: Victoria Transport Policy Institute, Comerica Bank.

*Place under windshield wiper*

---

ES 00376230 4

IMPORTANT: PLEASE READ CAREFULLY

Consider the man on horseback, and I have been a man on horseback for most of my life. Well, mostly he is a good man, but there is a change in him as soon as he mounts. Every man on horseback is an arrogant man, however gentle he may be on foot. The man in the automobile is one thousand times as dangerous. I tell you, it will engender absolute selfishness in mankind if the driving of automobiles becomes common. It will breed violence on a scale never seen before. It will mark the end of the family as we know it, the three or four generations living happily in one home. It will destroy the sense of neighborhood and the true sense of Nation. It will create giant-ized cankers of cities, false opulence of suburbs, ruinized countryside, and unhealthy conglomerations of specialized farming and manufacturing. It will make every man a tyrant.

– R.A. Lafferty

Mr.Lafferty's testimonial was written in the late nineteenth century. His views were considered alarmist and foolish in his day.

*Place on an offending vehicle*

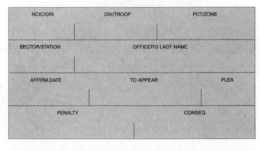

DO NOT WRITE BELOW THIS LINE

| NCIC/ORI | DIV/TROOP | PCT/ZONE |
| SECTOR/STATION | OFFICER'S LAST NAME | |
| AFFIRM.DATE | TO APPEAR | PLEA |
| PENALTY | CONSEQ | |

IF YOU DISPUTE THIS FINE, THE TRIAL WILL BE HELD IN YOUR OWN CONSCIENCE

---

cost of your marriage? Is it worth the cost of a divorce? Is your commute worth selling off tomorrow for the sake of breathing exhaust on a slow-moving highway today? To date, only a handful of economists have bothered to calculate costs like these. In a world where economic-speak is gospel, why are so many leading economists silent on our greatest inefficiencies? Let's figure it out … let's start understanding what the byproducts of our way of living are actually costing us and future generations … let's get economists to do some holistic work instead of pontificating about interest rates and Dow Jones swings at press conferences and on the daily news. Once we know what these social, economic and environmental costs are then we may actually start thinking differently about how we do things and live our lives.

# WHAT IS THE TRUE COST OF
# ONE CONTAINER MILE?

HOW CAN A THREE BY TEN INCH BOX OF CRACKERS
FROM PORTUGAL ONLY COST $1.50 AFTER BEING SENT
HALFWAY ACROSS THE OCEAN IN A FREIGHTER AND
THEN TRUCKED TO MY TOWN? I ASKED THE STORE
MANAGER AND HE DIDN'T KNOW EITHER.

**Manfred Max-Neef**

IT'S PRETTY AMAZING THAT
OUR SOCIETY HAS REACHED A POINT
WHERE THE EFFORT NECESSARY TO

EXTRACT OIL FROM THE GROUND
SHIP IT TO A REFINERY
TURN IT INTO PLASTIC
SHAPE IT APPROPRIATELY
TRUCK IT TO A STORE
BUY IT AND BRING IT HOME

IS CONSIDERED TO BE LESS EFFORT THAN WHAT IT TAKES
TO JUST WASH THE SPOON WHEN YOU'RE DONE WITH IT

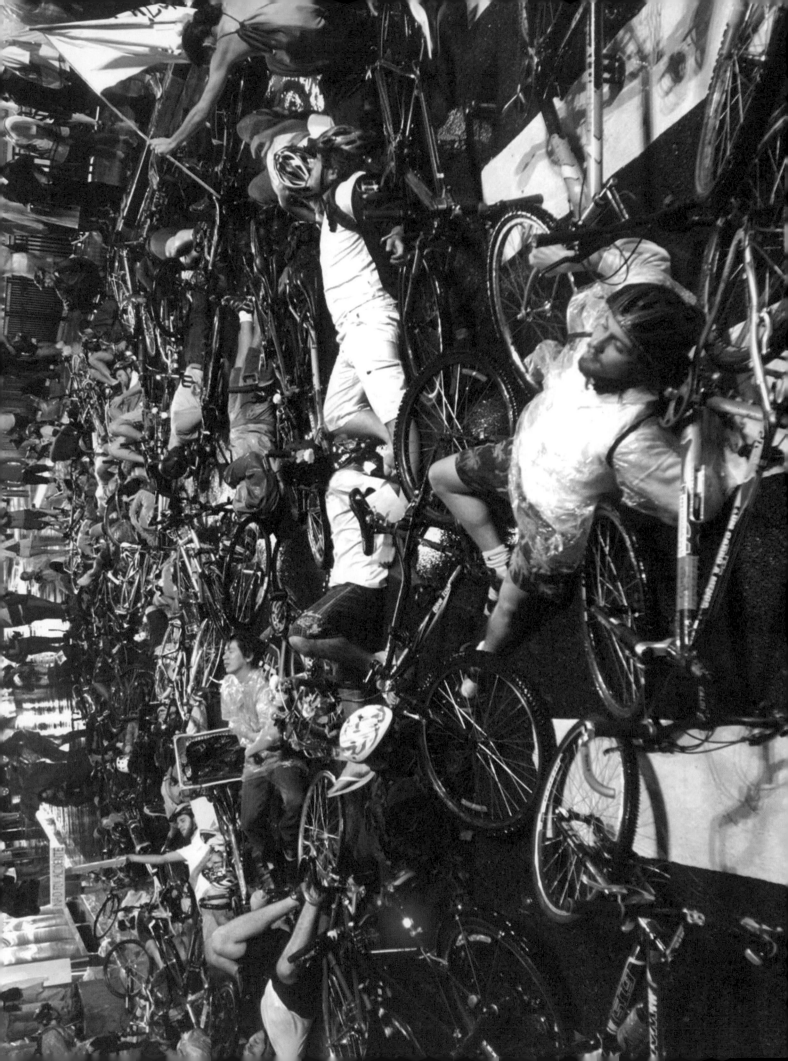

This is the project for
the next generation
of economists:

# To calculate and internalize all the costs of our way of doing business.

And then to create a global marketplace
in which the price of every product tells
the ecological truth.

CRT

RCIAL

RE

# PSYCHO

# NOMICS

# CHAPTER SIX

## Alright you pill poppers and anxiety wrecks out there,

An epidemic of mental illness is sweeping the globe. Could consumer capitalism be one of its root causes? Is advertising just a benign way of stimulating the economy or does this trillion dollar a year worldwide industry represent something more ominous for our economic and mental wellbeing? Could the nonstop noise and emotional blackmail—3,000 marketing messages injected into your brain every day whether you like it or not—be the source of the anxieties, mood disorders and depression so many of us suffer? What does your professor have to say?

Sitting at the center of economics right now is a pathetic parody of a human being called the "Rational Utility Maximizer" who runs around making perfectly predictable choices within perfectly functioning markets. This creature is never depressed, never sickened by pollution, never emotional, never a dreamy wanderer, never in love … but of course real human beings are not like that … we fly off on wild tangents, have altruistic impulses, do crazy things. We feel guilty when we overindulge, get depressed when we lose our jobs, seek revenge when people do us wrong … and we often refuse to buy something just because our values don't jibe with those of a corporation. And we routinely go against our "rational self-interest" by pulling off remarkable feats of compassion and teamwork. But such impulses fall outside today's standard model … Neoclassical economics has achieved its coherence as a science by amputating most of human nature.

An interdisciplinary groundswell is now bubbling up. Its goal: Put full-blooded human beings back into the driver's seat of economics. Its practitioners have stepped down from the ivory towers of perfect rationality, drawn inspiration from psychology, sociology, anthropology, mythology and neuroscience and started taking some baby steps into whole new worlds of emotion, social relations, empathy, religion, morality and virtue. These "psychonomists" have done their homework in the streets, in Zuccotti Park, in the slums and favelas of the world … they know what it feels like to go hungry, to lose a home, to not have enough money to pay for a life-saving drug. And they have come to a stunning conclusion: When the chips are down, cooperation rather than selfish interest is the key to survival. Out of this vital area of inquiry, a new branch of economics—a psychonomics—is being born.

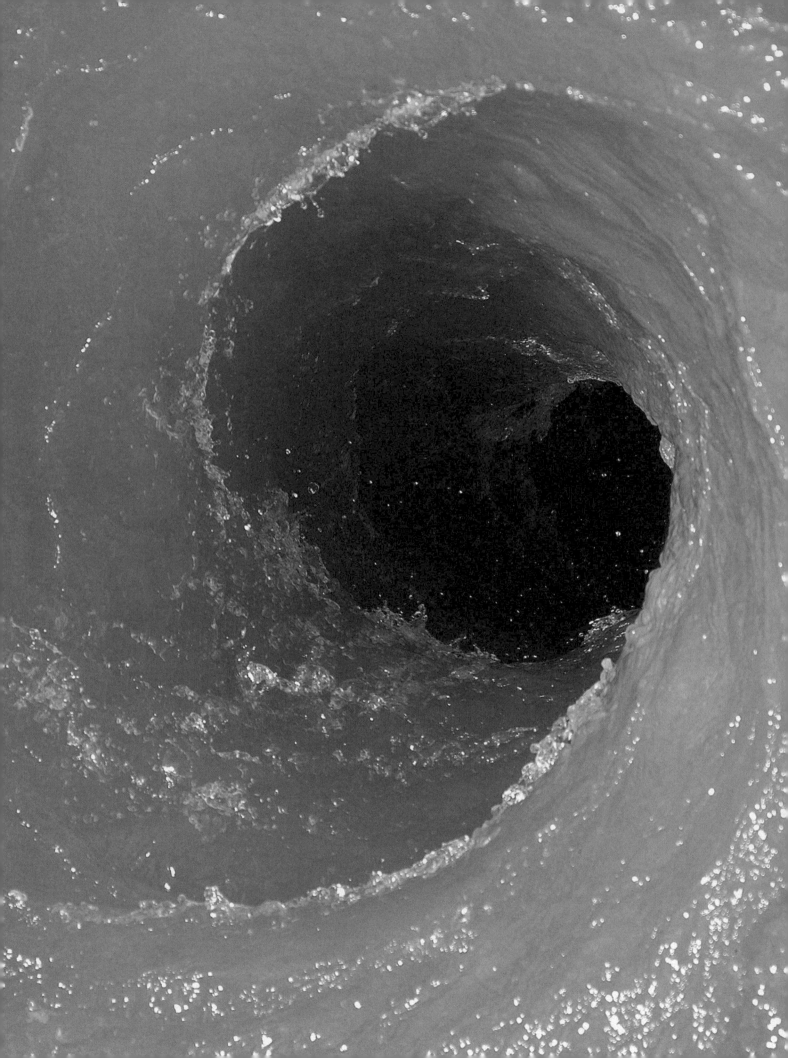

Climate disruption's assault on all we believed—endless progress, a stable future, our capacity to control the natural world with science and technology—will corrode the pillars that hold up the psyche of modern humanity. It will be physiologically destabilizing in a way exceeded in human history perhaps only by the shift to agriculture and the rise of industrial society. Already we find psychiatrists and psychologists issuing guidelines on how to respond to emotional and psychological distress associated with awareness of climate change, although the leading therapeutic recommendation of "be optimistic about the future" suggests that the mental health professionals have yet to grasp the seriousness of the threat posed by global warming. We can expect that, for a time, the loss of faith in the future and in our inability to control our lives will see a proliferation of mental disturbance characterized by depression, withdrawal and fearfulness.

MOOD DISORDERS

Clive Hamilton, *Requiem for a Species*

When you cut off arterial blood to an organ, the organ dies. When you cut the flow of nature into people's lives, their spirit dies. It's as simple as that.

WE ARE BLINDED ,
ENCHANTED AND FINALLY
ENSLAVED BY THE SPECTACLE.

*quiet space*

AVERAGE NUMBER OF ADS EXPOSED TO EACH DAY: 3000

ASK YOUR PROFESSOR:

How does the $1-trillion a year ad game factor into our study of economics?

THE PRO-DUCTION OF "FALSE IMAGES" IS A REQUIRE-MENT OF CAPITALISM

Olympic pole vaulter Tom Hintnaus posing for a Calvin Klein campaign, 1983. Photograph by Bruce Weber.

AD SPENDING PER PERSON
MAJOR MEDIA AD SPENDING PER CAPITA

| 1986 | | 2011 |
|---|---|---|
| | UNITED STATES | |
| $276 | | $498 |
| 9¢ | CHINA | $22 |
| $30 | WORLDWIDE | $67 |

BECAUSE YOU'RE WORTHLESS

For each and every one of us living in the so-called "Developed World," a very personal, almost Faustian dilemma presents itself: What's the point of living in one of the most advanced, dynamic and affluent nations on Earth if we're feeling stressed out and anxious all of the time? Have we gained our affluence, power and wealth at the price of—let's just say it—a piece of our soul? After thousands of years of struggling to survive, have we finally filled the hole in our stomachs, only to discover a new hole in our heads?

**ASK YOUR PROFESSOR:**

**What is the economic cost of the epidemic of mental illness now sweeping the globe?**

The rat-bastard Capitalist scum
who are telling you to
"reach out and touch someone"
with a telephone or "be there!" *(where? Alone in front of a goddam television?)* —
these lovecrafty suckers are
trying to turn you into
a scrunched-up,
blood-drained,
pathetic, crippled little cog
in the death-machine of the
human soul *(and lets not have any theological quibbles about what we mean by "soul"?)*. Fight them—
by meeting with friends,
not to consume or produce,
but to enjoy friendship—
and you will have triumphed *(at least for a moment)*
over the most pernicious conspiracy
in EuroAmerican society today—
the conspiracy to turn you into
a living corpse galvanized
by prosthesis and the
terror of scarcity—
to turn you into a spook
haunting your own brain.

Hakim Bey

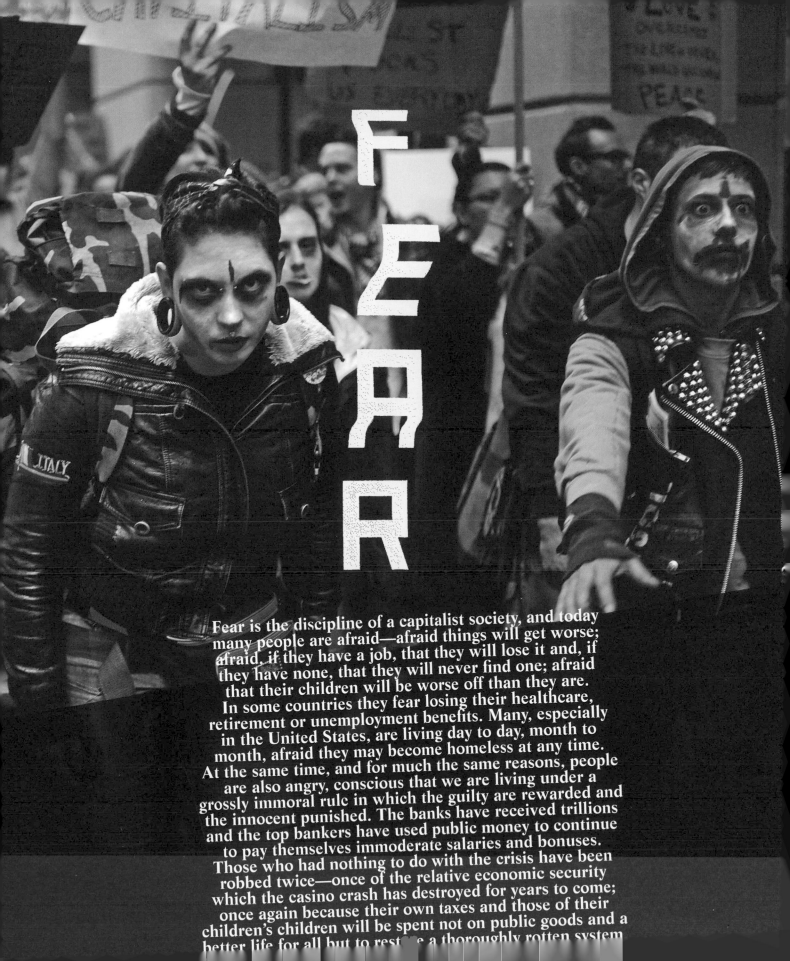

# FEAR

Fear is the discipline of a capitalist society, and today many people are afraid—afraid things will get worse; afraid, if they have a job, that they will lose it and, if they have none, that they will never find one; afraid that their children will be worse off than they are.

In some countries they fear losing their healthcare, retirement or unemployment benefits. Many, especially in the United States, are living day to day, month to month, afraid they may become homeless at any time.

At the same time, and for much the same reasons, people are also angry, conscious that we are living under a grossly immoral rule in which the guilty are rewarded and the innocent punished. The banks have received trillions and the top bankers have used public money to continue to pay themselves immoderate salaries and bonuses.

Those who had nothing to do with the crisis have been robbed twice—once of the relative economic security which the casino crash has destroyed for years to come; once again because their own taxes and those of their children's children will be spent not on public goods and a better life for all but to restore a thoroughly rotten system

# TIMOTHY MORTON

Timothy Morton is a key thinker in the emerging philosophical field of Object-Oriented Ontology. He is the author of *The Ecological Thought* (Harvard University Press, 2010), *Ecology without Nature* (Harvard University Press, 2007) and seven other books. He blogs regularly at ecologywithoutnature.blogspot.com.

# "WHAT IS LEFT? INTIMACY"

Nature is the featureless remainder at either end of the process of production. Either it's exploitable stuff, or value-added stuff. Whatever: It's basically featureless, abstract, gray. It has nothing to do with nematode worms or orangutans, organic chemicals in comets or rock strata. You can scour the Earth from the mountaintops to the Marianas Trench. You will never find Nature. That's why I put it in capitals. I want the reader to see that it's an empty category looking for something to fill it. Gray goo.

Capitalism did away with feudal and pre-feudal myths such as the divine hierarchy between classes of people. In so doing, however, it substituted one heck of a giant myth of its own: Nature. Nature is precisely the lump that preexists the capitalist labor process. Martin Heidegger has the best term for it: Standing reserve, Bestand.

Bestand means "stuff," as in the old ad from the 1990s, "Drink Pepsi: Get Stuff." There is an ontology implicit in capitalist production, then, that is strictly materialism as defined by Aristotle. Funnily enough, however, this materialism is not fascinated with material objects in all their manifold specificity. It's just stuff. This viewpoint is the basis of Aristotle's problem with materialism. Have you ever seen or handled matter? Have you ever held a piece of "stuff"? Sure, I've seen lots of objects: Santa Claus in a department store, snowflakes and photographs of atoms. But have I ever seen matter or stuff as such? Aristotle says it's a bit like searching through a zoo to find the "animal" rather than the various species such as monkeys and mynah birds. Marx says exactly the same thing regarding capital. "The 'expanded' form [of the commodity] passes into the 'general' form when some commodity is excluded, exempted from the collection of commodities, and thus appears as the general equivalent of all commodities, as the immediate embodiment of Commodity as such, as if, by the side of all real animals, there existed the Animal, the individual incarnation of the entire animal kingdom—or as if, to use an example from commercial capitalism, by the side of all real spices, there existed the Spice." As Nature goes, so goes matter. The two most progressive physical theories of our age, ecology and quantum theory, need have nothing to do with it.

What is bestand? Bestand is stockpiling. Gallon after gallon of oil waiting to be tapped. Row upon row of big box houses waiting to be inhabited. Terabyte after terabyte of memory waiting to be filled. Stockpiling is the art of the zeugma—the yoking of things you hear in phrases such as "wave upon wave" or "bumper to bumper." Stockpiling is the dominant mode of social existence. Giant parking lots empty of cars, huge tables in restaurants across which you can't hold hands, vast empty lawns. Nature is stockpiling. Range upon range of mountains, receding into the distance. The Rocky Flats nuclear bomb trigger factory was sited precisely to evoke this kind of mountainous stockpile. The eerie strangeness of this fact confronts us with the ways in which we still believe that Nature is "over there"—that it exists apart from technology, apart from history. Far from it. Nature is the stockpile of stockpiles.

So again, I ask, what exactly are we sustaining when we talk about sustainability? An intrinsically out of control system that sucks in gray goo at one end and pushes out gray value at the other. It's Natural goo, Natural value. Result? Mountain ranges of inertia, piling higher every year, while humans boil away in the agony of uncertainty. Just take a look at *Manufactured Landscapes*: The ocean of telephone dials, dials as far as the eye can see, somewhere in China. A real ocean—it lies there at this very moment.

Societies embody philosophies. Actually, what we have in modernity is much, much worse than just instrumentality. Here we must depart from Heidegger. What's worse is the location of essence in some beyond, away from any specific existence. To this extent, capitalism is itself Heideggerian! Whether we call it scientism, deconstruction, relationism or just good old-fashioned Platonic forms, there is no essence in what exists. Either the beyond is itself nonexistent (deconstruction, nihilism), or it's some kind of real away from "here." The problem, then, is not essentialism but this very notion of a beyond. Think of what Tony Hayward said. He said that the Gulf of Mexico was a huge ocean, and that the spill was tiny by comparison. Nature would absorb the industrial accident. I don't want to quibble about the relative size of ocean and spill, as if an even larger spill would somehow have gotten it into Hayward's thick head that it was bad news. I simply want to point out the metaphysics involved in Hayward's assertion, which we could call capitalist essentialism. The essence of reality is capital and Nature. Both exist in an ethereal beyond. Over here, where we live, is an oil spill. But don't worry. The beyond will take care of it.

Meanwhile, despite Nature, despite gray goo, real things writhe and smack into one another. Some leap out because industry malfunctions, or functions only too well. Oil bursts out of its ancient sinkhole and floods the Gulf of Mexico. Gamma rays shoot out of plutonium for 24,000 years. Hurricanes congeal out of massive storm systems, fed by the heat from the burning of fossil fuels. The ocean of telephone dials grows ever larger. Paradoxically, capitalism has unleashed myriad objects upon us, in their manifold horror and sparkling splendor. Two hundred years of idealism, two hundred years of seeing humans at the center of existence, and now the objects take revenge, terrifyingly huge, ancient, long-lived, threateningly minute, invading every cell in our body.

Modern life presents us with a choice:
1) The essence of things is elsewhere (in the deep structure of capital, the unconscious, Being).
2) There is no essence. (At present I believe that the restriction of rightness and coolness to this choice is one reason why planet Earth is in big trouble right now. And I believe that the choice resembles a choice between grayish brown and brownish gray). That's why I believe in a third choice:
3) There is an essence, and it's right here, in the object resplendent with its sensual qualities yet withdrawn.

And that's why I believe we are entering a new era of academic work, where the point will not be to one-up each other by appealing to the trace of the givenness of the openness of the clearing of the lighting of the being of the pencil. Thinking past "meta mode" will at least bring us up to speed with the weirdness of things, a weirdness that evolution, ecology, relativity and quantum theory all speak about. This weirdness resides on the side of objects themselves, not our interpretation of them.

When we flush the toilet, we imagine that the U-bend takes the waste away into some ontologically alien realm. Ecology is now beginning to tell us of something very different: A flattened world without ontological U-bends. A world in which there is no "away." Marx was partly wrong, then, when in *The Communist Manifesto* he claimed that in capitalism all that is solid melts into air. He didn't see how a kind of hypersolidity oozes back into the emptied out space of capitalism, a hypersolidity I call here hyperobjects. This oozing real comes back and can no longer be ignored, so that even when the spill is supposedly "gone and forgotten," there, look! There it is, mile upon mile of strands of oil just below the surface, square mile upon square mile of ooze floating at the bottom of the ocean. The cosmic U-bend is no more. It can't be gone and forgotten – even ABC News knows that now.

When I hear the word "sustainability" I reach for my sunscreen.

## THE END OF THE WORLD

When Neo touches a mirror in *The Matrix* it adheres to his hand, instantly changing from reflective surface to viscous substance. The very thing that we use to reflect becomes an object in its own right, liquid and dark like oil in the dim light of the room in which Neo has taken the red pill. The usual reading of this scene is that Neo's reality is dissolving. If we stay on the level of the sticky, oily mirror, however, we obtain an equally powerful reading. It's not reality that dissolves, but the subject, the very capacity to "mirror" things, to be separate from the world like someone looking at a reflection in a mirror – removed from it by an ontological sheet of reflective glass. The sticky mirror demonstrates the truth of what phenomenology calls ingenuousness or sincerity (I'm thinking here of the work of Ortega y Gasset, Levinas and Graham Harman). Objects are what they are, in the sense that no matter what we are aware of, or how, there it is, impossible to shake off. In the midst of irony, there you are, being ironic. Even mirrors are what they are, no matter what they reflect. In its ingenuous sincerity, reality envelops us like a film of oil. The mirror becomes a substance, an object. Hyperobjects push the reset button on sincerity, just as Neo discovers that the mirror no longer distances his image from him in a nice, aesthetically manageable way, but sticks to him.

The beautiful reversibility of the oily, melting mirror speaks to something that is happening in a global warming age, precisely because of hyperobjects: The simultaneous dissolution of reality and the overwhelming presence of hyperobjects, which stick to us, which are us. The Greeks called it miasma, the way blood-guilt sticks to you.

Why objects, why now? The philosopher Graham Harman writes that because they withdraw irreducibly, you can't even get closer to objects. This becomes clearer as we enter the ecological crisis— "How far in are we?" This anxiety is a symptom of the emergence of hyperobjects. When you approach them, more and more objects emerge. It's like being in a dream written by Zeno. This strange paradox becomes clearer as we enter the age of ecological crisis—"Has it started yet? How far in are we?" is the question on all our lips, precisely because we are in it, precisely because it has started.

It's November 2010. You are waiting at a bus stop. Someone else ambles up. "Nice weather, isn't it?" she asks.

You pause for a moment. You wonder whether she is only saying that to distract you from the latest news about global warming. You decide she isn't.

"Yes," you say. But your reply holds something back— the awareness that for you it's not a particularly nice day because you're concerned that the heat and the moisture have to do with global warming. This holding back may or may not be reflected in your tone.

"Mind you," she says. "Oh, here it comes," you think. "Funny weather last week, wasn't it? I blame global warming."

We all have conversations that are more or less like that now. Just as after 9/11 objects to which we may have paid little attention—an X-Acto knife, some white powder—suddenly gained a terrible significance, so in an age of global warming the weather—that nice neutral backdrop that you can talk about with a stranger, in that nice neutral backdrop-y way we might call phatic (after Roman Jakobson)— has taken on a menacing air.

In any weather conversation, one of you is going to mention global warming at some point. Or you both decide not to mention it but it looms over the conversation like a dark cloud, brooding off the edge of an ellipsis.

This failure of the normal rhetorical routine, these remnants of shattered conversation lying around like broken hammers (they must take place everywhere), is a symptom of a much larger and deeper ontological shift in human awareness. Which in turn is a symptom of a profound upgrade of our ontological tools. As anyone who has waited while the little rainbow circle goes around and around on a Mac knows, these upgrades are not necessarily pleasant. It is very much the job of humanists such as ourselves to attune ourselves to the upgrading process and to help explain it.

What is the upgrading process? In a word, the notion that we are living "in" a world—one that for instance we can call Nature—no longer exists in any meaningful sense, except as nostalgia or in the temporarily useful local language of pleas and petitions. We don't want a certain species to be farmed to extinction, so we use the language of Nature to convince a legislative body. We have

a general feeling of ennui and malaise and create nostalgic visions of Hobbit-like worlds to inhabit. These syndromes have been going on now since as long as the Industrial Revolution began to take effect.

As a consequence of that revolution, however, something far bigger and more threatening is now looming on our horizon—looming so as to abolish our horizon, or any horizon, in fact. Global warming, the consequence of runaway fossil fuel burning (as we all know ad nauseam), has performed a radical shift in the status of the weather. Why? Because the world as such—not just a certain idea of world but world in its entirety—has evaporated. Or rather, we are realizing that we never had it in the first place.

We could explain this in terms of the good old-fashioned Aristotelian view of substance and accident. I'm sure you are familiar with the idea that for Aristotle, a realist, there are substances that happen to have various qualities or accidents that are not intrinsic to their substantiality. In section Epsilon 2 of the *Metaphysics*, Aristotle outlines the differences between substances and accidents. What climate change has done is shift the weather from accidental to substantial. Here's Aristotle:

Suppose, for instance, that in the season of the Cynosure [the dog days of summer] arctic cold were to prevail, this we would regard as an accident, whereas, if there were a sweltering heatwave, we would not. And this is because the latter, unlike the former, is always or for the most part the case.

But these sorts of violent changes are exactly what global warming predicts. So every accident of the weather becomes a potential symptom of a substance, global warming. So all of a sudden this wet stuff falling on my head is a mere feature of some much more sinister phenomenon that I can't see with my naked human eyes. I need terabytes of RAM and extreme processing speed to model it in real time (they were just able to do this in spring 2008).

There is an even spookier problem with Aristotle's arctic summer. If those arctic summers continue in any way, and if we can model them as symptoms of global warming, it is the case that there never was a genuine, meaningful (for us humans), sweltering summer, just a long period of sweltering that seemed real because it kept on repeating for say two or three millennia. Global warming, in other words, plays a very mean trick. It reveals that what we took to be a reliable world was actually just a habitual pattern—a collusion between forces such as sunshine

Depression can lift with the
joy arising from listening
to the song of a bird

and moisture and us humans expecting such things at certain regular intervals and giving them names, such as dog days. We took weather to be real. But in an age of global warming we see it as an accident, a simulation of something darker, more withdrawn—climate. As Harman argues, "world" is always presence-at-hand—a mere caricature of some real object. What Ben Franklin and others in the Romantic period discovered was not really weather, but rather a toy version of this real object, a toy that ironically started to unlock the door to the real thing.

Strange weather patterns and carbon emissions caused scientists to start monitoring things that at first only appeared locally significant. That's the old school definition of climate: there's the climate in Peru, the climate on Long Island, but climate in general, climate as the totality of derivatives of weather events—in much the same way as inertia is a derivative of velocity—climate as such is a beast newly recognized via the collaboration of weather, scientists, satellites, government agencies and so on. This beast includes the sun, since it's infrared heat from the sun that is trapped by the greenhouse effect of gases such as $CO_2$. So global warming is a colossal entity that includes entities that exist way beyond Earth's atmosphere and yet it affects us intimately, right here and now. Global warming is a prime example of what I am calling a hyperobject, an object that is massively distributed in space-time and that radically transforms our ideas of what an object is. It covers the entire surface of Earth and most of the effects extend up to five hundred years into the future. Remember what life was like in 1510?

You are walking on top of lifeforms. Your car drove here on lifeforms. The iron in Earth's crust is distributed bacterial excrement. The oxygen in our lungs is bacterial out-gassing. Oil is the result of some dark secret collusion between rocks and algae and plankton millions and millions of years in the past. When you look at oil you're looking at the past. Hyperobjects are time-stretched to such a vast extent that they become almost

impossible to hold in mind. And they are intricately bound up with lifeforms.

The spooky thing is, we discover global warming precisely when it's already here. It is like realizing that for some time you had been conducting your business in the expanding sphere of a slow motion nuclear bomb. You have a few seconds for amazement as the fantasy that you inhabited a neat, seamless little world melts away. All those apocalyptic narratives of doom about the "end of the world" are, from this point of view, part of the problem, not part of the solution. By postponing doom into some hypothetical future, these narratives inoculate us against the very real object that has intruded into ecological, social and psychic space.

If there is no background—no neutral, peripheral stage set of weather, but a very visible, highly monitored, publicly debated climate—then there is no foreground. Foregrounds need backgrounds to exist. So the strange effect of dragging weather phenomena into the foreground as part of our awareness of global warming has been the gradual realization that there is no foreground! The idea that we are embedded in a phenomenological lifeworld, for instance, tucked up like little hobbits in the safety of our burrow, has been exposed as a fiction. The specialness we granted ourselves as unravelers of cosmic meaning (Heideggerian Dasein for instance) falls apart since there is no meaningfulness possible in a world without a foreground-background distinction. Worlds need horizons and horizons need backgrounds, which need foregrounds. When we can see everywhere, when I can Google Earth the fish in my mom's pond in her garden in London, the world—as a significant, bounded, horizoning entity—disappears. We have no world because the objects that functioned as invisible scenery for us, as backdrops, have dissolved.

World turns out to be an aesthetic effect based on a kind of blurriness and aesthetic distance. This blurriness derives from an entity's ignorance concerning objects. Only in ignorance can objects act like blank screens for the projection of meaning.

"Red sky at night, shepherd's delight" is a charming old saw that evokes days when shepherds lived in worlds, worlds bounded by horizons on which things occurred such as red sunsets. The sun goes down, the sun comes up—of course now we know it doesn't, so Galileo and Copernicus tore big holes in that particular notion of world. Likewise, as soon as humans know about climate, weather becomes a flimsy, superficial appearance that is a mere local representation of some much larger phenomenon that is strictly invisible. You can't see or smell climate. Given our brains' processing power, we can't even really think about it all that concretely. You could say then that we still live in a world, only massively upgraded. True, but now world means significantly less than it used to—it doesn't mean "significant for humans" or even "significant for conscious entities."

A simple experiment demonstrates plainly that world is an aesthetic phenomenon. I call it *The Lord of the Rings* vs. *The Ball Popper* test. For this experiment you will need a copy of the second part of Peter Jackson's *The Lord of the Rings* trilogy. You will also require a Playskool Busy Ball Popper, made by Hasbro.

Now play the scene that I consider to be the absolute nadir of horror, when Frodo, captured by Faramir, is staggering around the bombed-out city Osgiliath when a Nazgul (a Ringwraith) attacks on a "fell beast," a terrifying winged dragon-like creature.

Switch on the ball popper. You will notice the inane tunes that the popper plays instantly undermine the coherence of Peter Jackson's narrative world.

The idea of world depends upon all kinds of mood lighting and mood music, aesthetic effects that by definition contain a kernel of sheer ridiculous meaninglessness. It's the job of serious Wagnerian worlding to erase the trace of this meaninglessness. Jackson's trilogy surely is Wagnerian, a total work of art or Gesamtkunstwerk in which elves, dwarves and men have their own languages, their own tools, their own architecture—this is done to fascist excess as if they were different sports teams. But it's easy to recover the trace of meaninglessness from this seamless world—absurdly easy, as the toy experiment proves.

Stupid Kids' Toy 5, Wagnerian Tolkien Movie Nil. What can we learn from this? "World," a key concept in ecophenomenology, is an illusion. And objects for sure have a hidden weirdness. In effect, the Stupid Kids' Toy "translated" the movie, clashing with it and altering it in its own limited and unique way.

In Lakewood, Colorado, residents objected to the building of a solar array in a park in 2008 because it didn't look "natural." Objections to wind farms are similar—not because of the risk to birds, but because they "spoil the view." A 2008 plan to put a wind farm near a remote Scottish island was, well, scotched, because residents of the island complained that their view would be destroyed. This is truly a case of the aesthetics of Nature impeding ecology, and a good argument for why ecology must be without Nature. How come a wind turbine is less beautiful than an oil pipeline? How come it "spoils the view" any more than pipes and roads?

You could see turbines as environmental art. Wind chimes play in the wind; some environmental sculptures sway and rock in the breeze. Wind farms have a slightly frightening size and magnificence. One could easily read them as embodying the aesthetics of the sublime (rather than the beautiful). But it's an ethical sublime that says, "We humans choose not to use carbon"—a choice visible in gigantic turbines. Perhaps it's this very visibility of choice that makes wind farms disturbing: Visible choice, rather than secret pipes, running under an apparently undisturbed "landscape" (a word for a painting, not actual trees and water). (And now of course there are wind spires, which do reproduce a kind of aesthetic distance common in landscape painting.) As a poster in the office of Mulder in *The X-Files* used to say: The truth is out there. Ideology is not just in your head. It's in the shape of a Coke bottle. It's in the way some things appear "natural"—rolling hills and greenery— as if the Industrial Revolution had never occurred. These fake landscapes are the original greenwashing. What the Scots are saying, in objecting to wind farms, is not "Save the environment!" but "Leave our dreams undisturbed!" World is an aesthetic construct that depends on things like underground oil and gas pipelines. A profound political act would be to choose another aesthetic construct, one that doesn't require smoothness and distance and coolness.

Standard ecological criticism depends upon different concepts of "world." Indeed, it derives this concept from philosophical thinking about climate, for instance in the proto-nationalist thinking of Humboldt and Herder, or from biological racism that says that I'm white because I was born in a northern climate. This concept is by no means doing what it should to help ecological criticism. Indeed, the more we see and know about ecology, as is inevitable in an era of ecological crisis, the more of that sheer meaninglessness we have. What an irony: The more data we have, the less it signifies a coherent world.

It's Heidegger, more than anyone else, who generates the concept of world for contemporary ecological philosophy and cultural analysis. In particular, in "The Question Concerning Technology" and "On the Origin of the Work of Art," world is what is created or "enframed" by equipment. This definition has given rise to the now pervasive doctrine of "worlding," whereby cultural artifacts embody the world in various ways: To a hammer, everything looks like a nail, as they say.

Now for a kick-off, there are many reasons why, even if world were a valid concept altogether, it shouldn't be used as the basis for ethics. Consider only this: witch-ducking stools constitute a world just as much as hammers. There was a wonderful world of witch-ducking in the Middle Ages. Witch-ducking stools constituted a world for their users in every meaningful sense. There is for sure a world of Nazi regalia. Just because the Nazis had a world, doesn't mean we should be preserving it. So the argument that "It's good because it constitutes a world" is, to use the technical term, bogus. The reasoning that one should not interfere with the environment because doing so interferes with someone's or something's world is nowhere near a good enough reason. It may even have pernicious consequences. So I'm afraid we must part with Donna Haraway, whose ethics insists that nonhumans are worthy of our care and respect because they constitute worlds, they are in the worlding business. I part company with Haraway here, just as she parts with me, since she thinks that what I'm proposing by contrast is "exterminism"—getting entities oven-ready for destruction. To which I reply, how can you get an entity that doesn't exist ready for destruction?

The second area of concern is historical, namely the way in which current ecological crises such as global warming and the sixth mass extinction event have thrown into sharp relief the notion of world. It is as if humans are losing their world, and their idea of world (including the idea that they ever had one), at one and the same time. This is at best highly disorienting. In this historical moment, the concept world is thrown into sharp relief by circumstances demanding conscious human intervention. Working to transcend our notion of world is important at this moment. Like a mannerist painting that stretches the rules of classicism to its breaking point, global warming has stretched our world to its breaking point. Human beings lack a world for a very good reason. This is simply because no entity at all has a world, or as Graham Harman puts it, "there is no such thing as a 'horizon.'"

Let's think about one way in which global warming abolishes the idea of a horizon. This would be the timescales involved—yes, timescales in the plural. There are three of them. We could call these, in turn, the frightening, the horrifying and the petrifying.

1) Frightening timescale. It will take several hundred years for cold ocean waters (assuming there are any) to absorb about 75 percent of the excess $CO_2$.

2) Horrifying timescale. It will then take another 30,000 years or so for most of the remaining 25 percent to be absorbed by igneous rocks. The half-life of plutonium is 24,100 years.

3) Petrifying timescale. The final 7 percent will be around 100,000 years from now.

There is a real sense in which "forever" is far easier on the mind than these very large timescales, what I call very large finitude. Hyperobjects produce very large finitude, scales of time and space that are finite and for that reason humiliatingly difficult for humans to visualize. Forever makes you feel important. But 100,000 years makes you wonder whether you can imagine 100,000 anything. It seems rather abstract to imagine that a book, for instance, is 100,000 words long.

The "world" as the significant totality of what is the case is strictly unimaginable, and for a good reason: It doesn't exist.

What is left if we aren't the world? Intimacy. We have lost the world but gained a soul, as it were—the entities that coexist with us obtrude on our awareness with greater and greater urgency. Our era is witness to the emergence of a renewed Aristotelianism, an object-oriented ontology that thinks essence is right here, not in some beyond. It's precisely the magical amazement of things like stones, beetles, doors, red hot chili peppers, Nirvana, Bob Geldof, quasars and cartoon characters in the shape of Richard Nixon's head that truly has to be explained, not explained away. Three cheers for the so-called end of the world, then, since this moment is the beginning of history… and the end of the human dream that reality is significant for humans alone.

Let us welcome the prospect of forging new alliances between humans and nonhumans alike, now that we have stepped out of the cocoon of the world.

PERCENTAGE
OF AMERICAN
HOUSEHOLDS

100

75

50

25

RADIO

AUTOMOBILE

TELEPHONE

1900          1915          1930          1945

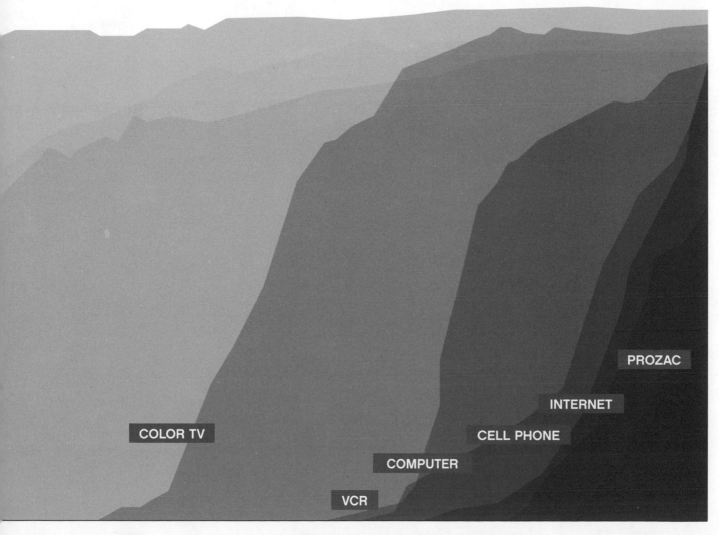

ARE
YOU
HAPPY
YET

?

PROZAC

INTERNET

CELL PHONE

COLOR TV

COMPUTER

VCR

1960    1975    1990    2005

darling!

let's get

deeply

into debt

# HAPPI N OMICS

The woman sitting opposite me on the #4 Powell bus is wearing a leather bomber jacket and stylized Armani glasses. Her fingers are crossed over the wooden handle of a corduroy shoulder bag. The words "PURL" and "KNIT" are tattooed across her knuckles in the same gothic lettering that Tupac Shakur used to tattoo "OUTLAW" on his forearm. I'm about to talk to someone who is, apparently, a gangster knitter.

I'm conducting an experiment designed by Canada's top subjective well-being researcher, Dr. John Helliwell. My assignment: To record my level of happiness and then get on a bus and initiate a conversation with a stranger. When I get off the bus, I will record my happiness level again. Helliwell's research has proven that the more positive social interactions we have, the higher our happiness levels. To test this claim, I have decided that my subjective happiness level is six out of ten. If Dr. Helliwell is correct, a conversation with the gangster knitter will raise my happiness level to seven.

I throw my best "what's up?" look across the aisle, but the gangster knitter's gaze, hooded by thick brown lashes, is fixed out the window. Her gaze drifts to the Full Throttle energy drink advertisement above my head, to the floor, to the yellow safety bars near the back door. I remember what Helliwell told me. "On a bus you think, 'I'm being nice to these people by not invading their space.' But research tells me that, in fact, if we shared a little more space, they'd be happier and I'd be happier. So who's the loser?"

Ten minutes later, the bus pulls up to my stop. At the door I turn and say, "I like your tattoos." She removes her iPod buds and looks up at me. (Hazel eyes. I love hazel eyes.) "Thank you," she says, a smile dancing at the edges of her lips. As the bus pulls away from the curb, I record a happiness level of seven into my logbook.

Dr. John Helliwell is the person who discovered the cash value of job satisfaction. (It takes a 40 percent increase in salary to counter balance a 10 percent drop in job satisfaction). His research has also shown that good governance is the most influential variable explaining happiness levels in different countries: The more trustworthy your government, the greater your chances of being happy. "The social context of well-being," he tells me. "That's my schtick."

It all started back in the 1990s when Helliwell became involved with the revolutionary field of social capital. Unlike mainstream economics, which assumes that well-being can be sufficiently measured by the production and distribution of goods and services, well-being researchers use direct measures of life satisfaction to discover the importance of social as well as economic circumstances. Thus Helliwell and other students of well-being ask, "How happy are individuals and societies, and why?"

One agency that collects data on subjective well-being is the World Values Survey Association (WVSA), a nonprofit collection of social scientists based in Stockholm. They claim to have polled over 350,000 people in countries home to 90 percent of the world's population. Their survey, called the World Values Survey (WVS), asks respondents to gauge their life satisfaction. "All things considered," the survey asks, "how satisfied are you with your life as a whole these days?" Through 250 cognitive and affect questions, scientific data and mathematical wizardry, the survey measures happiness on a four-point scale, one being "very happy," two being "rather happy," three being "not very happy" and four being "not at all happy." Helliwell and other researchers use this data to shed light on human behavior and society. The findings have even influenced public policy.

For simplicity's sake, I decided to use a ten-point scale (ten being high) instead of a four-point scale and clocked my own happiness level at six. As soon as I started considering my own happiness, a red danger light whirred up in my head. I wanted my number to be higher than the world average (five). I wrote down a six not because I necessarily felt I was a six, but because six was modestly, yet safely, above the world average.

## #7 NANAIMO STATION BUS, FEBRUARY 23

Crossing north on Vancouver's Granville Bridge, I engage four different strangers in a conversation about our bus's destination. "Do we turn right on West Pender or on West Hastings?" Amazingly, four people volunteer very helpful answers. Two minutes later I'm learning about software interfacing from my delightful neighbor with jet-black hair. My happiness level again blips up to a seven.

## THE GREAT $20 EXPERIMENT

"Defining happiness is like defining yellow," explains University of British Columbia (UBC) psychologist Elizabeth Dunn. She's referencing Daniel Gilbert, author of *Stumbling on Happiness.* "We all know what yellow is," she continues. "Asked if this is yellow, we can identify it. But asked to explain it, we get a little tongue-tied." Psychologists approach the question of ranking happiness levels very similarly to the WVS. "The emotional component," Dunn explains, "is how often do you experience positive feelings, and how often do you experience negative feelings?" The cognitive component asks, "looking at your life, how satisfied do you feel with it?"

In 2008 Dunn wanted to know if money could buy happiness. She gave a group of UBC students $5 or $20 and instructed them to spend the money on themselves. She gave another group of students the same amount of money and told them to spend it on others, in what Dunn calls "pro-social spending." The next morning, subjects were asked how happy they felt. Those who spent the money on others were overwhelmingly happier. (A correlation study was conducted with people spending their own money and the results were congruent. The study is also being replicated in Uganda, and the authors expect similar findings.) "If you use your money to promote social goals," Dunn explains, "it can make you happier." Dunn also found that the amount of money, $5 or $20, is inconsequential.

The really mind-boggling results came when participants were invited to predict the outcome of the survey. People thought that spending money on themselves would make them happier when, in fact, spending money on others is what makes them happier.

## 99 B-LINE BUS, MARCH 14

I'm sitting opposite a punk wearing a studded leather jacket, sporting a gelled Mohawk and reading Dante's *The Divine Comedy.* He seems interesting, but I'm too afraid to talk to him, to tell him I like his hair or ask if *The Divine Comedy* is good. Then I notice this other guy in a ball cap and T-shirt trying to make eye contact with me. He looks like the kind of guy that rides buses looking for people to talk to. I ignore him and start reading the Richmond Automall advertisement above his head. The punk to my left pulls out a baggie of snap peas and starts eating them like potato chips. Then the man in the ball cap says, "Snap peas?" "Yeah," the punk answers. "That's a really good idea. I should do that sometime." The punk looks up and they make eye contact. "They're amazing," says the punk. "They're so sweet. Sometimes, it's like I'm eating fruit."

For the rest of the journey into East Vancouver, the guy throws me these glances from under his ball cap, inviting me into their conversation. What do I do? I focus my attention on the Richmond Automall advertisement. Why is it so hard to talk to strangers when research shows that it will make me happier? Why not risk a simple "hello" that could nudge me into the sevens? I suggest to Elizabeth Dunn that humans act counterintuitively in the chase for happiness. They spend money on themselves instead of each other. They sit quietly on buses instead of talking to their neighbors. "There are two different mental systems that underlie a lot of our behavior," she explains. "So you can recognize on an intellectual level that you shouldn't eat lots of fatty foods and you should give a lot of money to charity, and then somehow you end up eating potato chips in front of your flat-screen TV. We recognize the value of something but we don't feel it. We don't internalize it."

## THE SOCIAL CAPITAL THEME SONG

I revisit Helliwell to discuss my experiment. I tell him that even though my happiness consistently increased, I continue to struggle to start conversations with strangers on buses, to push myself beyond my baseline level of happiness to achieve that delicious seven. Helliwell smiles and tells me about a recent conference at Toronto's Massey College. He got on stage in front of hundreds of fellow economists and sang an a cappella version of what he and his friends call "the social capitalist theme song." Without warning, he starts to sing: "The more we get together, the happier we'll be. Because your friends are my friends and my friends are your friends. The more …" He stops mid-sentence and focuses on me from behind his metal-rimmed glasses. "If the audience just sits there like you are, grinning, then I stop. And I say, 'You don't get it.' The whole point is it's not about me singing to you. It's not about being amused. It's not about being entertained. It's about us singing the song together. It's doing things together that makes us happy."

Back on the #4 Powell I realize that talking to the gangster knitter didn't just make me happier, it probably made her happier as well. Happiness is symbiotic. There is movement at the front of the bus. A woman in ankle boots carrying an oxblood shoulder bag gets on and, despite the absence of the driver, she swipes her bus pass and the machine beeps. She is walking towards me. She might not know it yet, but we each have something the other wants.

Ian Bullock is a high school social studies teacher and writer of fiction and non-fiction in Vancouver, Canada. He continues to find happiness in unexpected places.

I'm homeless

> Commercialized information delivery systems cannot be the fundamental organizing principle of a vibrant culture.

## JOLTS

A jolt is any "technical media event"—a shift in camera angle, a gunshot, a cut to commercial, a flashing pop-up window, an electronic alert, a click—that interrupts the flow of sound, thought or imagery. A jolt forces your brain to take notice and pump for meaning, even if there is none. In 1978, when Jerry Mander first defined "technical events" in his book *Four Arguments for the Elimination of Television*, regular TV programming averaged ten technical events per minute, twenty during commercials. Thirty years later these figures have more than doubled and now our computers and smartphones have their own more intimate and clandestine ways of getting us to take notice.

## INFOTOXINS

From the moment your alarm sounds in the morning to the wee hours of late-night TV and web surfing, micro-jolts of commercial pollution flow into your brain at the rate of about three thousand marketing messages per day. Every day, an estimated twelve billion display ads, three million radio commercials, more than two hundred thousand TV commercials and an unknown number of online ads, spam emails and marketing messages are dumped into our collective unconscious. Corporate advertising is the single largest psychological experiment ever carried out on the human race, yet its impact on us remains unstudied and largely unknown.

## NOISE

For most of human history the ambient noise was wind, rain, insects, birds, animals and people talking to each other. Now the soundtrack of our lives is the hum of computers, the chime of ringtones, the clicking of keyboards, the drone of appliances, the dull roar of traffic. Various kinds of noise—white, pink, brown, blue—are ever present. Trying to live your life above the noise of our wired world is like living next to a freeway: You get used to it, but at the cost of your mindfulness.

A factory dumps pollution into the water or air because that's the most efficient way to produce plastic or wood pulp or steel. A TV station, magazine or website dispenses sex and violence and "pollutes" the cultural environment because that's the most efficient way to produce audiences. It pays to pollute. The psychic fallout is just the cost of doing business.

## EROSION OF EMPATHY

The first time we saw a starving child on a Sunday morning TV ad we were appalled. Maybe we sent money. But as these images became more familiar, our capacity for compassion waned. Eventually these ads started to annoy us, even repulse us. The constant flow of pseudo-sex and violence renders us more voyeuristic, insatiable and aggressive. The commercially saturated mental environment is rearranging our neurons. Now nothing—not even genocide, torture or apocalypto-porn—shocks us anymore.

## ECOLOGY OF MIND

If psychologists learned how to measure the impact that mental pollutants like jolts, infotoxins and infoviruses have on our minds, then maybe we could pioneer a new science of "ecology of mind." Perhaps, as this new scientific enterprise progressed, we could establish safe pollution levels for our mental environment similar to the parts-per-billion environmental safety standards we have for our air, water and food. We could then learn how to measure the psychological risks posed by living in different kinds of mental spaces: Living in Mumbai vs. living in Geneva, raising your kids in a big city vs. raising them in a small country town, being a carpenter or plumber vs. being a graphic designer.

We may then be able to arrive at a Livability Index (LI) more revealing than the current indices that simply measure greenspace, smog levels and the quality of schools. With reliable Mental Environmental Indices (MEI), we could rate TV programs, films, videos and websites in terms of how many units of various kinds of mental pollutants per hour they manufacture, how much clutter they dump into the public mind and how this may be affecting our personal and cultural health.

LIFE UNDER CAPITALISM IS A SPIRITUAL BATTLE TO KEEP FEELING SOMETHING, TO STAY IN THE EMOTIONAL GAME, TO HANG ONTO YOUR EMOTIONAL HEARTLAND AS A FULLY FUNCTIONAL HUMAN BEING.

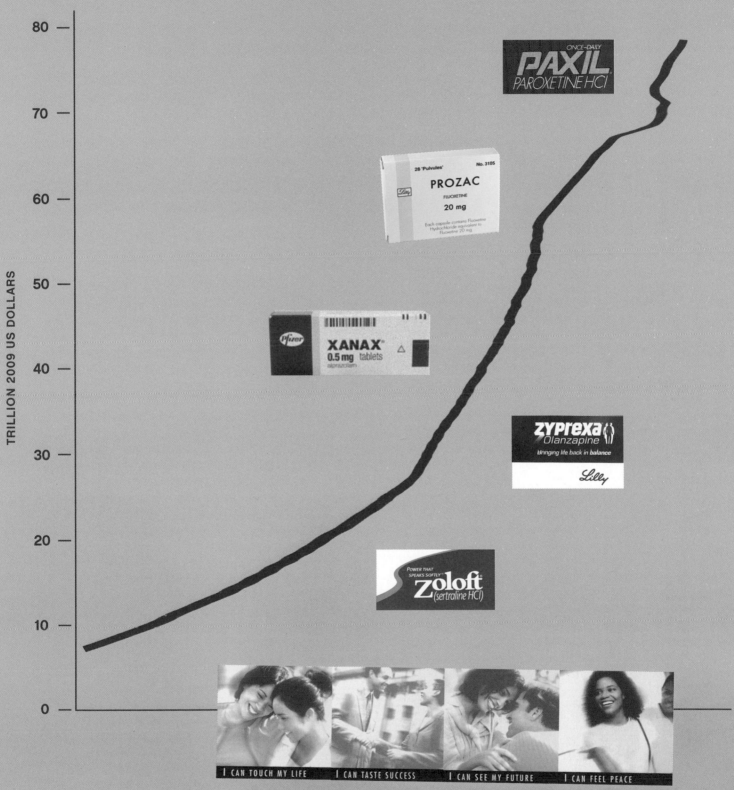

"I can" images from Paxil advertisement, *Archives of General Psychiatry*, January 2001.

# INNOCENCE

# &

# SPONTANEITY

**Hey all you left cortex diehards and rational maximizers out there,**

Ever since Lehman Brothers bit the dust back in 2008 we've been arguing nonstop about how best to pull the big macro policy levers and get the global economy back on track ... to get back to what we once called normal. We've reduced interest rates to almost zero, injected trillions of dollars of stimulus into the system, bailed out bankrupt megacorporations and had angry debates about whether to tax the richest one percent or not. All along we've believed that everything will be okay again once we get these fiscal matters right.

But maybe we're missing something. Maybe something much more profound is lurking under the surface. Maybe the idea that we can have a successful economy just by pulling the macroeconomic levers is a fiction—a cognitive illusion—a false belief that we intuitively accept as true.

Maybe the real trick of creating a vibrant economy is to manipulate the psychology, the sociology, the aesthetic and get the culture right ... to have small farms instead of big ... to have less consumption, not more ... to have ten cereal options instead of a thousand ... to attack the obesity problem and get the industrialized world thin again ... to rear more children in two-parent households ... get our kids off Ritalin ... our adults off Viagra, Zoloft and painkillers ... our youth off megacorps ... our citizens off automobiles ... our people off concrete, glass, mechanization, isolation and steel.

Maybe economic policy makers should stop obsessing so much about fiscal health and start obsessing more about cultural health. Maybe the Brazilians are doing so well right now because of their optimistic jazz-like entrepreneurial playfulness ... and the Chinese economy is thriving because they have a multi-thousand-year cultural wellspring of frugality, agility and hard work to draw from. Maybe the successful economies of the future will be less about interest rates, tax codes and money supplies and more about community, empathy, trust and a willingness to sacrifice for the common good.

Maybe innocence, spontaneity and playfulness are the bedrocks of economic well-being ... and when a culture grows cerebral and loses those virtues, it's done.

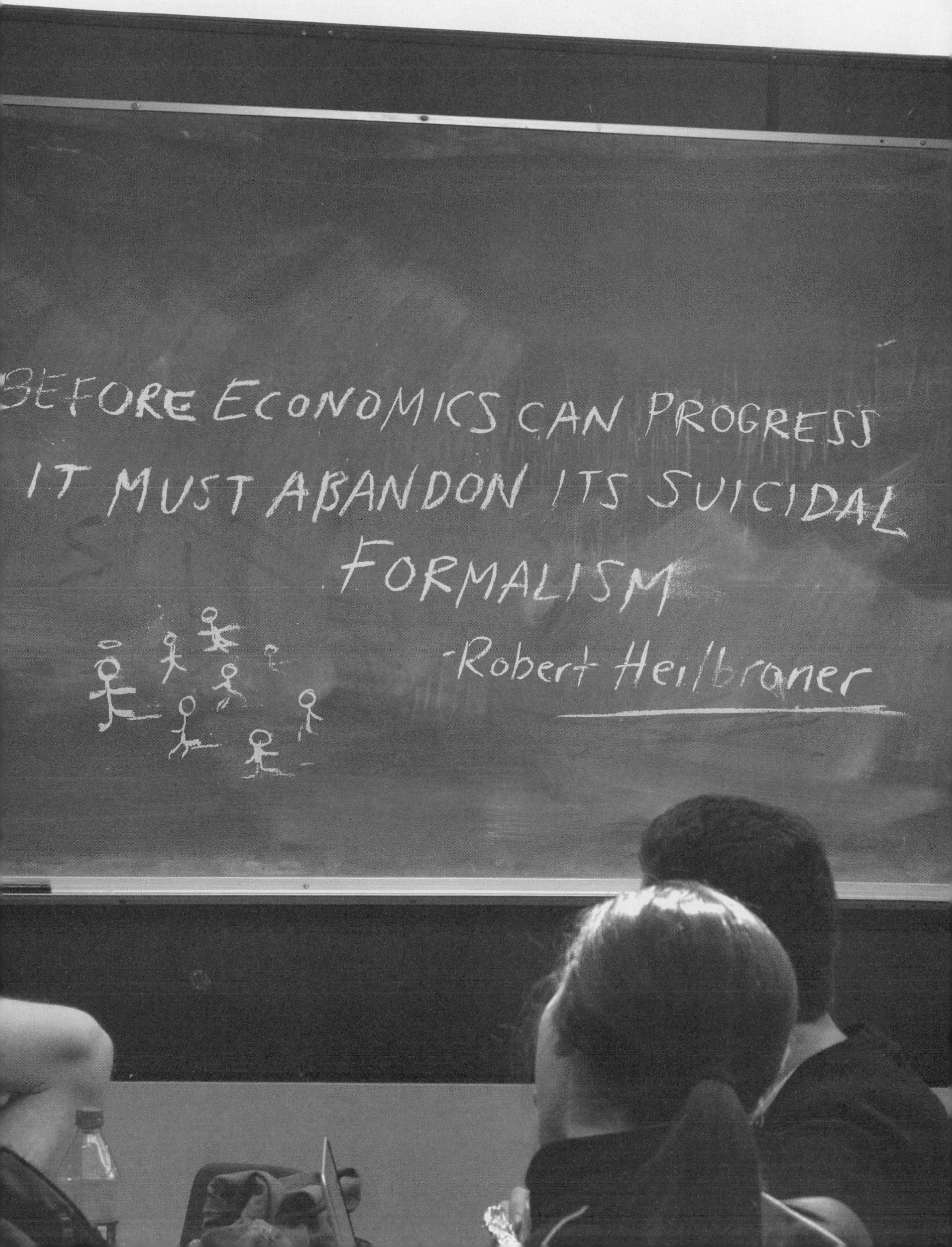
BEFORE ECONOMICS CAN PROGRESS
IT MUST ABANDON ITS SUICIDAL
FORMALISM
-Robert Heilbroner

THE BIG QUESTION:

IS ECONOMIC PROGRESS KILLING the PLANET?

# IE WAR
# ON CAMPUS

## Okay you paradigm shifters out there!

This is how scientific progress is supposed to happen: A theory, a paradigm, that has worked quite well for many years suddenly becomes problematic. Contradictions emerge; the theory no longer seems to predict reality. The scientific community senses the moment and rises to the occasion. A flurry of experiments are conducted, information shared, papers written and conferences held. Out of this intellectual turmoil, a hot new theory emerges. It is subjected to rigorous scrutiny and tested in a myriad of ways. Then, if it passes muster, it is finally accepted as the new theoretical framework, the new norm, the new "truth." The scientists who came up with the breakthrough are nominated for the Nobel Prize. The community settles back down, but now with a greater understanding of how the world really works.

*This is a myth.* What the scientific community and your university would like you to believe. Thomas Kuhn, in his seminal 1962 book, *The Structure*

THOUGHT CONTROL IN ECONOMICS

**BREAK FREE!**
KICKITOVER.ORG
TOXICTEXTBOOKS.COM
FOOTPRINTNETWORK.ORG
NEWECONOMICTHINKING.ORG
NEWECONOMICS.ORG
STEADYSTATE.ORG
DEGROWTH.NET
EUROECOLECON.ORG
ECOECO.ORG
UVM.EDU/GIEE
POSTCARBON.ORG
THESOLUTIONSJOURNAL.COM
PAECON.NET
EARTHECONOMICS.ORG
EARTHINC.ORG
HAPPYPLANETINDEX.ORG
NATIONALACCOUNTSOFWELLBEING.ORG
THEOILDRUM.COM

MY BOSTON | 2005 | PERFORMANCE | MUSEUM OF FINE ARTS | BOSTON USA

kickitover.org

*of Scientific Revolutions*, describes how paradigm shifts really happen. They are almost always nasty, messy, dirty affairs, very much like political revolutions. They unfold like vindictive putsches. The old guard protects its turf jealously. The dissenters are ignored, stonewalled, refused publication and tenure, ostracized and obstructed in every way.

Kuhn's most profound insight is that, contrary to the way scientific progress is supposed to happen, an old paradigm cannot be replaced by evidence, facts, or "the truth" ... it will not be thrown out because its forecasts are wrong, its policies no longer work, or its theories are proved unscientific. An old paradigm will only be replaced by a new one when a group of maverick scientists orchestrate a coup and throw the old-school practitioners out of power.

So the lesson we take from Kuhn is that if we really want a paradigm shift in the science of economics we have to move beyond our academic comfort zones and become meme warriors ... we have to occupy our school's economics department: Disrupt lectures, walk en masse out of classes, post a never-ending stream of posters and provocations in the corridors, nail manifestos to our professors' doors. We have to ridicule their theories in campus newspapers and on campus radio. We have to organize teach-ins and, in front of campus-wide audiences, demand to know how they factor forests, fish, climate change and ecosystem collapse into their macroeconomic models. We have to create a collective a-ha moment of truth when it becomes obvious that the professors in charge of educating the next generation of economic policy makers are unable to answer even the most fundamental questions: How do you measure progress, Mr. Professor? How do you know if we're going forward or backward? And if you don't know that then why are you so sure of what you're writing on the blackboard?

At critical moments throughout history, university students have catalyzed massive protests, called their professors and political leaders on their lies and thrust their nations in brave new directions. It happened in the 1960s on hundreds of campuses around the world, and more recently in South Korea, China, Indonesia, Greece, Spain, Egypt, Quebec, Chile and Argentina. Now in the wake of the 2008 financial debacle with climate tipping points looming prophetically on the horizon, we have reached another one of those critical moments when students of the world are called upon to play their catalytic card and trigger an overhaul of the political ideology and theoretical framework that has ruled the world since World War II.

A scientific revolution is brewing. Over the next few years, on campus after campus, a new breed of economists— open, holistic, human-scale—will chase the old goats out of power and begin the work of reprogramming the doomsday machine.

# DEBORAH CAMPBELL

# POST AUTIS—TIC

Deborah Campbell is an author and journalist who has written about international affairs for numerous publications including *Harper's* and the *Economist*. She teaches nonfiction writing at the University of British Columbia.

## ECONOMICS IS ABOUT PEOPLE, NOT CURVES

# PARIS, FRANCE, 2000

The university-aged children of France's ruling class ought to have been contentedly biding their time. They were, after all, destined to move into high-powered positions reserved for graduates of the elite École Normale Supérieure (ENS).

"The ENS is for very good students, and very good students aren't afraid to ask questions," said Sorbonne economist Bernard Guerrien.

It was early in the year 2000 and he was addressing a conference on the disconnect between mainstream neoclassical economics instruction and reality. Economics has an ideological function, he told them, to put forth the idea that the markets will resolve everything. In fact, he added, economic theory absolutely doesn't show that.

A group of economics students, their worst fears confirmed, approached Guerrien eager to "do something." A week later fifteen of them gathered in a classroom to hash out a plan of attack. Someone called the reigning neoclassical dogma "autistic!" The analogy would stick: Like sufferers of autism, the field of economics was intelligent but obsessive, narrowly focused and cut off from the outside world.

By June that year their outrage had coalesced into a petition signed by hundreds of students demanding reform within the teaching of economics, which, they said, had become enthralled with complex mathematical models that only operate in conditions that don't exist. "We wish to escape from imaginary worlds!" they declared. Networking through the internet and reaching the media through powerful family connections, they made their case.

"Call to teachers: Wake up before it's too late!" they demanded. "We no longer want to have this autistic science imposed on us." They decried an excessive reliance on mathematics "as an end in itself" and called for a plurality of approaches.

With that, autisme-économie, the Post-Autistic Economics (PAE) movement, was born.

Their revolutionary arguments created an earthquake in the French media, beginning with a report in *Le Monde* that sent a chill through the academic establishment. Several prominent economists voiced support, and a professors' petition followed. The French government, no doubt recalling the revolutionary moment of May 1968, when students led a ten-day general strike that rocked the republic to its foundations, promptly set up a special commission to investigate. It was headed by leading economist Jean-Paul Fitoussi, who also traveled to Madrid to address Spain's nascent "post-autistic" student movement. Fitoussi's findings: The rebels had a cause. Most important to the PAE followers, Fitoussi agreed to propose new courses oriented to "the big problems" being ignored by mainstream economics: Unemployment, the economy and the environment.

A backlash was inevitable. Several economists (notably the American Robert Solow from MIT), launched a return volley. What followed was an attempt to discredit the PAE by implying that the students were anti-intellectuals opposed to the "scientificity" of neoclassical economics. The accusations didn't stick: The dissenters were top students who had done the math and found it didn't add up.

Gilles Raveaud, a key PAE student leader, along with Emmanuelle Benicourt and Ioana Marinescu, saw the presiding faith in neoclassical economics as "an intellectual game" that, like Marxism and the Bible, purported to explain everything, rather than admitting there are many issues it hasn't figured out. "We've lost religion," said Raveaud, "so we've got something else to give meaning to our lives."

Benicourt described his hope for PAE as follows: "We hope it will trigger concrete transformations of the way economics is taught …. We believe that understanding real-world economic phenomena is enormously important to the future well-being of humankind, but that the current narrow, antiquated and naïve approaches to economics and economics teaching make this understanding impossible …. We therefore hold it to be extremely important, both ethically and economically, that reforms like the ones we have proposed are, in the years to come, carried through, not just in France but throughout the world."

# CAMBRIDGE, UNITED KINGDOM

Raveaud and Marinescu, key French PAE student leaders, visited the Cambridge Workshop on Realism and Economics in the UK. "It must have been the right time," said Phil Faulkner, a PhD student at Cambridge University. That June he and twenty-six other disgruntled PhD students issued their own reform manifesto, called "Opening Up Economics," that soon attracted 750 signatures. Economics students at Oxford University who had been at the same workshop followed with their own "post-autistic" manifesto and website. Similar groups linked to heterodox (as opposed to orthodox) economics began emerging elsewhere in Europe and South America.

The Cambridge rebellion "was prompted by frustration," said Faulkner, but they hadn't expected such a positive reception from fellow students. "If anyone were to be happy about the way economics had gone, we'd expect it to be PhD students, because if they were unhappy with it, they simply wouldn't be here. In fact, that wasn't the case."

As expected, Cambridge ignored them. Their efforts, Faulkner explained, were meant to show support for the French students and to use their privileged position at the esteemed economics department to demonstrate to the rest of the world their discontent. Some of the signatories worried that speaking out could have dire consequences, and the original letter was unsigned. "I think it's more future possibilities, getting jobs, etc., that [made them think] it might not be smart to be associated with this stuff," said Faulkner. For himself, he already knew that his research interests meant he would have to work outside of the mainstream: "There was nothing to lose really."

Edward Fullbrook, a research fellow at the University of the West of England, had already launched the first Post-Autistic Economics Newsletter in September 2000. Inspired by the French student revolt and outraged by stories emerging from American campuses that courses on the history of economic thought were being eradicated (which he viewed as an effort to facilitate complete indoctrination of students), Fullbrook battled hate mail and virus attacks to get the newsletter off the ground. Soon prominent economists such as James Galbraith stepped up to offer encouragement and hard copy. The subscriber list ballooned from several dozen to 7,500 people around the world.

Fullbrook edited *The Crisis in Economics*, a book based on PAE contributions that was eventually translated into Chinese. Textbook publishers, always hunting for the next big thing, have inquired about PAE (now called Real World Economics) textbooks ever since. It made sense, said Fullbrook, since enrollments in standard economics classes have been dropping, cutting into textbook revenues. In other words, students just aren't buying it. Ironically, Fullbrook said, "market forces are working against neoclassical economics."

One of the movement's first contributors was Australian economist Steve Keen, who led a student rebellion in 1973 that instigated the formation of a political economy department at Sydney University. "Neoclassical economics has become a religion," said Keen. "Because it has a mathematical veneer, and I emphasize the word veneer, they actually believe it's true. Once you believe something is true, you're locked into its way of thinking unless there's something that can break in from the outside and destroy that confidence."

The neoclassical model still reigns supreme at Cambridge. Faulkner now teaches at Clare College, but is limited to mainstream economics—the only game in town. "If you're into math, it's a fun thing to do," he said. "It's little problems, little puzzles, so it's an enjoyable occupation. But I don't think it's insightful. I don't think it tells these kids about the things it claims to describe: Markets or individuals."

# HARVARD, USA

Sitting in an overcrowded café near Harvard Square, talking over the din of full-volume Fleetwood Mac and espresso-fueled chatter, Gabe Katsh described his disillusionment with economics teaching at Harvard University. The red-haired twenty-one-year-old made it clear that not all of Harvard's elite student body are the "rationally" self-interested beings that Harvard's most influential economics course pegs them as.

"I was disgusted with the way ideas were being presented in this class, and I saw it as hypocritical—given that Harvard values critical thinking and the free marketplace of ideas—that they were then having this course which was extremely doctrinaire," said Katsh. "It only presented one side of the story when there are obviously others to be presented."

Before Gregory Mankiw took the helm, Harvard's introductory economics class was dominated for two decades by one man: Martin Feldstein. It was a *New York Times* article on Feldstein titled "Scholarly Mentor to Bush's Team," that first lit the fire under the Harvard activist. Calling the Bush economic team a "Feldstein alumni club," the article declared that he had "built an empire of influence that is probably unmatched in his field." Not only that, but thousands of Harvard students "who have taken his, and only his, economics class during their Harvard years have gone on to become policy makers and corporate executives," the article noted. "I really like it; I've been doing it for 18 years," Feldstein told the *Times*. "I think it changes the way they see the world."

That was exactly Katsh's problem. As a freshman, he'd taken Ec 10, Feldstein's course. "I don't think I'm alone in thinking that Ec 10 presents itself as politically neutral, presents itself as a science, but really espouses a conservative political agenda and the ideas of this professor, who is a former Reagan advisor, and who is unabashedly Republican," he said. "I don't think I'm alone in wanting a class that presents a balanced viewpoint and is not trying to cover up its conservative political bias with economic jargon."

In his first year at Harvard, Katsh joined a student campaign to bring a living wage to Harvard support staff. Fellow students were sympathetic, but many said they couldn't support the campaign because, as they'd learned in Ec 10, raising wages would increase unemployment and hurt those it was designed to help. During a three-week sit-in at the Harvard president's office, students succeeded in raising workers' wages, though not to "living wage" standards.

After the living wage "victory," Harvard activists from Students for a Humane and Responsible Economics (SHARE) decided to stage an intervention. This time they went after the source, leafleting Ec 10 classes with alternative readings. For a lecture on corporations they handed out articles on corporate fraud. For a free trade lecture they dispensed critiques of the WTO and IMF. Later they issued a manifesto reminiscent of the French post-autistic revolt, and petitioned for an alternative class. Armed with eight hundred signatures, they appealed for a critical alternative to Ec 10. Turned down flat, they succeeded in introducing the course outside the economics department.

Their actions followed on the Kansas City Proposal, an open letter to economics departments "in agreement with and in support of the Post-Autistic Economics Movement and the Cambridge Proposal" that was signed by economics students and academics from twenty-two countries.

Harvard's then-president, Lawrence Summers, illustrated the kind of thinking that emerges from neoclassical economics. Summers is the same former chief economist of the World Bank who sparked international outrage after his infamous memo advocating pollution trading was leaked in the early 1990s. "Just between you and me, shouldn't the World Bank be encouraging MORE migration of the dirty industries to the ldcs [Less Developed Countries]?" the memo inquired. "I think the economic logic behind dumping a load of toxic waste in the lowest wage country is impeccable, and we should face up to that. ... I've always thought that underpopulated countries in Africa are vastly UNDER-polluted ..."

Brazil's then-Secretary of the Environment, José Lutzenburger, replied: "Your reasoning is perfectly logical but totally insane. ... Your thoughts [provide] a concrete example of the unbelievable alienation, reductionist thinking, social ruthlessness and arrogant ignorance of many conventional 'economists' concerning the nature of the world we live in."

Summers later claimed the memo was intended ironically, while reports suggested that it was written by an aide. In any case, Summers devoted his 2003/2004 prayer address at Harvard to a "moral" defense of sweatshop labor, calling it the "best alternative" for workers in low-wage countries.

"You can't ignore the academic foundations for what's going on in politics," said Jessie Marglin, a Harvard sophomore with SHARE. The organization didn't want a liberal class with its own hegemony of ideas. It wanted "a critical class in which you have all the perspectives rather than just that of the right." Without an academic basis for criticism, other approaches "aren't legitimized by the institution," she said. "It becomes their word versus Professor Feldstein, who is very powerful."

Harvard economics professor Stephen Marglin, Jessie's father, teaches the Ec 10 alternative. A faculty member since 1967, Marglin was at the tail end of a generation formed by the Great Depression and World War II. "This generation," he said, "believed that in some cases markets could be the solution, but that markets could also be the problem."

Going for a decade now, his course uses the Ec 10 textbook, but includes a critical evaluation of the underlying assumptions. Marglin wanted to provide balance, rather than bias.

"I'm trying to provide ammunition for people to question what it is about this economic [system] that makes them want to go out in the streets to protest it," he said. "I'm responding in part to what's going on, and I think the post-autistic economics group is responding to that. Economics doesn't lead politics, it follows politics. Until there is a broadening of the political spectrum beyond a protest in Seattle or a protest in Washington, there will not be a broader economics. People like me can plant a few seeds, but those seeds won't germinate until the conditions are a lot more suitable."

Is it possible that these seeds are now germinating?

After leaving Harvard, Larry Summers was invited to serve as Barack Obama's chief economic advisor, crafting the administration's response to the financial crisis of 2008. It would later be revealed that Summers received $5 million in salary that year from a hedge fund and a further $2.7 million in speaking fees from the same Wall Street firms that had received government bailout money. As of 2012, Summers was again teaching at Harvard. In one of his most recent opinion pieces he cited the "dramatic rises in the share of income going to the top 1 and even the top .01 percent." That article is titled, "Why Isn't Capitalism Working?"

A slogan emblazoned on a wall on a campus in Madrid, where mass protests against the undue influence of financial institutions over global policy have spread around world, may provide him with an answer: "¡La economia es de gente, no de curvas!"—"Economics is about people, not curves!"

March 12, 2012. An Occupy economics display outside the Sauder School of Business, University of British Columbia, Vancouver.

SAUDER
School of Busines
ROBERT H. LEE
GRADUATE SCHOOL
OCCUPY
ECON 101
THE BIG QUESTION:
IS ECONOMIC PROGRESS
KILLING

# GILLES RAVEAUD

# NEOCON INDOCTRINATIO — THE MANKI

Gilles Raveaud is currently assistant professor of economics at the University of Paris 8. He is cofounder of the Post-Autistic Economics movement (paecon.net). He has a blog: www.alternatives-economiques.fr/blogs/raveaud and can be reached at gillesraveaud@gmail.com.

You might not have heard of N. Gregory Mankiw. The Harvard economics professor and former adviser to George W. Bush is one of the most gifted economists of our generation. He is also one of the most effective and talented propagandists of our times. His target: Young economics students. His field of operation: The world's universities. His weapon: The bestselling economics textbook in the world. It includes thirty-six chapters and eight hundred pages of color illustrations, graphs, stories and interesting asides. Don't worry if you or your kids don't speak English; Mankiw's text surely exists in your language.

# WAY

What is most worrisome about this scenario is not Mankiw's ideas themselves, but that his text presents economics as a unified discipline, one entirely committed to the neoliberal agenda. "Most economists" is one of the dominant phrases throughout his impressive text. One of the first things you'll learn in its pages is that Mankiw believes markets are the solution to almost everything—and it seems by way of his text he would like students to believe likewise. Species extinction? Not a problem. Privatize endangered beasts to keep them alive. It worked for cows, chickens and pigs. Why not rhinos, elephants and blue whales? You can read about it in chapter eleven.

According to Mankiw, if a problem persists, it can only be for one of two reasons: The market is imperfect, or it is nonexistent. No other explanation for persisting economic or social problems is ultimately permitted. And the externalities now engulfing humanity, well these are trade-offs humans make for living well. This devil's bargain is the first maxim on his top ten list of key principles that begin the book.

Being an unfunded post-doc at Harvard in 2005 and 2006, I worked as a teaching fellow for Mankiw. The experience was nearly unsustainable: If macro, although bad, was bearable, micro was a neoliberal caricature. Each week, I was drawing supply and demand curves on the board. Whatever the question, unemployment, consumption or housing, I had to repeat the same mantra: Perfect competition leads to a "social optimum." Except in the notable case of pollution, no intervention from the state can improve well-being. And as the market rewards the most productive, inequalities cannot be an issue.

Unemployment is an example of the market being imperfect. For Mankiw, if unemployment exists, it is only because of human interventions such as unemployment benefits, trade unions and minimum wages. Without these interventions, he maintains, there can be no unemployment. Mankiw presents this as a consensual view among economists—chapter six. In fact quite a few of them admit that the labor market is a very special "market" indeed, where the price—the wage—is not set the same way as the price of other "goods." As Alan Krueger put it, "it is a gross oversimplification to say that 'wages are set by the competitive forces of supply and demand' or that there is a unique, market-determined wage."

This specificity in the way wages are set is one of the reasons why six hundred economists (including stars like Kenneth Arrow, Robert Solow and Joseph Stiglitz) have argued in favor of an increase of the US minimum wage. But when students and workers at Harvard asked for a "living wage," Mankiw opposed it. As he told *Harvard Magazine* in 2001, even a modest raise in the minimum wage for janitors at Harvard would "compromise the university's commitment to the creation and dissemination of knowledge." No kidding. Of course, Mankiw does not discuss the possibility that the salary of tenured professors might be above its "equilibrium" value; not to mention the very existence of tenure, which goes against the principles of a perfectly competitive labor market.

While unemployment is an example of an imperfect market for Mankiw, pollution is an example of the nonexistent market. He admits that, in some cases, markets do not ensure that the environment is clean, and the result is excessive pollution (what economists call a "negative externality"). But what is the solution to pollution? According to Mankiw, it is to define property rights to pollute. Public authorities would issue "pollution permits" to polluting companies (who then cannot pollute more than the amount covered by the permits they hold). Companies then buy and sell these permits on the market, depending on how much they will pollute in a year. The fewer the permits, the higher their price and the higher the incentives for firms to reduce their pollution. This system is not stupid. Indeed, there are instances where such permit systems might work to solve simple pollution problems. But the problem is that, to the amazement of some of his students (but unfortunately by no means all), Mankiw rarely mentions self-restraint. This would defy introductory maxim number four—people respond to incentives. And despite climate change being such a critical issue today, caused by ever-growing economic activity, it merits only one index entry in Mankiw's book. Where the reference appears, the author outlines how Obama missed the boat on the Carbon Tax.

When I published a version of this piece in *Adbusters* in 2007, Mankiw replied in his blog that he "presents, as honestly as possible, the consensus of the profession." According to him, the economic mainstream is "right of center" and "more market-friendly than the typical literature professor." Mankiw has since been rejoined in his assessment of the economic profession by his political opponent, and laureate of the Prize in Economic Sciences of the Bank of Sweden in 2008, Paul Krugman.

In his famous *New York Times* article, "How Did Economists get it so Wrong," Paul Krugman explains that the most renowned economists could not foresee the crisis because they believed in the rationality of individuals and the efficiency of free markets. A crisis was beyond the realm of the possible. On this point both Mankiw and the critical Krugman share something in common: They overlook their "heterodox" colleagues. As it happens, many of them were suspicious of an impending crash and therefore much better at predicting the current crisis than the stars of the discipline. In his piece called "Who are these Economists, Anyway?" economist James K. Galbraith mentions the case of Dean Baker, head of the Center for Economic and Policy Research, who, as early as 2002, saw the housing bubble coming. As Galbraith notes,

Baker understood what was going on because he knew the normal level of prices on the housing market. As Galbraith analyzes, "market institutions and relationships are generally stable, in the sense that normal values exist." As a consequence, when the price of houses is much higher than its historical value, the existence of a bubble is "the most likely thing." Not rocket science, but difficult to see through dark shaded neoliberal goggles. That is because in Mankiw's world, there are no bubbles, no disequilibria, no crises. Mankiw's world is one where markets work smoothly, where fairness prevails as everybody gets what they deserve. It is a world where the magic of markets, private enterprise and property rights work wonders. In this world, standards of living rise constantly, people are in better health, live longer, are happier. A beautiful world … if only it existed.

Some of my former students at Harvard have described Mankiw's course to me during private conversations as "massive conservative propaganda." One of them told me he thought Mankiw had managed to "indoctrinate a whole generation." In 2003 a protest against a similar course proposed by professor Martin Feldstein, an ex-adviser to President Reagan, led to the creation of an alternative intro economics course taught by radical economist Steve Marglin. But while Mankiw's course gives the required credits to economics majors, Marglin's does not. As a result, Mankiw has around eight hundred students, and Marglin one hundred. Not to mention the more than a hundred thousand students around the globe who learn from Mankiw's textbook.

According to Mankiw, since markets are a good way to organize economic activity, supply and demand is just about all you need to know in economics. Whatever you desire, you can pay for in the market: Tomatoes, healthcare, housing, a car. That's demand. On the other side of the market, firms compete to supply consumers with the latest cool clothes, mobile phones and housing. That's supply. When supply is higher than demand, the price falls (holiday travel to a country at war). When demand is higher than supply, the price rises (a war in Ivory Coast reduces the supply of cocoa). And supply and demand apply to absolutely every issue you can imagine, including organ scarcity. But Mankiw's text is all about

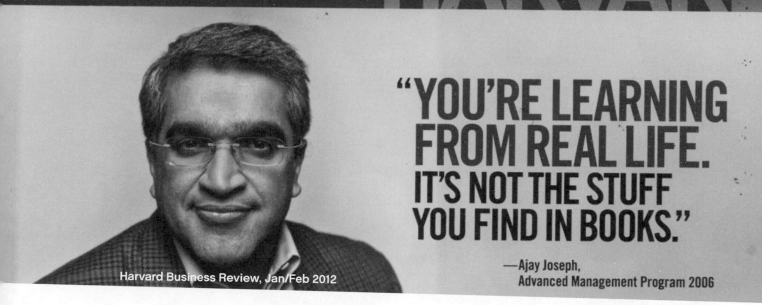
Harvard Business Review, Jan/Feb 2012

trivial choices, such as how many slices of pizza you are willing to give up to buy yourself an extra can of Coke. This method is extremely effective in hiding the magnitude of what is at stake. The reactions of the students would be different if the textbook addressed how much healthcare people have to give up to be able to buy basic food. Also, the very notion of "need" is absent from Mankiw's text. One may wonder how students would feel if we discussed the fact that a millionaire's desire for a yacht will always be met because it is backed by money, while a poor family's need for a roof won't. But such discussions are avoided. By repeating trivial examples, Mankiw accustoms students to ideological rather than reality-based understandings of individual choices and preferences. The words "poor" and "rich" are rarely used. But more surprisingly, there is also no mention of the power of corporations to shape tastes. This is because Mankiw's world is a world of small firms operating in perfectly competitive markets. "Corporate America" is not part of the picture. No McDonald's, no Nike, no Microsoft.

Mankiw also downplays inequality despite the growing gap between rich and poor in the US over the last decade that has commanded the attention of more and more American economists, even within the mainstream. But Mankiw is not one of them. True, he admits there is more disparity in the US than in Europe (even if he forgets to mention that this was not the case in the 1960s). But he goes on to remark that there is less disparity in the US than in Brazil and China. And this growing gap is not caused by right-wing policies intentionally designed to give the rich more money over the same time period, but rather by the impact of new technologies on the workforce and globalization.

If Harvard and other universities fail to equip their students with a broad and critical understanding of economics, their actions are more than likely to harm the society at large. It is time for professors to start using the C-word again—capitalism—instead of "free markets." While Mankiw's text is easy for professors to use, it oversimplifies economic theory and omits the ways in which markets can degrade human well-being, undermine societies and threaten the planet. Each year tens of thousands of students go out into the world with Mankiw's biases as a road map to the future. But we know that the neoliberal agenda is more and more disputed outside universities. Within universities alternative textbooks are flourishing. One can thus hope that these new textbooks, with their greater relevance to real-world problems and better acknowledgment of the diversity and complexity of economic thought, will soon out-compete Mankiw's bible. As a believer in competition, Professor Mankiw could only consider this to be fair game.

# DAVID ORRELL

# "YOU CAN GO IN AND BREAK THE MACHINE"

David Orrell studied mathematics at the University of Alberta, and obtained his doctorate from Oxford on the prediction of nonlinear systems. This excerpt is from his book *Economyths: How the Science of Complex Systems is Transforming Economic Thought*. He is also the author of *The Future of Everything: The Science of Prediction*.

Neoclassical economics owes its continued existence in large part to university academics, who keep it buffed and maintained and protected for the next generation. This involvement goes well beyond the economics departments. Universities divide subjects into minute specialties and have traditionally tried to keep them separate. (There are signs that this is beginning to change.) Economics decisions affect most aspects of life in one way or another though, so everyone else should at least have an opinion.

Some pending questions:
How does the physics department feel about economic ideas masquerading as laws of nature? Do the humanities departments agree with the story that society is made up of individuals who act independently? If not, how is that being reflected in the education of future business leaders?
Is the mathematics department OK with the kinds of models used in economics classes? Are assumptions of things like stability plausible? What do mechanical engineers think of the safety margin used by "financial engineers"? Is the gender studies department cool with the definition of Homo economicus? Do sociologists agree that societies always behave rationally? Do neoclassical tools make sense in an increasingly networked society in which one of the most valuable commodities – information – can be distributed at near zero cost? Are political scientists sure that economics is politically neutral?
Are historians convinced that neoclassical economics is an objective science and not a cultural artifact shaped by a certain period of history? What will be the impact of the rising consumer power of women? Of non-Western countries with different political and economic ideas and agendas?

Do ecologists think the environment is taken seriously enough in economic textbooks? If they seriously believe we are in danger of a huge survival-threatening environmental crisis, is the introductory economics class at their institution increasing or decreasing the risk? What does the psychology department think about the definition of utility or about the economics of happiness?
Are the philosophers in agreement that markets can make ethical decisions?
And finally, how do elite institutions like Harvard University, Oxford University, Massachusetts Institute of Technology and the California Institute of Technology feel about the fact that in 2007, 20 or 30 or more percent of their graduates went straight into the financial sector? Are these institutions being used as a filter to select talented students for this overpaid and socially underproductive area? If that is the case, shouldn't the universities at least try to revise their teaching to better reflect new theories and approaches, not to mention ethics?
Until university departments break down the artificial divisions that separate their subjects, the Neoclassic Logic Piano will be safe. The best hope for change probably comes not from university administrators but from the ones with the most at stake: the students. They are the ones who are being fed the story about the economy. If they decide not to buy in, then that will be it. One excuse heard for the lack of progress in economics is that academia changes slowly. But that isn't true at all. Nothing much happens for a long time, but when change comes, it is often sudden and violent, like an earthquake … or indeed a financial crash. Early in the last century, physics was completely rewritten in the space of a few years. Recent technological advances such as the human genome project have revolutionized biology.

Harvard students walking out of Professor
Gregory Mankiw's Ec 10 class.

Harvard attracts the brightest and most analytical minds in America. Depending on how you count their academic affiliations, the school has produced anywhere between 46 and 107 Nobel laureates, 16 of them in economics. It even produced the most recent President of the United States. Many students who enter Harvard don't ever fathom a Wall Street career in their future. But after a heavy dose of recruiting and Harvard culture, almost half the student body find themselves on the other side of their degree, not chasing their youthful dreams of changing the world, but working at Goldman Sachs, JP Morgan, Bank of America and the like. *NPR* reported that in 2010, 49 percent of Harvard grads went on to work in consulting and the financial sector after graduation. How does this happen?

The funneling starts in Gregory Mankiw's year-long Economics 10, the most popular course in one of the most popular disciplines at Harvard, a prerequisite for many degrees, not just economics. The class's alumni disproportionately clutter the halls of the IMF, the World Bank, the White House and Wall Street; some alumni, like Larry Summers, have worked at three of the four. The leading architects and planners of the 2008 financial crisis have all done their tours at Harvard, or similar Ivy League schools with similar econ curriculums, as students, teachers and presidents. Their influence ranges from the price of the

shares in your mutual fund portfolio to the words on the pages of almost everything you'll ever read in mainstream economics. Today, no matter where you are, if you're interested in economics you're only a few degrees of separation from Harvard's Ec 10.

November 2, 2011, is the day that one of the most widely reported, poorly attended protests in recent American history took place. Five months out of high school and two months into their Harvard education, teenagers Rachel J. Sandalow-Ash and Gabriel H. Bayard led a column of seventy students in a walkout on Dr. Mankiw, demanding a more balanced curriculum.

"Sure I'm an introductory economics student, but I would like to get both sides of this," says Bayard of the reasoning behind the protest.

"I was afraid that the students in the class, including me, who didn't go on in economics and didn't pursue deep understandings of this, were just going to get this cursory knowledge of economics but yet were going to become important players in the field of economic policy."

For their concern they were heckled and jeered by the seven hundred-odd classmates who remained behind. A handful of students even waged a counter walk-in in support of their favorite professor. A chorus of "We love Mankiw!" serenaded the occupiers' otherwise silent departure.

The walkout was reported in the mainstream media as an absurd one percent protest of the one percent. Most of it vilified the protestors as spoiled and naïve brats. Even Harvard's own student newspaper, *The Crimson*, roasted it, calling the protestors ignorant, unaware and ideological. Their editorial was titled "Stay in School: Protesting a class's ideology damages free academic discourse." *Fox News* questioned why resume-polishing students were walking out of a balanced middle-of-the-road introductory course. *The Huffington Post* highlighted that the lecture topic of the day was income inequality and that this was ironic. And Mankiw himself, though moved by the protestors' passion, wrote in the *New York Times* that he was saddened how "poorly informed" the students were and that "most" economists believe that mainstream economics is ideology-free. As it turns out, the liberal use of the word "most" in Ec 10 lingo is one of the student's core complaints.

"There is debate in the economic community so why shouldn't that debate be reflected in our education?" says Bayard.

The idea for the walkout was a hasty and impromptu affair, hatched about forty-eight hours earlier at an Occupy Harvard meeting to coincide with a much larger Occupy Boston rally. Once the action was agreed upon, organizers stayed up to the wee hours of the morning drafting a manifesto, "An Open Letter to Greg Mankiw," which they sent out to the *Harvard Political Review*.

"Today, we are walking out of your class, Economics 10, in order to express our discontent with the bias inherent in this introductory economics course," it read.

"As Harvard undergraduates, we enrolled in Economics 10 hoping to gain a broad and introductory foundation of economic theory that would assist us in our various intellectual pursuits and diverse disciplines, which range from economics, to government, to environmental sciences and public policy, and beyond. Instead, we found a course that espouses a specific—and limited—view of economics that we believe perpetuates problematic and inefficient systems of economic inequality in our society today."

The letter highlighted Harvard's connection to the current financial system, problems with the class textbook, the purpose of an economics education, a lack of diverse opinions and the monopoly Ec 10 has as a gateway course to further studies in economics at Harvard. The letter was also riddled with questionable examples from the course and the type of idealistic ramblings you'd expect from a handful of eighteen-year-olds living out of home for the first time. These misgivings in the manifesto were attacked soon enough. But despite their follies, the intention was nonetheless rooted in an honest and undeniable suspicion: Are we being taught science or ideology? That question is at the core of the debate that erupted on campus and around the world.

"People never used to discuss the content of Ec 10 before. They discussed what the answer was to question number five on the problem set and how stressed they were about the upcoming midterm. But now they're actually discussing the substance, the ideas behind what is being said," says Sandalow-Ash.

A decade ago, a similar protest by students in Europe, the Post-Autistic Economics movement, radically changed the curriculum and ideological stance of European economics departments. Now called Real World Economics, the movement made a brief foray into England and America too but for the most part fizzled out at the gates of Harvard Yard. Could the Mankiw walkout be the beginning of a similar movement in America, one that this time could stick? Or is it just a flash in the pan?

"We are going to be fighting our peers as much as we are going to be fighting structures of power," says Fenna Krienen, a member of Occupy Harvard and fifth-year graduate student in neuropsychology.

ASK YOUR PROFESSOR:

**Is economics a cold theoretical game**

**or …**

**a profoundly personal discipline that goes to the heart of who we are as human beings?**

Krienen sat in on Mankiw's class that day and was part of the walkout. One of the more interesting caveats of the scene at Occupy Harvard is that the vast majority of their members aren't undergraduates. And while the walkout was the brainchild of Occupy Harvard's few undergraduate sympathizers, graduate students outside the discipline of economics make up the core of the movement. Within economics in fact, there is scant a whiff of Occupy, at least not publically. Krienen insists that there is an undercurrent of support behind the scenes, but that many students and faculty are just too afraid to speak out, to endorse something so drastically unpopular with Harvard culture. Many, she says, are still waiting to see how it all unfolds.

"These are students who are not conditioned to challenge authority, quite the opposite. They define their ideas of success and self-worth in terms of what authority thinks of them," says former Harvard grad and Pulitzer Prize winning author Chris Hedges.

"However capable they are, and they are capable, they're not conditioned to challenge power. They pay deference to power and that makes them, in that sense, easily malleable and is why corporations like Goldman Sachs go in and recruit in places like Harvard."

In the weeks following the walkout, Hedges spent a night camping out in Harvard Yard. While he was there about fifty occupiers attempted to attend a Goldman Sachs recruiting session. Protestors were denied entry, but the protest itself didn't go unnoticed. Goldman Sachs canceled subsequent hiring sessions at Harvard and several other nearby schools. *The Crimson* again wrote an impassioned editorial against Occupy, this time defending Goldman Sachs by calling the protest against the Wall Street corporation "myopic and unoriginal." Their pleas on behalf of those who don't consider Goldman Sachs, or those who work there, as primary actors in the 2008 crash weren't enough to get the firm to reinstate its canceled

events. On campus today, occupiers say taking a job at one of the nations major financial firms has lost some of its sheen.

"I really think there are a lot of students for whom the messaging did resonate," says occupy supporter Sandra Korn, 20, who was part of the Goldman Sachs action.

"I'll overhear conversations in the dining hall, people will say 'Oh yeah, I just got that job at JPMorgan, and their friends instead of congratulating them, (before everyone would say 'Congratulations, that's so awesome, I'm so proud of you'), now people say 'Oh no, your selling you're soul, why are you doing that, what a shame, why aren't you doing that thing you always wanted to do?'"

Heterodox Harvard economist Stephen Marglin says that an assault on mainstream economics has to begin with an assault on mainstream politics. He was one of the few members of Harvard's economics faculty to openly support Occupy's underpinned intentions. His most recent title, *The Dismal Science: How Thinking Like an Economist Destroys Community*, is a progressive diamond in the neoclassical rough.

"This is not about Greg Mankiw. It's about a much more pervasive ideology. The striking thing about economics texts across the board, mainstream economics, is how similar they are, not how different they are," he told students at an Occupy sponsored teach-in in the weeks following the walkout.

"The ideology is Republican, it's Democrat, it is a faith in markets that is unshaken by any encounters with reality."

That message is one that Ec 10 students rarely hear. And while Marglin says it is still to early to tell, he thinks Occupy could be the beginning of a political push that dislodges the current stranglehold neoclassicism has on American classrooms.

**Darren Fleet**

Post everywhere
**kickitover.org**

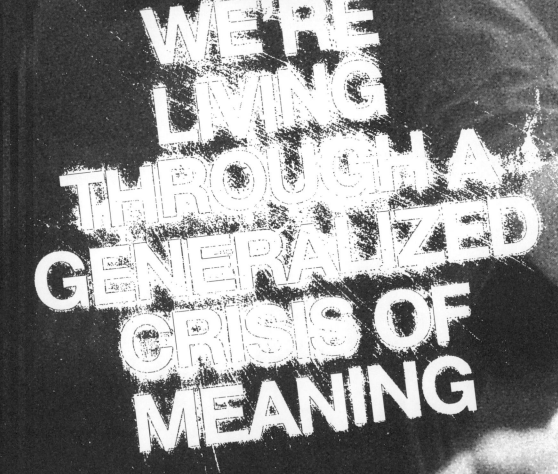

HEY MR. PROFESSOR,

**Do you think the economic and political framework which has ruled the world for the past fifty years is about to heave?**

neoclassical economics

THE ONLY WAY OF ACHIEVING "SUSTAINABILITY" IS TO TRANSFORM THE VERY IDEA AND INSTITUTIONS OF MONEY ITSELF.

Alf Hornborg

# PETER STALKER

# "IT'S TIME TO DEVISE A NEW FINANCIAL ARCHITECTURE"

Peter Stalker is a freelance writer and editor based in the UK. He authored *The No-Nonsense Guide to Global Finance* and has written three books on international migration. He is a former co-editor of the *New Internationalist*, has edited the UN Development Programme's "Human Development Report" and now works as a consultant to a number of UN agencies.

## PRUNE THE EXOTICA

The meltdown of 2008 and the ensuing economic recession it triggered can be laid firmly at the door of speculators in banks, hedge funds and other institutions who had created a shadow financial system, operating with intertwining and overlapping derivatives. Not only were these barely comprehended, even by those using them, the ways in which they would interact were almost impossible to predict. Some derivatives are useful; others are largely vehicles for speculation. All should be presented for inspection by the financial authorities and only those approved should be used—and traded on public exchanges so that everyone is aware of who owns what and which institution is exposed to what risk. Trading in unapproved derivatives would be stifled if these were legally unenforceable.

Among the most dangerous derivatives are credit default swaps, currently valued at around $55 trillion—an indirect and opaque form of insurance that could yet sink many more lenders. These should be banned, requiring lenders to take full responsibility for the credit they offer and denying speculators this particular form of get-rich scheme.

Also in line for pruning should be the hedge funds. At present these are largely unregulated since it was wrongly assumed they were a risk only to themselves. One way to reduce the damage would be to prevent short-selling by banning other institutions from lending them the shares they need for this purpose.

## TAX THE TRANSACTIONS

Distortions and bubbles of all kinds are encouraged by electronic trading, which can see shares or currencies or bonds changing hands continuously at lightning speed. This encourages "momentum" trading which has nothing to do with underlying values and more to do with what other traders will do in the subsequent seconds or minutes. One of the most promising ways of addressing this, but as yet untried thirty years after it was proposed by Nobel laureate James Tobin, would be to tax every transaction. At present only around 5 percent of currency trades, around $3 trillion per day, are linked to actual trade. The rest is speculation which can wreak havoc with national budgets, especially for developing countries.

Applying a sales tax of around 0.2 percent on each trade would skim off much of the speculative froth—while also generating valuable revenue. Assuming the annual trade were cut to a more reasonable level of $100 trillion this would yield tax revenues of $200 billion for public purses. The same principle could be applied to stock exchanges, which would have the merit of stifling some of the endless churning of stocks in hedge funds which achieve little other than to enrich traders and brokers.

## MATCH RISKS AND REWARDS

The most repulsive aspect of the 2008 financial crisis is that even disgraced chief executives of failed banks walked away with huge bonuses, as reward for failure. This is because the incentive systems encouraged employees to take bets on the markets that would produce short-term gains, in risky deals and crazy loans that would later turn toxic, by which time the trader of chief executive would have collected millions of dollars. This is akin to betting against a number coming up on a roulette wheel—you can take quite a few spins before being caught out, by which time you could have moved on to a different game. When chief executive Stan O'Neal was ousted from Merrill Lynch in October 2007, he was comforted with a $160-million payoff, in part based on a rise in the share price that had yet to reflect his dangerous strategies. The pay for bankers and others should be based instead on continuous assessment of their performance and, where appropriate, reflect the full implications of their activities, even if these may not be known for several years. This will mean devising new contracts, so now's a good time while the bankers are looking for jobs and are not so picky about the perks.

## CLOSE TAX HAVENS

The world's tax havens serve no purpose other than to boost corporate profits and rich individuals at the expense of regular tax payers. The British government bears much of the responsibility since it is in a position to exert direct control over some of its own territories. But there are other measures that could be taken to lift the veil of secrecy under which many companies and individuals operate, as they shuffle money from one dubious jurisdiction to another. This would involve, for example, demanding that companies declare their profits, losses and taxes they pay in every country they do business. Just as important would be to end banking secrecy and ensure that tax authorities in each country are able to exchange the necessary information.

## A FRESH START

The 2008 financial meltdown has had huge costs, not just for taxpayers in the rich countries but also for millions of people in developing countries who are suffering from a global economic crisis. But it also represents an opportunity for a fresh start—looking again at the most basic assumptions under which our financial systems operate.

The corporate lobbyists are, of course, busy preparing their arguments as to why it would be dangerous to react to the latest drama by stifling the creativity of financial markets. They claim that the latest crisis is simply a part of a cycle of creative destruction, a Darwinian process that will permit the survival of the most robust financial models and sweep away those that have proved useless or dangerous.

But we now know the true cost of this free-for-all. The financial markets are not to be trusted. They expect to be given free rein to make huge profits while the sun is shining, but hasten to the shelter of the state when the skies darken. Never again. We now know better. Time to devise a new financial architecture.

From *People First Economics*, New Internationalist Publications, 2009.

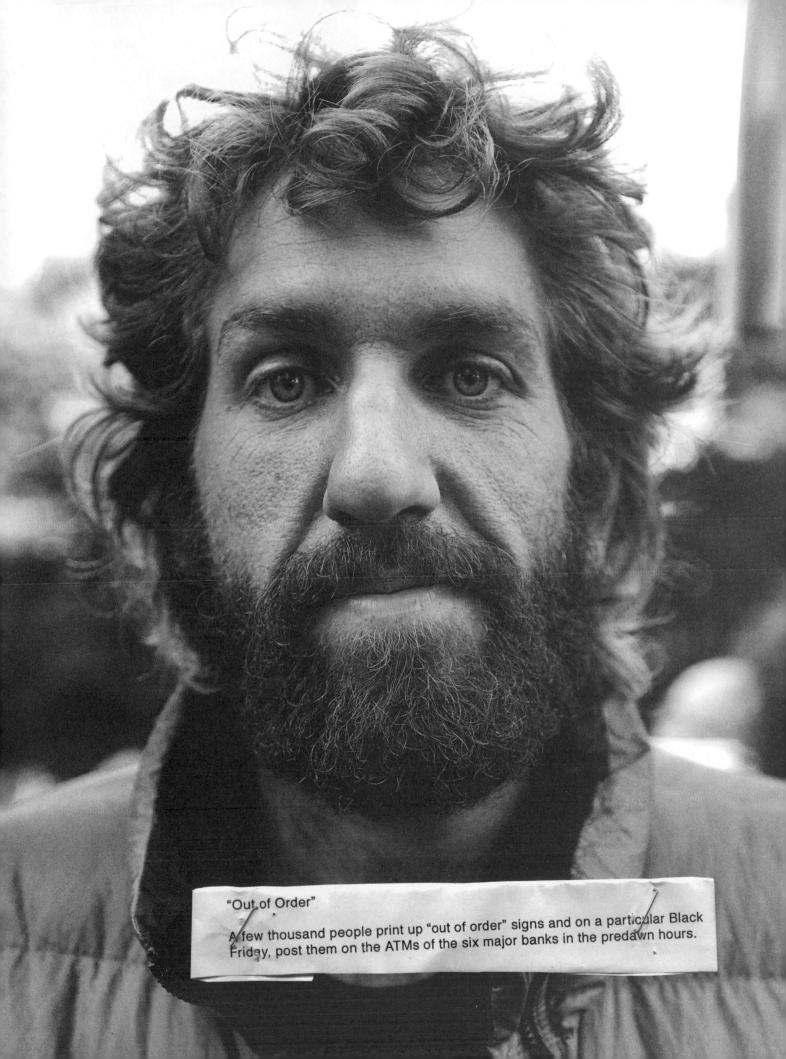

"Out of Order"

A few thousand people print up "out of order" signs and on a particular Black Friday, post them on the ATMs of the six major banks in the predawn hours.

## With summer drawing to a close,

the sea of eager students shuffle into the main lecture hall for the first class on Microeconomic Analysis. While everyone takes their seats and the lecturer attaches the microphone and prepares the overheads, the typical introductions unfold. As my attention drifts from the monotony of administration and protocol, I am abruptly brought back to consciousness by an abhorrent passing remark. The lecturer, in a blasé manner, notes that this intermediate unit will not and cannot incorporate any aspect of the environment, political influence or "irrational" behaviour—for they are considered "externalities," and such subjects are a "concern for other disciplines."

I am astonished. Not so much by the lecturer's dogmatic abnegation of an economics which includes the natural world—for as I have come to recognize, that is to be expected; nor am I shocked by his lack of concern or resolution; what astounded me was, that out of a lecture hall of four hundred people, not one other student so much as flinched after he spat these outworn credos.

Has this generation of economics students conformed to the neoclassical theories? Or is there something more insidious and profound at play—a generation silent and unwilling to confront the discontents of economics and its ubiquitous impacts?

Economics is largely a self-fulfilling psychology. It effectively constructs a model of behavior, to a model for behavior; whereby such models educate us to think how we're "supposed" to think. As a result, this pseudoscience has maintained a heavy reliance upon seeking numerical legitimacy and mathematical reassurance for justifying assumptions of rationality. While other disciplines, such as physics (which largely influenced traditional economic theory), have continued to stride forward with the integration of external variables, economics remains stagnant, promulgating the incessant drone of outworn slogans and obsolete assumptions. Moreover, university economics textbooks freely discuss assumptions of Homo Economicus, rationality and utility-maximization as if they were a certainty; however, counter arguments and opposing ideologies are rarely discussed in economic textbooks and classrooms alike. These arguments appear only to be presented in political economy and social science units. Such topics are often therefore neglected, as modern economics students rarely pursue such subjects due to their

qualitative and philosophical focus. It is the mathematical analysis and quantitative elements of the discipline which have become the appeal for those studying economics.

Certainly, mathematics is an integral part of economics, and it is a role in which it should maintain. The failure of economics, however, lies in its inability to include functions of the natural world and its reluctance to incorporate findings from other disciplines. In fact, if research results are not consistent with the foundational assumptions and models, even if it is presented by other acclaimed economists, it is immediately denounced. This is no more evident than with the research conducted by David Card and Alan Krueger. Their work largely disproved with empirical evidence the standard labor market model that has plagued neoclassical theory regarding the minimum wage. In each of the myriad of cases they researched, their work found that increases in the minimum wage lead to increases in pay, but no loss in jobs. These unprecedented findings were swiftly dismissed and referred to as an "anomaly" by neoclassical economists.

Still, with all these known problems, people increasingly pursue economics without question. Each year students grapple with the convoluted theories and the complicated formulas which accompany modern economics. Yet, as students belabor with the theory, few seem to recognize that their efforts are in vain, for their studies surround an idealized, assumptive economy independent of the world.

We as students are not helpless before this task, or hopeless of its success. Through exercising our curiosity and challenging economics' archaic conventions, we can shine a light on the fractures and fissures associated with the dry crust of this so-called "autistic discipline." Let us raise the level of debate within this subject and reinvigorate a multidiscipline approach to resolving its omnipresent flaws. This would leave a legacy any generation would be proud of.

For economics to advance and therefore contribute to improving the quality of life, it must incorporate externalities and societal findings from other disciplines into their models. Until then, economics is ultimately not human nature described; but human nature assumed.

And this generation of economics students are not saying enough about it …

Nik Dawson is a graduate of the economics and political science program at Sydney's Macquarie University.

#OccupyHarvard, November 2011

ASK YOUR PROFESSOR:

**Will our econ 101 curriculum change?**

# VIII.

I see us free, therefore, to return to some of the most sure and certain principles of religion and traditional virtue—that avarice is a vice, that the exaction of usury is a misdemeanor, and the love of money is detestable, that those walk most truly in the paths of virtue and sane wisdom who take least thought for the morrow. We shall once more value ends above means and prefer the good to the useful. We shall honor those who can teach us how to pluck the hour and the day virtuously and well, the delightful people who are capable of taking direct enjoyment of things, the lilies of the field who toil not, neither do they spin.

**JOHN MAYNARD KEYNES**

# CHAPTER EIGHT

# EARLY PIONEERS

## WE STAND ON THEIR SHOULDERS

### Alright all you history buffs out there,

The emerging new science of economics, whatever we eventually decide to call it—bionomics? psychonomics? ecological economics?—stands on the shoulders of a small group of pioneering thinkers who had the courage to occupy the fray.

They are a quixotic bunch of intellectuals who each in their own way had grandiose, down-to-earth, out-of-the-box ideas about how the world really works … about entropy, thermodynamics, chaos theory and the possibility of never-ending growth and long-term survival within a closed system nurtured only by the sun.

They thought big and questioned what we all thought were sacrosanct axioms of economic science. They dared to poke at the unspoken assumptions. They made the skeletons rattle.

These sojourners will be remembered as the revolutionary pioneers who transformed economics much like Copernicus transformed astronomy, Freud psychology and Einstein Physics.

# FREDERICK SODDY

## "STOP CREATING MONEY OUT OF NOTHING!"

Frederick Soddy, born in 1877, was an individualist who bowed to few conventions and who is described by one biographer as a difficult, obstinate man. A 1921 Nobel laureate in chemistry for his work on radioactive decay, he foresaw the energy potential of atomic fission as early as 1909. But his disquiet about that power's potential wartime use, combined with his revulsion at his discipline's complicity in the mass deaths of World War I, led him to set aside chemistry for the study of political economy— the world into which scientific progress introduces its gifts. In four books written from 1921 to 1934, Soddy carried on a visionary campaign for a radical restructuring of global monetary relationships.

He offered a perspective on economics rooted in physics—the laws of thermodynamics, in particular. An economy is often likened to a machine, though few economists follow the parallel to its logical conclusion: Like any machine the economy must draw energy from outside itself. The first and second laws of thermodynamics forbid perpetual motion, schemes in which machines create energy out of nothing or recycle it forever. Soddy criticized the prevailing belief of the economy as a perpetual motion machine, capable of generating infinite wealth—a criticism echoed by his intellectual heirs in the now emergent field of ecological economics.

A more apt analogy, said Nicholas Georgescu-Roegen (a Romanian-born economist whose work in the 1970s began to define this new approach), is to model the economy as a living system. Like all life, it draws from its environment valuable (or "low entropy") matter and energy—for animate life, food; for an economy, energy, ores, the raw materials provided by plants and animals. And like all life, an economy emits a high-entropy wake—it spews degraded matter and energy: Waste heat, waste gases, toxic byproducts, apple cores, the molecules of iron lost to rust and abrasion. Emissions include trash and pollution in all their forms, including yesterday's newspaper, last year's sneakers, last decade's rusted automobile.

Matter taken up into the economy can be recycled, using energy; but energy, used once, is forever unavailable to us at that level again. The law of entropy commands a one-way flow downward from more to less useful forms. An animal can't live perpetually on its own excreta. Thus, Georgescu-Roegen, paraphrasing the economist Alfred Marshall, said: "Biology, not mechanics, is our Mecca."

Following Soddy, Georgescu-Roegen and other ecological economists argue that wealth is real and physical. It's the stock of cars and computers and clothing, of furniture and French fries that we buy with our dollars. The dollars aren't real wealth but only symbols that represent the bearer's claim on an economy's ability to generate wealth. Debt, for its part, is a claim on the economy's ability to generate wealth in the future. "The ruling passion of the age," Soddy said, "is to convert wealth into debt"—to exchange a thing with present-day real value (a thing that could be stolen, or broken, or rust or rot before you can manage to use it) for something immutable and unchanging, a claim on wealth that has yet to be made. Money facilitates the exchange; it is, he said, "the nothing you get for something before you can get anything." Problems arise when wealth and debt are not kept in proper relation. The amount of wealth that an economy can create is limited by the amount of low-entropy energy that it can sustainably suck from its environment—and by the amount of high-entropy effluent from an economy that the environment can sustainably absorb. Debt, being imaginary, has no such natural limit. It can grow infinitely, compounding at any rate we decide.

Whenever an economy allows debt to grow faster than wealth can be created, that economy has a need for debt repudiation. Inflation can do the job, decreasing debt gradually by eroding the purchasing power, the claim on future wealth, that each of your saved dollars represents. But when there is no inflation, an economy with overgrown claims on future wealth will experience regular crises of debt repudiation—stock market crashes, bankruptcies and foreclosures, defaults on bonds or loans or pension promises, the disappearance of paper assets.

It's like musical chairs—in the wake of some shock, holders of abstract debt suddenly want to hold money or real wealth instead. But not all of them can. One person's loss causes another's, and the whole system cascades into crisis. Each and every one of the crises that has beset the American economy in recent years has been, at heart, a crisis of debt repudiation. And we are unlikely to avoid more of them until we stop allowing claims on income to grow faster than income.

Soddy would not have been surprised at our current state of affairs. The problem isn't simply greed, isn't simply ignorance, isn't a failure of regulatory diligence but a systemic flaw in how our economy finances itself. As long as growth in claims on wealth outstrips the economy's capacity to increase its wealth, market capitalism creates a niche for entrepreneurs who are all too willing to invent instruments of debt that will someday be repudiated. There will always be a Bernard Madoff or a subprime mortgage repackager willing to set us up for catastrophe. To stop them we must balance claims on future wealth with the economy's power to produce that wealth.

Soddy distilled his eccentric vision into five policy prescriptions, each of which was taken at the time as evidence that his theories were unworkable. The first four were to abandon the gold standard, let international exchange rates float, use federal surpluses and deficits as macroeconomic policy tools that could counter cyclical trends, and establish bureaus of economic statistics (including a consumer price index) in order to facilitate this effort. All of these are now conventional practice.

Soddy's fifth proposal, the only one that remains outside the bounds of conventional wisdom, was to stop banks from creating money (and debt) out of nothing. Banks do this by lending out most of their depositors' money at interest—making loans that the borrower soon puts in a demand deposit (checking) account, where it will soon be lent out again to create more debt and demand deposits, and so on, almost ad infinitum.

If such a major structural renovation of our economy sounds hopelessly unrealistic, consider that so too did the abolition of the gold standard and the introduction of floating exchange rates back in the 1920s. If the laws of thermodynamics are sturdy, and if Soddy's analysis of their relevance to economic life is correct, we'd better expand the realm of what we think is realistic.

Eric Zencey is the author of *Virgin Forest: Meditations on History, Ecology and Culture* and a novel, *Panama*. Excerpted from *The New York Times*, April, 2009. © *The New York Times*. Used by permission.

# NICHOLAS GEORGESCU-ROEGEN

# "EXISTENCE IS A FREE GIFT FROM THE SUN."

The Strip, Las Vegas, 1965

Nicholas Georgescu-Roegen's experiences in life permeated his economic thought. He was a political dissident, a refugee and a committed scholar who took pride in his humble roots, vowing never to forget his troubled homeland—even though it almost cost him his life.

Born in 1906 to a Romanian army officer father and a seamstress mother, there is a strong chance we never would have heard of Roegen had it not been for a generous government scholarship that allowed him to escape Romanian poverty and study mathematics abroad, first in Paris, then London and eventually the United States.

Roegen made his mark early on in mathematics and statistical theory. His 1927 Sorbonne doctoral thesis improved upon existing analytical models to understand random occurrences within systems. His expertise was finding glitches, statistical untruths and false variables. Famed Harvard economist Joseph Schumpeter used Roegen's research in his text *Business Cycles* and brought him to Harvard in the early 1930s. Schumpeter hoped Roegen's statistical genius could help kick-start the stalling world economy.

Roegen believed the predictive qualities of the leading economic theories of his day were limited by the fact they assumed human wants were equal as opposed to hierarchical. Individuals desire different things for different reasons he said, and therefore multiple theories, multiple explanations and multiple models are needed for each problem. Just as the discipline of physics embraced Niels Bohr's observation that the electron has both wave and particle qualities, (a contradiction explainable by divergent theories), Roegen thought economics should also embrace contradictions instead of creating ideological assumptions to excuse them. He also held that classifications like currency, commodities and expectations were abstractions, not absolutes, and therefore could never be fully captured in economic formulas. Roegen's call for multiplicity marked one of the first key methodological critiques of neoclassical economics.

At the beginning of his rise in America, and to the detriment of his career, Roegen returned to Romania in 1937 only to be forced to spend a decade in the service of various violent national governments. He was eventually reduced to poverty and threatened with death by the ruling communists. Roegen published little over the next decade. In 1948, he secretly escaped Romania and headed back to the United States, where he accepted a position at Vanderbilt University and produced his most lasting work.

Like Frederick Soddy before him, Roegen challenged the foundational assumptions of neoclassical economic theory using the laws of thermodynamics. His landmark text, *The Entropy Law and Economic Process*, 1971, expanded on Soddy's often-overlooked work.

The second law of thermodynamics, also known as the entropy law, posits that energy, once used, can never be recovered—you can't make a cow from a hamburger. The modern economy is built almost entirely on fossil fuels, burning low entropy materials and producing high entropy waste. This process, turning "free" energy into "bound" energy, is mistakenly called growth. Roegen argued that such growth was actually an illusion and that present generations were living on borrowed time. He believed that entropic laws and energy conservation ought to be paramount in economic theory. "If we understand well the problem, the best use of our iron resources is to produce plows or harrows as they are needed, not Rolls Royces, not even agricultural tractors."

Roegen also took economists to task for overlooking key physical truths: "Had economics recognized the entropic nature of the economic process, it might have been able to warn its co-workers for the betterment of mankind—the technological sciences—that 'bigger and better' washing machines, automobiles and superjets must lead to 'bigger and better pollution.'"

According to entropy laws, the foundational neoclassical premise—indefinite material substitution for exhausted resources—is a fallacy. New technologies cannot stop the flow of free energy to bound energy for which we all depend for survival. It is simply a matter of time, Roegen said, until the price system devours every source of free energy on Earth until only the sun is left. While not as hopeful as his protégés about humanity's future, Roegen believed that with a radical paradigm shift, life on Earth could be expanded from its bleakly small forecasts to near infinity. His work is considered the foundation of bioeconomics.

**Darren Fleet**

# HOWARD ODUM

"THE STRUGGLE BETWEEN ORDER AND DISORDER, BETWEEN ANGELS AND DEVILS, IS STILL WITH US."

1955 Ford Thunderbird

Few economists—love for scientific rigor notwithstanding—understand how concepts like chaos theory and the laws of thermodynamics could possibly impact their work. For Howard Odum, however, scientific principles were central to both the study of economics and life in general. As he saw it, "The struggle between order and disorder, between the angels and devils, is still with us."

Odum was a prominent figure in the vanguard of the ecological economics revolution. Throughout his long career, Odum wrote extensively about the biological limits to economic activity, the role fossil fuels play in international relations and net energy analysis. He applied the laws of thermodynamics to demonstrate that energy use has to be measured not only in terms of usage but also of waste. Generating nuclear power, for example, requires a massive amount of energy. By Odum's measures, more energy is consumed in its creation than produced. So why, he asked, would we do it? Odum was among the first to conceptualize energy as currency, demonstrating the differences between the ecological impact of natural versus manufactured processes. He also pioneered the field of "ecological engineering," the management and restoration of ecosystems to account for the demands of both human activity and the natural environment.

His 1971 text, *Environment, Power and Society*, blew the lid off of comfortable understandings that hydrocarbons were the elixir of humanities salvation. "Few people realize that their prosperity comes from the great flux of fossil fuel energies and not just from human dedication and political design," he wrote. This directly challenged the growing orthodoxy in economics that human exception, not energy determinism, was the root of industrial prosperity. Using energy as a framework to understand environmental, mechanical and social phenomena, Odum showed that human organization is directly related to the type of energy a society relies upon: "When resources are in excess, maximum power is achieved by the uncontrolled overgrowth of a few species specialized for quick capture of energy and materials."

In this way, modern human civilization is no different from weeds colonizing a clear-cut logging patch, optimizing unhindered access to the sun; or millions of sea crabs populating deep Atlantic heat vents in an otherwise barren underwater wasteland; or an idea permeating a society when free speech is suddenly acceptable, like free markets in the East after the fall of the USSR.

As part of his analysis, Odum posited two unique phases in human civilization defined by energy systems: Solar society and fossil society. Because of its weak and varied flow, solar energy creates parochial, small and biologically diverse communities. On the other hand, fossil fuel energy creates large, dependent and biologically narrow societies.

What Odum offered was not just an economic theory of the need for energy conservation in the process of contemporary capitalism, but a new way of understanding human limits and the role of energy in our lives—a new paradigm of thinking about progress. Megacities are not technological marvels but a response to a massive overflow of hydrocarbons. Modern agricultural inputs are not an advancement of Earth's photosynthetic process, but a diversion of it.

"A whole generation of citizens thought that higher efficiencies in using the energy of the sun had arrived. This was a sad hoax, for people of the developed world no longer eat potatoes made from solar energy … the food reaching humans is produced mostly by the energy subsidies in support of all the human services required. People are really eating potatoes partly made of oil."

He also observed that greater energy consumption in industrial societies leads to diminishing acknowledgement of energy dependence. A rural dweller in central Africa knows the work it takes to get water from the ground with a hand-pump and therefore conserves energy appropriately. Meanwhile, because a wealthy Westerner takes a twenty-minute hot shower with the simple turn of a wrist, they cannot appreciate the work cost and literally pour energy down the drain.

Late in life, Odum and his wife Elizabeth devoted their time to warning of an imminent ecological collapse if our patterns of consumption remained unchanged. In their 2001 book, *A Prosperous Way Down*, they argued that humans must wean themselves off fossil fuels in light of rapidly shrinking reserves. Among other things, the pair suggested redistributing the world's wealth more equitably, curbing population growth, streamlining energy use, promoting lower intensity agriculture and modifying capitalism to make it less focused on growth. Doing so gradually, they claimed, would allow a "soft path down" that would make the world more prosperous after a global economic descent.

Succumbing to cancer in 2002, Odum ended his career as he began it—as a sentinel at the very forefront of revolutionary economic thought. He spent his final days working on a new edition of *Environment, Power and Society* that was published posthumously in 2007.

Rotary dial telephone, 1947

a quiet temple pond
frog jumps in
plop!

Basho

# KENNETH BOULDING

# "ANYONE WHO BELIEVES EXPONENTIAL GROWTH CAN GO ON FOREVER IS EITHER A MADMAN OR AN ECONOMIST."

Packard-Bell Radio, 1952

Kenneth Boulding was an economist known for having a way with words and refusing to mince them. His most biting criticisms were reserved for the myopia of his own discipline: "Anyone who believes exponential growth can go on forever in a finite world is either a madman or an economist," and "Mathematics brought rigor to economics. Unfortunately it also brought mortis."

Boulding earned the right to speak his mind by serving as president of the American Economic Association and authoring *Economic Analysis*, 1941, the authoritative textbook of neoclassical-Keynesian economic synthesis. "Economic Analysis established my respectability," Boulding said, "so I have been able to be disreputable ever since."

His thought evolved radically over his career. He was a poet, philosopher and peace activist who argued that desirable economic outcomes should be determined with ethical, religious and ecological concerns in mind. This big picture thinking was no doubt influenced by his life-long spiritual identification as a Quaker, a breakaway sect of Anabaptism, with strong beliefs on pacifism, community and redistribution of wealth.

For a time he was a card-carrying Republican, but was driven away from the party by Reagan's hard-right politics. He was especially put off by the president's supply-side deregulation economics and unbridled military spending. Boulding advocated a less hawkish stance toward the Soviet Union and publically mocked Reagan's communist paranoia.

Beyond his advocacy for peace, Boulding was an environmentalist who argued that economics needed to show a greater reverence for nature. In 1958, he asked, "Are we to regard the world of nature simply as a storehouse to be robbed for the immediate benefit of man? ... Does man have any responsibility for the preservation of a decent balance in nature, for the preservation of rare species or even for the indefinite continuance of his race?" He called the growth model a "cowboy economy," which treats nature as inexhaustible and rewards "reckless exploitative, romantic and violent behavior." Boulding proposed an alternative paradigm, a "spaceman economy," that likened the Earth to a self-contained spaceship. With limited resources, members of a spaceman economy have a decided incentive to save rather than consume. "The image of the frontier is probably one of the oldest images of mankind, and it is not surprising that we find it hard to get rid of," he said. The sum of his argument was that without statist intervention, cowboys are destined to defer the consequences of their production, sacrificing the future for the present.

Boulding also broke the mold with his theory of *Psychic Capital*, the idea that human happiness, the ultimate goal of the economics profession, is dependent on the quality of external inputs rather than the quantity. The neoclassical consumption model encourages rapid cycling of cheap goods which, in order to be profitable, must replace existing goods. This process creates consumers who become increasingly dependent on the market for their satisfaction, a market that can only offer weaker forms of the original mental satisfaction. Boulding's less-is-more concept, first articulated in 1950, stands as one of the earliest attempts to expand economics to include observations from medical and social sciences.

Writing in an era of infinite resource frontiers and economic confidence, Boulding was a heretical voice. While others of his stature were praising the benevolence of growth, he argued for prudence and thrift, for an economics more akin with actual human happiness and not just Gross World Product. And with *Psychic Capital*, he challenged his peers to find ways to measure the satisfaction quotient of the "stock" (quality) of things and not just the "flow" (amount).

Above all, Boulding sought truth in economics. He wanted to construct just, sustainable models that reflected the complex interconnectedness of the world. The conclusion of his poem, "A Ballad of Ecological Awareness," puts it this way: "So cost-benefit analysis is nearly always sure/To justify the building of a solid concrete fact/While the Ecologic Truth is left behind in the Abstract."

# E. F. SCHUMACHER

# "SMALL IS BEAUTIFUL."

E. F. Schumacher didn't mind when fellow economists dismissed his unorthodox ideas and called him a crank. He chose to take it as a compliment, reasoning that "the crank is the part of the machine which creates revolution and it is very small. I am a small revolutionary!" Schumacher would in fact build his legacy around the idea of small, which in the world of economics is a revolutionary feat indeed.

Born in Germany in 1911, Schumacher studied in England as a Rhodes scholar and later taught economics at Columbia University and Oxford. A protégé of John Maynard Keynes, Schumacher influenced his eminent mentor's proposal for the postwar currency system that would become the International Monetary Fund. After World War II he aided the British government in the effort to reconstruct the collapsed German nation. From there he moved to *The Times* newspaper—the heart of the British establishment—where he penned editorials criticizing the Labour government's ambitious nationalization plans. In addition to all his endeavors in the private sector, Schumacher served as chief economist for the National Coal Board for twenty years.

Early in his tenure at the Coal Board, Schumacher was sent on a mission to Burma to teach its citizens how to achieve progress by following the Western model of economic growth. Once there, he quickly surmised that the Burmese were better served drawing from their own traditions rather than from Western ones. He coined the term "Buddhist economics" to describe a model that, in complete opposition to its Western counterpart, didn't allow for unlimited growth and consumption but emphasized the use of renewable resources and regarded employment as a path to personal fulfillment, not a sacrifice of time in exchange for income. In a Buddhist economy, work must always be regarded above the product and employment integrated into a broader value system aimed at limiting wants. By treating labor as a market abstraction, a commodity to be subtracted and added for maximum efficiency, modern economics overlooked its fundamental commitment to the individual.

"While the materialist is mainly interested in goods, the Buddhist is mainly interested in liberation," Schumacher wrote. "From an economist's point of view, the marvel of the Buddhist way of life is the utter rationality of its pattern—amazingly small means leading to extraordinarily satisfactory results."

At the time, this Burmese focus on thrift and leisure was heretical to the psychological tenets of classical economics that unlimited pursuit of profits and maximization of effort was the surest way to human happiness. To those who questioned the relevance of Eastern philosophy to economics, Schumacher replied: "Economics without Buddhism, i.e., without spiritual, human and ecological values, is like sex without love."

He later returned to the Coal Board, but working at one of the largest commercial organizations of the day contributed to Schumacher's deep-seated conviction that large-scale technologies were dehumanizing. His experiences led him to conclude: "man is small and, therefore, small is beautiful." It was this syllogism that inspired the title of his 1973 treatise *Small Is Beautiful: A Study of Economics as if People Mattered*, a sweeping indictment of the neoclassical model. The work introduced Schumacher's concept of "natural capital" and outlined an alternative economy based on human-scale, decentralized and appropriate technologies.

"Modern man does not experience himself as a part of nature but as an outside force destined to dominate and conquer it," he wrote. "He even talks of a battle with nature, forgetting that, if he won the battle, he would find himself on the losing side."

Schumacher sought to correct his economist peers about the fundamental difference between income and capital. Income is the wealth earned by producing goods and services and selling them. Capital is the material and wealth it takes to produce income. Since the beginning of the economics discipline, economists (left and right) have put Earth's resources in the wrong category, selling off capital and calling it profit. This, Schumacher said, is a "suicidal error," a Ponzi scheme gambling with the fate of the planet. Until economists corrected their models to account for the loss of natural systems—natural capital—economics wasn't fit to call itself an academic discipline, let alone a science.

To the very end of his life, Schumacher lived by his own prescriptions. He baked his family's weekly bread supply with locally procured organic wheat that he ground himself in a hand-operated flour mill. Schumacher died in 1977 but his followers still advance his prescient economic vision through societies founded in his honor. The Intermediate Technology Development Group (ITDG), founded by Schumacher, continues his work by promoting poverty reduction in the developing world through sustainable technology. Today ITDG continues to demonstrate the wisdom of Schumacher's words, proving that small is not only beautiful ... it has the potential to be prosperous.

# The Endless Summer

On any day of the year it's summer somewhere in the world. Bruce Brown's latest color film highlights the adventures of two young American surfers, Robert August and Mike Hynson who follow this everlasting summer around the world. Their unique expedition takes them to Senegal, Ghana, Nigeria, South Africa, Australia, New Zealand, Tahiti, Hawaii and California. Share their experiences as they search the world for that perfect wave which may be forming just over the next Horizon. **BRUCE BROWN FILMS**

Poster for the 1966 American surfing
documentary classic *Endless Summer*.

# HERMAN DALY

Herman Daly's parochial Texan beginnings defy his stature as the world's preeminent thinker in ecological degrowth economics. He was raised, maybe even born, with an anti-intellectual streak. His father, a devote Irish Catholic, was amazed at how "dumb certain educated people could be."

Daly's parents were uneducated southerners. And while they respected education, they had occasional misgivings about their son's book learning aspirations. They made sure that his primary education was cataloging inventory and serving customers at their small Houston hardware store. Born on the eve of WWII in 1938, he worked in the family business until the day he left for college. "It was as good of an education as any," Daly says of his shelf-stocking days. "Everybody comes into a hardware store for something. So you have to deal with people. That's your job. To be nice and to sell them something and show them how it works and learn how if you don't."

That idea of understanding something before prescribing a solution was key in Daly's leanings towards economics. Growing up in Texas in the 1940s and 1950s, he was no stranger to poverty and the plight of migrant workers from Mexico in the United States. He learned Spanish as a teen and as a final send-off from high school went on a road trip from Houston to Mexico City, a voyage that changed the course of his life. He saw the destitution of the poor in the border towns but also the lavish and cultured lifestyles of the refined enclaves within Mexico City. He decided to dedicate his life to making life better for the poor across Latin America.

"The field of economic development in the 1950s was new and exciting. The whole idea was 'let's raise the world out of poverty.' I wanted to do that and economics wanted to do that with economic development. And a big part of development was simply growth. So I was originally a growth economist."

It didn't take long for Daly to fall out of step with the dominant thinking of his time. His doctoral research at Vanderbilt University took him to Uruguay and eventually Brazil in the late 1960s, where as an advisor to local policy managers he began to question the underlying philosophy he'd trained in. There he saw first hand the mass destruction of the Brazilian rainforest to make room for rapid economic development and population expansion. His Houston hardware store math told him this model couldn't go on forever, that unlimited growth would eventually gobble up the entire natural world.

If one word defines Herman Daly, it's limits. Not the negative-no-hope-dogma type, but the kind based in the realism of biology, the laws of physics and the sobriety of Methodist theologians—the Christian faith he is most close to today. It's the kind that says if you spend more money than you earn, you'll go broke; that if you stay up too late in the evening you'll be tired the next day; that action leads to reaction. It's also the kind of limits that says a child stricken with polio, like Daly was at the age of eight, might have to amputate one of their arms.

# "GROWTH MAY COST MORE THAN IT'S WORTH."

"There is a balance between the old John Wayne American view of you-can-do-anything-if-you-set-your-mind-to-it, nothing is impossible, all dreams can be fulfilled if you just do it ... [and the reality that] there are certain things that are impossible," he says.

These competing visions—sober limits vs. American optimism—played out in the family discussions over his health and his future, his protestant German mother leaning more to the John Wayne side of things. An economist through and through, Daly talks about his childhood malady in the language of projections and curves. "That taught me the notion of opportunity cost. For every hour you waste in some crackpot treatment or therapy to recover a paralyzed arm, that's an hour you could have spent doing something else that would have given you more."

The wisdom Daly gained from his battle with polio would surface again later in life during his tenure at Louisiana State University when he penned his first musings about uneconomic growth—that the cost of unlimited economic activity would eventually undermine its utility. Before publishing *Steady-State Economics*, the text that launched bioeconomics as a discipline in 1977, Daly studied under the famed neoclassicist-turned-thermodynamic-obsessed Nicholas Georgescu-Roegen, who until the day he died toiled mercurially over a not-yet-proven fourth energy law of physics. Under Roegen's statistical genius, Daly got a heavy dose of the entropy law, the principle that energy once used cannot be regained. This law became the basis of Daly's broader theory that economics is a subsystem of the ecosystem, not vice versa, and that to avoid future economic and environmental collapse economies need to stop growing.

"The idea comes right out of classical economics and is most clearly expressed by John Stuart Mill in his writing on the stationary state economy or on the stationary state. He made the argument so simply and beautifully that it just overwhelmed me. I remember reading it and thinking 'Wow! This is very important,'" Daly says.

He paired Mill's nineteenth-century idea with the highly influential Leontief input/output models, that all economies are intrinsically interdependent. But instead of applying Leontief strictly to the economy, he expanded it to the natural world in which the economy operates.

Daly was influenced by some of the most radical economic thinkers of his time. His voice erupts with admiration at the mention of Kenneth Boulding and E. F. Schumacher, whose works he followed closely. As an undergraduate economics student in the 1950s, the ideas of Kenneth Boulding and Paul Samuelson competed for classroom dominance. Daly admits that Boulding's normative analysis didn't stir him but that it was Boulding's examinations of human satisfaction that captured his mind. "He just kind of turned a lot of things on their head and that really impressed me," Daly says about reading Boulding's more radical work.

In his essay "Income or Welfare," Boulding attempted to measure human happiness as an intersection between goods and leisure. The idea that human happiness was dependent on stock of goods rather than the flow of income, that less is often more, was key to Daly's formation of steady state economics. Because current satisfaction models are pegged to constantly increasing GDP, stock of goods must be constantly replaced by an increased flow of income in order to get more goods. Thrift or satiation is the ultimate enemy of this model. If people are happy with what they have in the natural environment or the technological innovations of their time, if people stop upgrading and replacing existing stock, GDP goes down.

Daly also found himself attracted to E. F. Schumacher's search for equitable economic principles in spirituality, first in Buddhism and then in Catholicism. Schumacher argued that the best practices of all faiths place limits on growth. Daly says he felt a tremendous kinship with Schumacher, especially his ideas about faith-based, Earth-first economics. And although Daly hesitates when calling himself a Christian, (because, he says, of the many environmental and economic ills done in the name of Christianity today), he does believe that faith can have a role in combating the religion of our age, economic growth. "What is sufficient for a good life is the philosophical question that we've been wrestling with throughout history. Economics has not dealt seriously with the concept of sufficiency. It's always more, and more efficient ways to get more and more."

Like most ecological economists, Daly has found himself pushed to the fringe of mainstream economics. This began at Louisiana State University in the 1980s he says, when the institution began to hire a new wave of Chicago school economists. He watched as his supply of doctoral students dried up and the economics faculty moved towards Reaganomics. "It became rather uncomfortable because any student who wanted to write a dissertation with me was sort of automatically suspect and considered unsound. It put my students in an impossible position and it put me in an impossible position."

In 1989, after two decades of teaching economics at LSU, Daly left academia and joined the World Bank as a sustainable development economist. The move coincided with the fall of the Berlin Wall, marking the unchallenged ascension of neoclassical economics to the pulpit of econ departments across the world. Admittedly, it was a difficult time for a degrowth thinker to enter the bastion of Western economic liberalism, but he did it anyway, thinking he could nudge the organization in a different direction. "I was a bridge between the small number of ecologists and environmentalists at the bank and the large number of economists ... a kind of translator between these two things."

For six years Daly battled to have sustainability and environmental conservation linked to development projects and cash loans; he had little luck combating the growth-first, environment-second orthodoxy. "Eventually it just became clear that all of this [sustainability] was pretty much window dressing and it was business as usual with a tiny bit of recycling at the end."

With Harvard economist Larry Summers as the Chief Economist, Daly resigned. As a parting gift his colleagues gave him the opportunity to address the organization in a public speech in 1994. "Don't waste time trying to censor some little staff economist who, in his theoretical writings, deviates from the Bank's party line favoring free trade, NAFTA, or anything else," Daly said. "Without deviance there can be no change."

He then suggested the bank take a dose of antacids and laxatives to help cure some of the pressure of the top down structure, and prescribed a hearing aid and eyeglasses so the bank could see and experience the external world as it really is. He outlined four core policy moves needed to reform the Word Bank: Stop counting the consumption of natural capital as income; tax labor and income less and tax resource throughput more; maximize the productivity of natural capital in the short run, and invest in increasing its supply in the long run; move away from the ideology of global economic integration by free trade.

Having so openly critiqued one of the most dominant growth organizations in the world, Daly's prospects of finding another position in a leading economics department were limited. He eventually found a home at the Institute of Public Policy at the University of Maryland, a position he held until retiring in the late 2000s. There he was a major influence on many of the key degrowth and ecological economists today including Robert Costanza and Joshua Farley.

The snail's pace at which his degrowth steady state economic model has percolated into mainstream economics is not surprising. The philosophy of limits is about as un-American as an Al-Qaeda Christmas party. Degrowth doesn't just challenge the fundamental precepts of neoclassical economics, it offends the most basic values of the great American myth: Permanent opportunity.

"I had rather hoped that the 2008 financial crisis might have provided enough of a kick in the head to stimulate a degrowth type of rethinking ... but the crisis has put growth first and center even more," Daly laments.

Growth is the dominant preanalytic vision of our time, Daly says. It's the lens through which even the majority of critics, let alone supporters, see the world. After more than five decades of research, numerous awards, countless books and hundreds of peer-reviewed articles, Daly says he's not that optimistic for the future. Global warming, economic anxiety, the continued dogma of growth, environmental degradation, population expansion, increasing inequality and expanding global free-trade are just a few of the things that cause him to worry. Yet in that paradoxical John Wayne sense of his Protestant mother, he is hopeful. "As a rational expectation I am not optimistic, but as an existential attitude, I am hopeful. I think you have to be hopeful as a way of getting through the world."

**Darren Fleet**

## MARTIN LUTHER

was one of the most devout Catholics
of his time. He profoundly believed
in the benevolency of the Papacy and
the sacredness of the apostolic lineage.
He went to Rome believing that if the
Pontiff only knew the depravity of
indulgences and the extent of church
corruption, he would intervene. But
the Pope only wanted to hear one
word from Luther:

**Recant.**

# KICK IT OVER MANIFESTO

## WE, THE ECONOMICS STUDENTS OF THE WORLD, MAKE THIS ACCUSATION:

THAT YOU, THE TEACHERS OF NEOCLASSICAL ECONOMICS AND THE STUDENTS THAT YOU GRADUATE, HAVE PERPETUATED A GIGANTIC FRAUD UPON THE WORLD.

YOU CLAIM TO WORK IN A PURE SCIENCE OF FORMULA AND LAW, BUT YOURS IS A SOCIAL SCIENCE, WITH ALL THE FRAGILITY AND UNCERTAINTY THAT THIS ENTAILS. WE ACCUSE YOU OF PRETENDING TO BE WHAT YOU ARE NOT.

YOU HIDE IN YOUR OFFICES, PROTECTED BY YOUR JARGON, WHILE IN THE REAL WORLD FORESTS VANISH, SPECIES PERISH, HUMAN LIVES ARE RUINED AND LOST. WE ACCUSE YOU OF GROSS NEGLIGENCE IN THE MANAGEMENT OF OUR PLANETARY HOUSEHOLD.

YOU HAVE KNOWN SINCE ITS INCEPTION THAT YOUR MEASURE OF ECONOMIC PROGRESS, THE GROSS DOMESTIC PRODUCT, IS FUNDAMENTALLY FLAWED AND INCOMPLETE, AND YET YOU HAVE ALLOWED IT TO BECOME A GLOBAL STANDARD, REPORTED DAY BY DAY IN EVERY FORM OF MEDIA. WE ACCUSE YOU OF RECKLESSLY SUPPORTING THE ILLUSION OF PROGRESS AT THE EXPENSE OF HUMAN AND ENVIRONMENTAL HEALTH.

YOU HAVE DONE GREAT HARM, BUT YOUR TIME IS COMING TO ITS CLOSE. THE REVOLUTION OF ECONOMICS HAS BEGUN, AS HOPEFUL AND DETERMINED AS ANY IN OUR HISTORY. WE WILL HAVE OUR CLASH OF PARADIGMS, WE WILL HAVE OUR MOMENT OF TRUTH, AND OUT OF EACH WILL COME A NEW ECONOMICS — OPEN, HOLISTIC, HUMAN SCALE.

ON CAMPUS AFTER CAMPUS, WE WILL CHASE YOU OLD GOATS OUT OF POWER. THEN, IN THE MONTHS AND YEARS THAT FOLLOW, WE WILL BEGIN THE WORK OF REPROGRAMMING THE DOOMSDAY MACHINE.

### Sign the manifesto at kickitover.org

Our 10,000 year old
civilization bet is now hedged
completely on one throw:

*singularity*

In one sweeping global moment
we change the direction of our future forever.

*Nightfall*

The new 1,000 year Dark Age begins.

sea levels are expected
to keep rising for the
next thousand years
and beyond . . .

WHO ARE WE?

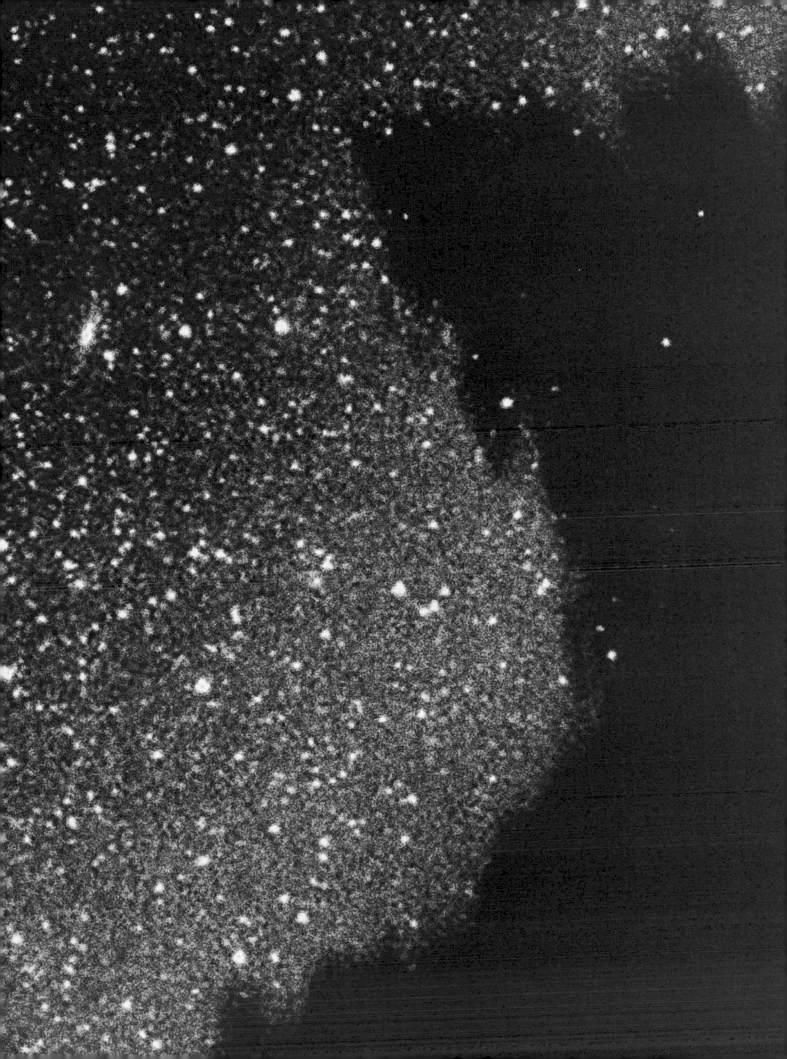

# WHERE ARE
# WE GOING?

# The Angel of History

A Klee painting named *Angelus Novus* shows an angel
looking as though he is about to move away from something
he is fixedly contemplating. His eyes are staring, his mouth
is open, his wings are spread. This is how one pictures the
angel of history. His face is turned toward the past. Where
we perceive a chain of events, he sees one single catastrophe
which keeps piling wreckage upon wreckage and hurls it in
front of his feet. The angel would like to stay, awaken the
dead, and make whole what has been smashed. But a storm
is blowing from Paradise; it has got caught in his wings
with such violence that the angel can no longer close them.
The storm irresistibly propels him into the future to which
his back is turned, while the pile of debris before him grows
skyward. This storm is what we call progress.

Walter Benjamin

EXHAUSTED

## Ok all you crash survivors out there,

How are you?

We've spent the last month, like everyone, wondering what the hell happened after that terrible week when everything collapsed. But we regrouped, and now we're back … and forging ahead as best we can.

Most of us are still in shock, trying our best to move from anger/depression toward some kind of acceptance. But what does it mean to be an adbuster in a world without ads; a culture jammer when there's no consumer culture left to jam? Well, we put out the word that we were working on a postcrash issue of Adbusters, and the word spread. And the letters started flooding in from all over the world. This issue is a compilation of your poignant, freaky, angry thoughts. Like us, you are starting to make sense of this crazy new world.

Looking back now on "the good old days," it sure feels like we activists did protest too much. We were always anti-everything and pro very little. We kept on saying, "A New World Is Possible," but we didn't have the vision and guts to build it. I remember how just about every "progressive" magazine I read before the crash was stuffed full of lefty whining, without a single action or solution proposed.

But not everyone here is raking over the ashes of history. A few bright sparks are running around saying: "Fuck your postmortem … OK, so capitalism crashed, the megacorps we hated so much are gone, and you can't buy a can of Coke anymore. So what's your problem? Isn't this the world we always dreamed about? Isn't this what we were fighting for all along?"

These fired-up young anarchists will be our new leaders. They have an almost pathological, taboo-like disgust for the old world and—Coke or no Coke—they're determined to never let it rise again. The price was too high, for all of us, for everything. Their world is about bioregions, true-cost farming, keeping every corporation on a very tight leash and building a new media that delivers truth. And they swear they'll never again let national governments or global institutions tell them what they can or cannot do in their communities.

We'll try to put out another issue soon. Keep your letters and stories rolling in. We've just had a collective near-death experience, but with it has come a powerful new urge to live. Every day, more and more of us are finding something very real, very concrete to fight for and maybe, even, to die for. That old Situationist slogan, "Live Without Dead Time," really means something now.

So, *Adbusters*, I hope you're finally satisfied. Issue after issue you proclaimed the system dead or dying, and now things have gone your way. So where is the revolution? I don't see any rainbows in the sky or people dancing in the streets. Yes, there's a redistribution of wealth, or should I say a near-total elimination of it. But I can't quite see how this is going to change the world in a positive way.

Where I live the water is now undrinkable and people can't get their medicine. The old guy next door was attacked and stabbed for his groceries, something once unheard of in my neighborhood. All of my family have lost their jobs. Living in fear and surviving just to get by is not a liberating experience. It kills the soul. We will survive, trust me, but not by reading *Adbusters*. It's kinda ironic: You morons lived to see the big day but now have nothing to say. I used to love your little spoof ads. Now you're the spoof ad.

Peter Lawson
Detroit, Michigan

**Before the crash I was a psychologist. Given the excruciating demands for survival now, private practice has turned into public practice. What else is there to do but pitch in?**

I just came back from LA to my home in the Sierras. That city's dying like starved cancer. Some sick part of me craved to see the heart of the suffering, wanted to see the consumers pay. You wouldn't believe how bad the stink is. There's still people leaving any way they can.

Abandoned cars were everywhere, even ditched on the freeways, where people were walking around the stalled traffic and trying to laugh off the hot sun, rummaging around in the vehicles for treasures left behind—batteries, bulbs, a pack of cigarettes . . . But just think, no more road rage.

Across the flat, dry horizon I saw the blue smoke of cookfires trail up from rooftops, and clotheslines hung from building to building in a colorful array. Something powerful was happening here: Amid all the brown lawns, violence and cries of the hungry and dying, people began to plant seeds—in boots, TV monitors, jewelry boxes, flocking with spades and other implements to anywhere dirt could be found. They were already growing.

Love, Terry
South Lake Tahoe, California

Beyond the necessity of developing workable food and sanitation systems, I'd say our most pressing problem is psychological. When people's belief in immunity from catastrophe is stripped, the first reaction is to look to the outside world for help; the realization that none is coming can catalyze unbearable abandonment. And with it, anger at God. Paralyzing grief. The revival of childhood separation anxieties. Numbing. Panic. Preoccupation with death. And, for some, total breakdown. Thankfully, the breakdowns have been rolling, touching in on different families like a random plague. In the beginning many of the older and already-sick folks died, I presume, from fright. I lost my father.

I've been working round the clock. Last moon I finally got beyond seat-of-the-pants emergency response and set up a network of "psychic nurses." We now have a cadre of eighty-nine serving our community of fifteen thousand, their skills varying from pastoral counseling and Twelve Steps to "being a mother."

I keep ruminating about how it must have been for our ancestors in the Ice Age when—like us, against all odds—everyone was challenged to make survival happen. We are struggling to make it work.

Sincerely, Dr. Sasha White,
Chimayo, New Mexico

The sun is shining, I'm lying back on my rear deck, shaded by a giant pine, drinking homegrown apple juice. I love how the tables have turned. I'm happy because I'm not coming down off any of the perpetual highs that most everyone's been riding for the past many years. Off the grid, I wasn't addicted to constant rush, the 24-hour news cycle and constant email and text messages. I didn't miss primetime TV or the surrogate emotions of the big screen. Genuinely hooked on nature, I'm not withdrawing from any of the toxic psychiatric meds. Nor am I scrambling to keep caffeine and nicotine coursing through my body. Last week when I took a trip to the city, I saw a whole society unable to maintain its multisensory dependencies. Perhaps the masses will shake off their addictions and realize just how indulgent, wired and hoodwinked they have become. Maybe then we can get back to being nice to each other. Either way, I'm happy.

Ellen Harding
Chilliwack, British Columbia

Explanations for the collapse cannot be summed up in a single idea or one catastrophic event. The truth lies somewhere deeper down. What went wrong started going wrong a long time ago, perhaps as far back as the start of our evolution as human beings, certainly at the start of our own cultural evolution. Deep in the recesses of our minds and societies, there exist structures that govern our ways of thinking and being. These structures, built over centuries as a dialectic between inner mind and outer world, have a destructive power that still remains hidden from view. We must become aware of these structures and tear down all that remains of them. This is the next evolutionary step.

**I was in the middle of a PhD in economics when the crash hit. So I remember watching firsthand as my profs defended their ideology until the severity of the economic meltdown made their proclamations embarrassingly comical. Before the university officially closed, I walked away. There was no point carrying on with the charade.**

I was never certain I would get back home, but thanks to a few Good Samaritans and a healthy dose of serendipity, I made it. And on account of my academic background, I was immediately asked to join a group of local community leaders who were trying to configure an alternative economy. It was damage control, really. We wanted to protect ourselves from the more catastrophic effects of the collapse.

Due to patchy supply lines and the end of cheap long-haul transport, we knew we would have to be more self-sufficient and distinguish needs from wants. Food was an obvious starting point. We only have minimal capacity to import food so we got all the local farmers to agree that no food will leave the community until local needs have been met. Other resources are kept local through the formal bartering network we have established. We buy cooperatively even though it means fighting over how long we use particular items. We recycle so much that we rarely use the term "waste." Almost everything holds value. And it's been a struggle, but I think I've managed to convince people to loan each other resources without charging interest. The way I see it, no one should profit off someone else without laboring for it. And I'm not alone. The sacred texts of Jews, Christians and Muslims all condemn the charging of interest.

Now that we're slowly getting to our feet, we've put feelers out to other communities to see what they're doing. Many of them are excited by our prescriptions and have asked us for advice. We may try to create regional alliances. But as the new economy grows, we'll fight to ensure that our original vision is never abandoned. We're taking full responsibility for our economy now that governments and corporations have dropped the ball. It's not easy. We don't always agree and not all of our ideas have worked. The new economy involves a considerable degree of sacrifice, but people are used to sacrifice now. We're committed to creating a sustainable, holistic, human-scale economy designed for the long term. It'll be built on the model of a true-cost market in which the price of every product tells the ecological truth. Progress will be measured by our social and environmental well-being as well as the sum of how much we produce and consume. Our waterways, forests and grasslands will be valued as natural capital that does not need to be harvested to be worth something. And we'll restore the historical taboo against charging interest.

This time we simply have to get it right.

Janneken Drange

In the chaos I found power
I was ruler of a kingdom of one
Life was adventure, mystery
The map was burned
Rules meaningless
In the morning, there came a sun
And under it I saw my shadow
For the very first time

TIP: PRESERVE FOOD USING NATURAL INGREDIENTS. FOR FISH, RUB PLENTY OF SALT INTO IT; FOR VEGETABLES, BOIL THEM IN WATER WITH LEMON OR LIME JUICE. TO MAKE FISH PEMMICAN, SOFTEN COOKED FISH WITH YOUR HANDS, WORK IT INTO POWDERY PIECES, ADD BERRIES AND OTHER SEASONINGS, ROLL INTO CLUMPS THE SIZE OF GOLF BALLS, THEN LEAVE IN THE SUN TO HARDEN. IT WILL REMAIN EDIBLE FOR YEARS.

# Hmmph, city boy. You want coffee or what?

I know it's cold out here, but I haven't passed a coffee shop. Look, I've got some coffee that I looted from a Starbucks and I've got a stove, so we'll boil some up right quick. Grab me that soup can—yeah the big one . . . and a small one, too.

We're going to put sand in the bottom of the big can. You know, insulation. Next time you have a grease fire you'll appreciate it. Just pick up the stove and tip the sand and fire together: Instant fire extinguisher. Doesn't seem brilliant now, but if it's freezing and you're living in a wood lean-to, the last thing you want to do is burn it down.

Twist some coat hangers. Got something sturdier? Well, use it. Interlock them in the bottom of the can and pour sand on top. Find a heavy rock for extra stability. Put the small soup can in the big one for your fuel burner, then surround it with more sand. If you have liquid fuel, use an aluminum pop can. Cut the edge of the can into triangle shapes, then bend them into the middle of the can. That way the fuel will lick upward in separate flames instead of being a big cup just burning away. It's the sort of thing that you can use any liquid fuel for. Steal some denatured alcohol, maybe some white gas . . . whatever it takes. I want my cup of coffee.

If you don't have liquid fuel, use a regular soup can for your burner. Anything you can find to burn will work. Hell, if you have to use dung, use it: Won't smell nice but it'll work. Just remember that this isn't an 80,000 BTU, six-burner range with two ovens: This is a camp stove, boy. You'll boil water, just don't think it'll happen in seconds.

Which brings us to our second device, our "luxury" option. If you've got electricity, make an immersion heater. It's dead simple science: Electricity passing through metal with high resistance makes heat. We're not talking wires you ripped out of a wall; we're looking to waste electricity and cram it through metal to slow it down and get it fucking hot.

Find a percolator with a narrow bottom and smash it to get the heating element (the old spring elements are common, but if you find a solid element, just mount it differently). That way you've got a heater to stick in any old pot of water, even in a tub of water for a bath. You can't take a bath in a percolator.

Take the cord from the same percolator and wrap electrical tape around one end of the coil and an exposed end of wire. Repeat with the other end. Main thing is, it's electricity. Any metal that touches it will be charged. Mount it to ceramic so that you can touch it while it's plugged in. Your best bet will be to find a ceramic tube; even the neck off an old teapot would be okay. Oh yeah, water conducts electricity, too, so remember that it's easy to make a dead-funny mistake and leave yourself, well, dead. Yeah yeah, it's dangerous, but I hear there's a guy a couple clicks away with a generator. And damn, some days I just want my cup of coffee now, you know?

Julian Killam

Analog is back, and rightly so. Just as distant planets move along their orbits and the Earth on its axis, so should vinyl spin on your turntable and hands spin on the face of your watch. No longer is the digital world warm enough or human enough. Four DNA bases, the synapse, twenty-six letters, zero and one. The brute, lifeless order of things has its constituent parts, but the whole transcends those parts: Living organisms, consciousness. We can't be blamed for wanting things to be whole again. We want to see the moving parts. Something we can wind up. We want to look at the orbits and axes on high, not the protons and electrons deep down below.

CAPITALISM IS A DEAD DOG

The Guess Jeans billboard near my apartment, the one that made me gag in the mornings on my way to work, has now become a site for sexual catharsis. It's toppled, smashed and ripped apart. Both of Paris Hilton's suggestive eyes have big $$s etched into them. And spray-painted across her tanned forehead: "You fucked the system!"

The rage toward this lingering effigy of our fallen economy isn't directed at Paris, or even at Guess. More like years of needless sexual desire suddenly finding a violent release. Remember that old sex-infused economy? Those sultry body parts of celebrities that became more familiar than your own? Remember your imaginary body? Breasts by Heidi Klum, butt by Gisele Bündchen, legs by Paris Hilton, abs by Usher, fat wallet and fat lifestyle by Donald Trump. Sex was the magic manna energizing it all.

But an economy that sold naughty fantasies doesn't completely explain why Paris's face has been on the receiving end of rocks and aerosol paint. For that, you need to ponder what we rarely questioned before the crash: what does it mean to construct an entire system of exchange on sex?

After supply and demand were jettisoned as our economic axis, irrational desire fueled by personal inadequacies and sold at Wal-Mart prices took over. This arousal machine sent out constant sexual shocks to keep us spending. Reduced to responding to sexual stimulation, corporations and consumers became pimps and johns.

It wasn't in the store where sex sold, it was in the mind. The purchase was the final moment of an intricate come-on. The product hardly mattered. If Brand X's toothpaste made teeth whiter, but Brand Y's had sex appeal, we bought Brand Y like horny sheep. Sexy ads replaced our natural understanding of love and beauty with unobtainable ideals that fed on our esteem. Sullen and depressed, we bought to feel the excitement and lust of the flesh surrounding us.

When Maslow put the physiological requirements of food, water and sex at the base of his hierarchy of needs, he meant physical sex. But the physical wasn't on offer in the virtual economy. It was all tease and no penetration. Marketers piqued base sexual appetites, yet never fed them. Still, numbed by television, repetitive jobs, and easy, thoughtless lives, sexual fantasy offered wild escape. We allowed ourselves to be swallowed whole into the cultural spectacle, and the further we slipped into the virtual, the less physical sex we had.

The crash was both psychological and structural. Our ordering of desires over needs was sent into painful reversal. So many insulated lives full of needless desire were abruptly exposed to a wilderness of real needs—for food, water and shelter. In an instant, sexual fantasy was destroyed. Countless industries built upon the shrine of the flesh, from cars to fashion, music and entertainment, fell to dust along with it. And then the whole structure buckled. We prayed our economic house could weather the shocks, but ultimately, the veil was off. A fantasy economy based on desire was meaningless when desire itself was an impossible fantasy.

And so we revolt against the old signs of the system, the steamy looks and pouted lips and buxom breasts of life in a secure little bubble. Paris Hilton represents everything that was wrong with the old economy, where few of us could accept that the sexy carrot at the end of the stick was not meant to be eaten. As George Gilder said, "Real poverty is less a state of income than a state of mind." We destroyed the Earth, and our souls, in the process. That's what economics built on sex finally meant.

Timothy Querengesser

I LOVE YOU

"free at last, free at last from the tyranny of style"

**Dear Adbusters,**

Well, here I am sitting on my cabin porch at the eastern foot of the Three Sisters volcanoes in the Cascades Mountains of Oregon. I'm a seventy-five-year-old geezer with bad digestion, blurred vision, and only a few of my original teeth. Ma Nature can take me out as soon as She wishes. I've had a good life, and there are plenty of young, strong, innovative folks who can use the scarce food supplies better'n me.

If you want to know the truth, I'm feeling okay about this civilization going under. Always did think that we *Homo sapiens* took a wrong turn back when we threw our lot in with agriculture and the inevitable cities, and with them, concentrated people and pollution, stashes of goods and armies to raid other cities' stashes of goods.

This beautiful planet could probably get along fine with several hundred million of us on board, living simply off the land. But we've succeeded so well at increasing our numbers and taking over every corner of the place that She's overloaded. With civilization down for the count, our numbers can slide back south toward some reasonable level.

I can't imagine our species not reinventing civilization after a while, but maybe we've learned something from the previous go-round. I'm sure many of you will make it through, carrying forward your creative ideas and our collected wisdom from the past ten thousand years on what does and doesn't work. Be sure and enjoy every step of the way, too, okay? Goodbye, and best of luck.

Billy Stevens
Sisters, Oregon

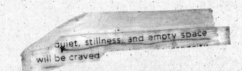

quiet, stillness, and empty space
will be craved

I CAN'T GO TO WORK, I'M HAVING
    AN EMOTIONAL  BREAKDOWN

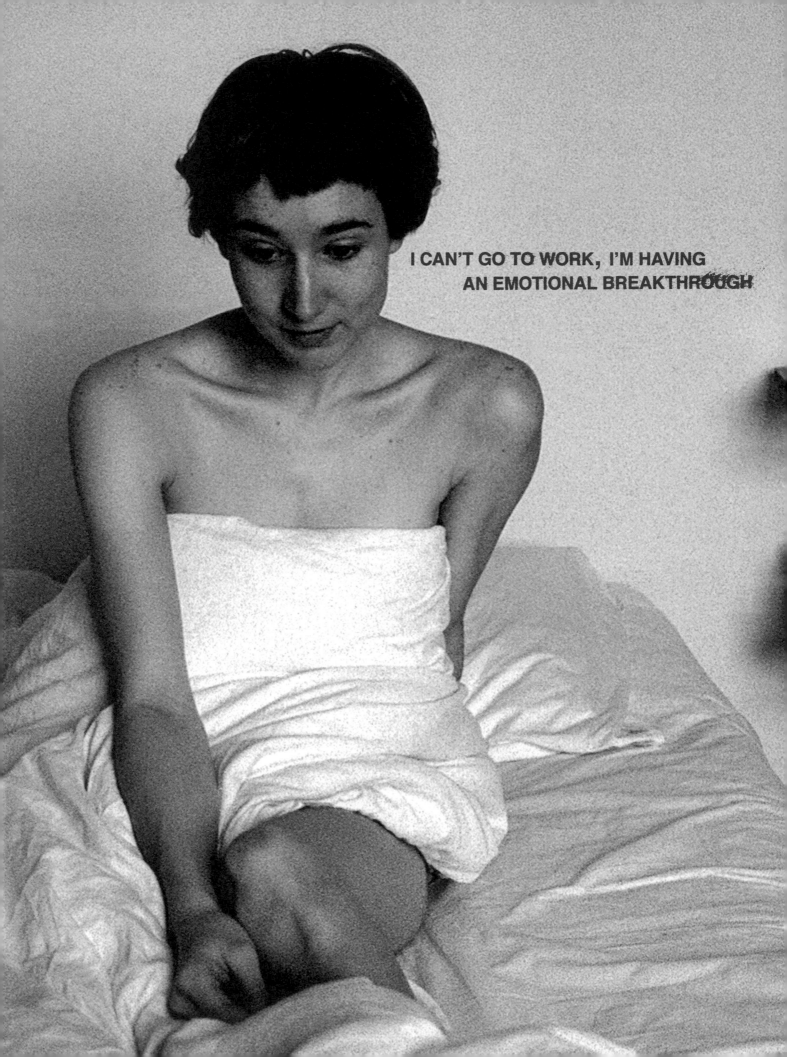

I CAN'T GO TO WORK, I'M HAVING
AN EMOTIONAL BREAKTHROUGH

1

A few people start breaking their old patterns,

embracing what they love (and in the process discovering
what they hate), daydreaming, questioning, rebelling. What
happens naturally then, according to revolutions past, is
a groundswell of support for this new way of being, with
more and more people empowered to perform new
gestures unencumbered by history.

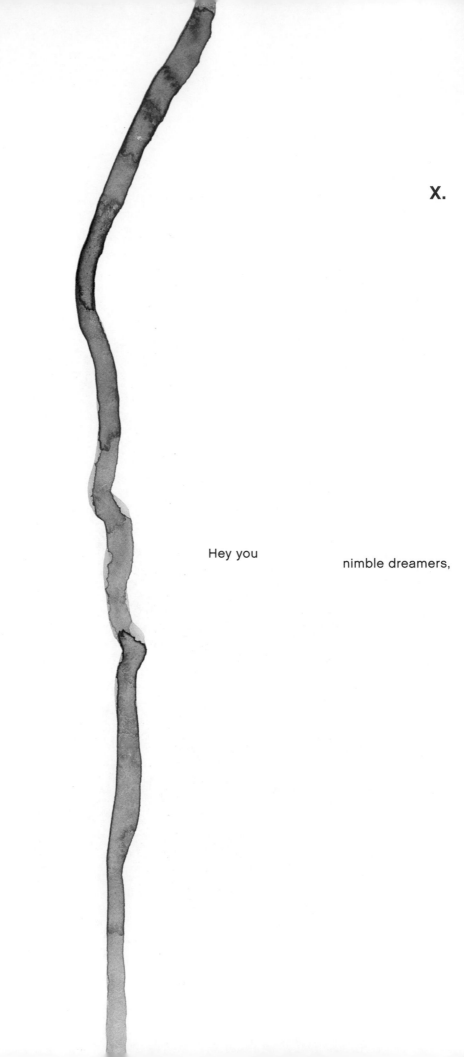

**X.**

Hey you

nimble dreamers,

# A          NEW AESTHETIC

redeemers

and horizontals out there!

You know, we're going to have to go through a
rite of passage ... a civilizational singularity ...
a global "shi" moment ... if we're going to get
through the next thousand years. We'll have to
come up with a new narrative, a new story ... a
new tone, style, feeling, mood ... a new aesthetic
... a new way of "being" in the world.

And then of course we'll have to find the courage
to live fearlessly without dead time and launch
a global drive—a spiritual insurrection ... we'll
have to creatively destroy the old world, the old
corpo-commercial aesthetic and give birth to a
new sense of loveliness ...

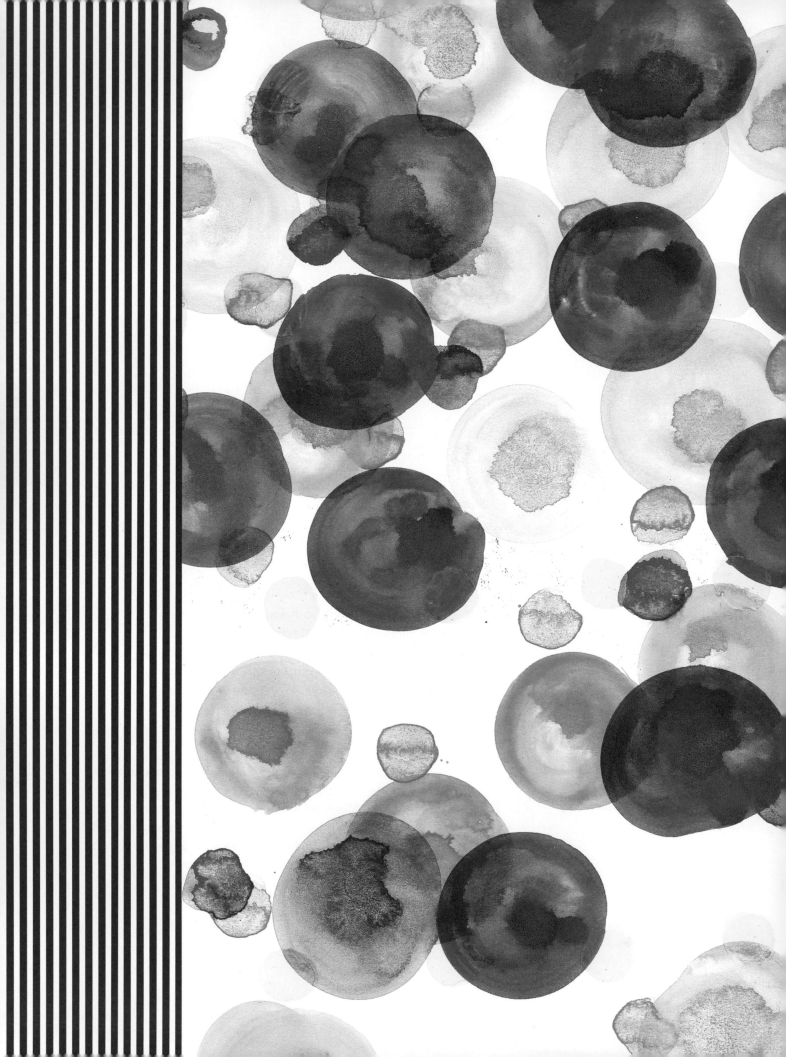

this page
is a living
surface

The perspective—the aesthetic—of our sustainable future has yet to take hold, but it's a simple, honest way of living. It follows organic cycles and mimics nature's ways. It's not so much about being moral or "good" as being a little bit wild and fiercely determined, like crabgrass growing through cracks in the concrete. It's about "being" rather than "having" and "process" rather than "form." As this new way of experiencing the world seeps into our imaginations, it begins to change our clothes, our houses, our shops, streets, food, music.

The straight line is Godless and immoral.

Friedensreich Hundertwasser

Why do straight lines haunt economic theory?

The answer has a lot to do with one of the basic notions of economics, the belief that society is no more than the sum of its parts ... that to understand the whole, all you have to do is connect the dots ... that the interactions between human beings are either zero or negligible. This is the recurring nightmare of the straight line that the next generation of economists will have to wake up and move on from.

**Economics wasn't always the science it now claims to be.**

In fact, not so long ago what now is called big E economics was once magical, mysterious and altogether profound. John Maynard Keynes, the architect of America's recovery from the Great Depression and champion of the welfare state, believed that at its core, economics is ruled by "animal spirits." That is to say that the free, equal and rational mind of consumers in the Locke/Smith economic paradigm does not sufficiently explain human action in the marketplace; that economies operate more according to Freudian animal heritage, or esoteric and emotional impulses, than reason. Other thinkers from this formative economic era, like Joseph Schumpeter, sensed that a violent, warlike impulse of "creative destruction" lurked at the heart of capitalism. And Karl Marx, the great dreamer, proposed that economic theory, rather than empowering and rewarding the selfish gene, could instead create a better social realm in which every person gave according to his abilities and received according to his needs.

But around the 1950s, when the logical positivists were strutting their philosophy of strict rationality, applying scientific method to social phenomena, economists started distancing themselves from psychological and sociological considerations. They liked to think of themselves as real scientists, and over the next few generations they rationalized human behavior, sanitized their theories and models, and tried to transform economics into a mathematically driven exact discipline on the model of physics.

THE NEW SPIRIT OF ECONOMICS

As the global economic and ecological crises bear down upon us, positivists are being forced to admit that their understanding of nonlinear, real-world systems is frail at best and that their mathematical models have very limited value.

This is the perfect moment to give the logic freaks one final push into the dustbin of history. We the heterodox economists, ecological economists and not-so-radical professors and students at universities around the world can kick over the old neoclassical paradigm and pave the way toward a new kind of economics—a psychonomics, a bionomics, a barefoot economics—a wide-ranging, multifaceted, human-scale discipline full of magic, mystery and animal spirits once again.

% saying this is "very important" or "essential"

100

80

60

40

20

0

1965 1970 1975 1980 1985 1990 1995 2000 2005 2010 2015

Developing a meaningful life philosophy

Being very well-off financially

All the joy the world contains
Has come through wishing happiness for others
All the misery the world contains
Has come through wanting pleasure for oneself

—Shantideva, *The Way of the Bodhisattva*

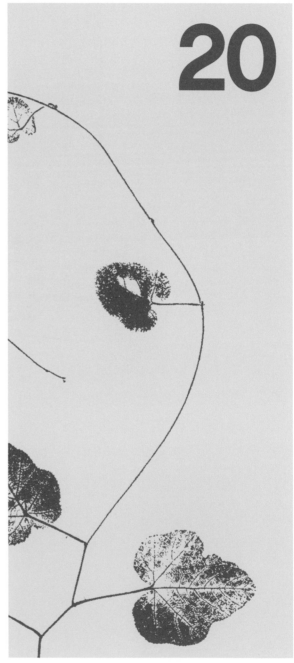

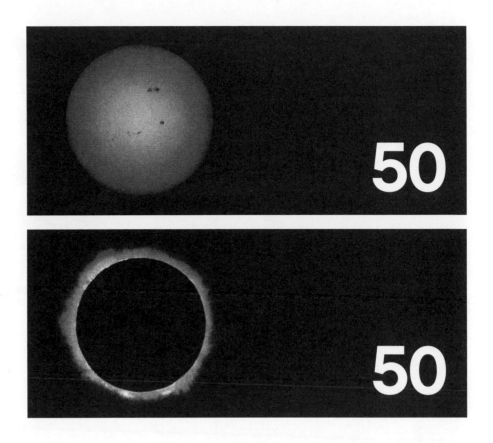

The money of the future

will not have

famous men, architectural triumphs,
Masonic symbolism—no pyramid, an all-seeing eye of
providence or god ...

nor will it reflect the anonymity, the
faceless modern scientific aesthetic, the abstract
emptiness of the current crop of Euro notes ...

these gloriously old
fashioned designs will give way to snow-capped mountain
peaks, salmon river runs, caribou herds, towering glaciers,
breathing forests, teaming jungles, vibrant plains ...

it will reflect the mind shift from     anthropocentric to ecocentric ...

from     individual to communal ...     from political to spiritual ...

and from concrete to  nature ...  which is the ultimate source
of survival of this human experiment of
ours on Planet     Earth.

# ecological civilization

## as a

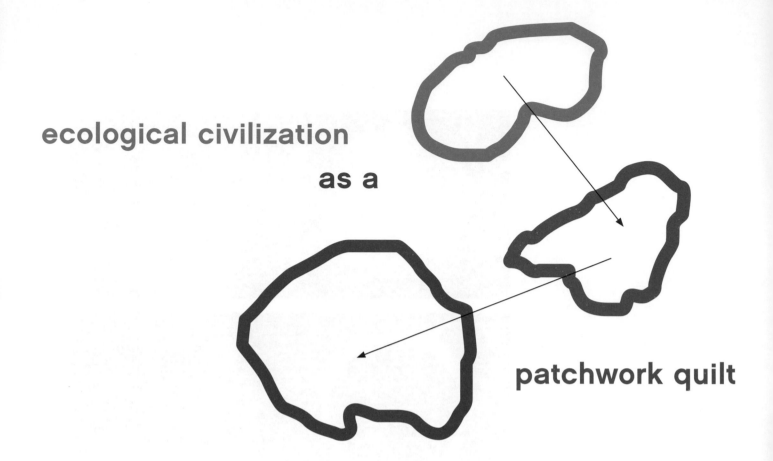

## patchwork quilt

Imagine a patchwork quilt of coevolving ecological societies. They support each other through the differences between them and thereby together make up ecological civilization.

Within each patch, values, knowledge, organization and technology are coevolving with nature. The patches are "lightly coupled" in the sense that transfers of traits, or culturgens can occur between cultures but do not occur so frequently that the cultures lose their distinctiveness achieved through their separate histories.

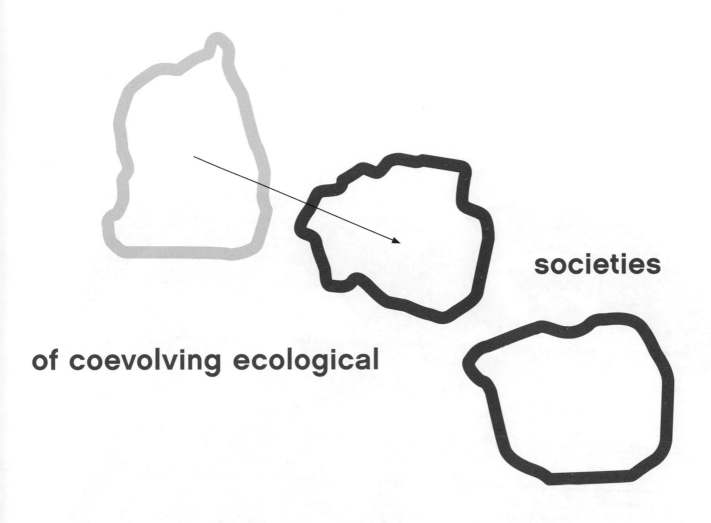

**societies**

**of coevolving ecological**

For the maintenance of diversity, there are appropriate and inappropriate levels of connectivity, and there is little question that the connectivity of globalized industrial civilization is reducing diversity and experimentation in ways of valuing,

understanding, organizing and relating to the environment. Industrial civilization and its globalization have all been rooted in the rationale of efficiency, a logical rationale to follow when a Newtonian mechanical understanding of systems dominates the knowledge system. A coevolutionary ecological civilization would place much more emphasis on understandings of systems stemming from Darwin.

Richard B. Norgaard, *A Coevolutionary Interpretation of Ecological Civilization*

**successful**

# bioeconomies of the future

## Hey kids,

after the crash, the global economy will fracture into dozens of bioregional economies—small, economic communities that survive by tuning in to the specific opportunities and needs of the ecosystems in which they live.

## They will mimic nature at every step.

A new breed of "barefoot" economists, deeply embedded in their bioregions, will take over from the abstract money crunchers. They will pioneer new indices of economic progress and broadcast them on the web like the weather.

Ancient taboos against usury and waste will resurface. The old parasitic professionals—tax lawyers, money brokers, financial consultants—will be turned into economically productive eco-consultants, permaculture advisors and energy planners.

## The corporation will reinvent itself as a cyclical entity,

whose products, in the words of heterodox economist Paul Hawken, "either literally disappear into harmless components, or … are so specific and targeted to a specific function that there is no spillover effect, no waste, no random molecules dancing in the cells of wildlife."

The new global economy will reemerge, this time as an across-the-board true cost market regime in which

## the price of every product tells the ecological truth.

The successful bioeconomies will recycle their unsustainable "sunset" industries into productive "sunrise" ones. The fossil-fuel-based auto industry—previously subsidized by future generations to the tune of hundreds of billions of dollars a year—will be culled back to its "natural" size. The single occupancy vehicle will become a thing of the past. Cities will hum with the conversations of birds, greenery, inventors and artisans.

Bit by bit we will move toward that ultimately fair and level playing field … the one between generations.

**product**

**calming**

Design could be the rapture
creativity of the post-growth era
and designers its superstars ...

a future
without
artifice?

# INDIGEN∆†E!

Indigenation is the most important concept to emerge from permaculture, a kind of reimagination of the "old way," in tandem with "appropriate" technology, defined as technology that strives for harmony with the Earth and community.

To get to reindigenation, we must cultivate a tribal awareness of the life cycle of communities and Earth. We very much need to integrate the concepts of community-supported agriculture and food sovereignty into our messaging and lives, such that the basis of our freedom and livelihood is rooted in the natural systems, the Earth, the strength of our backs and hands and the harmony of our systems approach to the hierarchy of needs.

Green building, sustainable agriculture, artisanal apprenticeship, social entrepreneurship; these are the gateways to a revitalized capacity to create the new model Buckminster Fuller heralded:

## "To change something, build a new model that makes the existing model obsolete."

We know that we need a new model of governance on Earth; we know we need a new model of economics, of social ecology, of mythology, cosmology, spirituality.

In the effort to manifest these visions, we must ground our effort in concerted action to produce friendly environments for ourselves— warm, welcoming, naturally conducive places where we can restore our bodies and minds with friendship and nourishment from the heart and hearth.

I have three acres that my landlord, the deputy mayor of a local village, gave me permission to farm and the local teamster will be showing up this spring to prepare the soil with his team of black Percherons. Drop on by.

Down the road, my friend has 130 acres on which we are preparing to create a CSA farm and orchard. Twenty-five acres of apple trees, five thousand organic trees need pruning and care, and await your hands at harvest. New York alone has seven million acres of prime farmland, most of it planted to feed animals, and feed them poorly at that.

We must resist the temptation to remain an intellectual and political movement. We must understand that the true task is to create a model of civilization which successfully solves for homemaking, sustenance, creativity and culture. Succeeding at this, we can make a legitimate bid for the hearts and minds of all, knowing that we prepare for each other a place of love, goodness, future and possibility.

**Leland Lehrman**

Climb Mount Fuji
O snail,
    but slowly, slowly

Basho

There are many promising directions for the reinvention of economics, which is halfway between a science and an art.

In this time of darkness, as we lose species and languages daily, as we teeter on the edge of climatic collapse, we must remember that our very human capacity for beauty and wholeness remains intact and binds us to the most fundamental processes of the universe.

Stuart Cowan, *The Structurist*

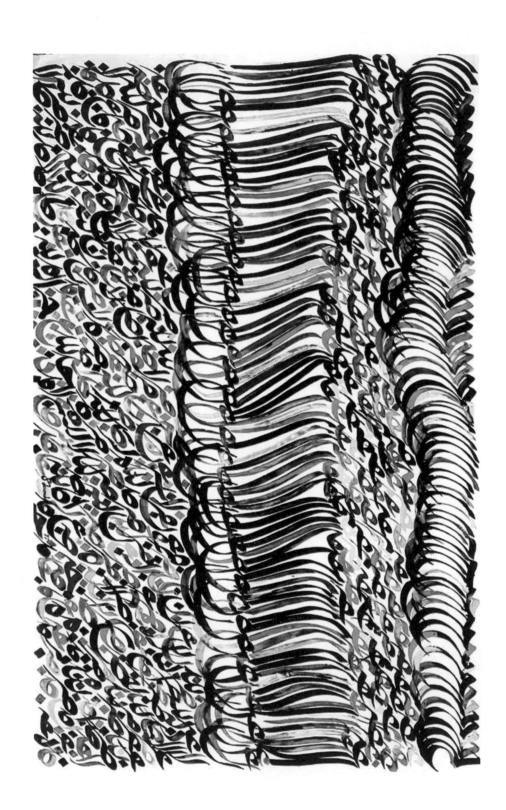

# a tree grows from the New York Stock Exchange

With the financial markets in the gutter, and the trickle-down effect starting to be seen in many of our daily lives—friends and neighbors losing jobs (I especially see it around here in New York)—now seems like a good time to reflect on our financial culture here in the West.

A lot of us probably hate the idea of finance, think it's a sleazy profession motivated by greed. But in many ways the developments in finance in Europe over the past five hundred years have been a crucial part of our success, helping to make possible a huge array of innovations, from the first clothing factories in England at the end of the eighteenth century, to the development of the iPod at the end of the twentieth. Despite the gains facilitated by finance, the benefits to society have always been coupled with a wild irregularity, a boom-bust cycle, which Marx described as part of the inherent contradictions of capitalism, contradictions which would eventually lead to its demise. We've never really grounded our financial ideas in solid principles, other than the sole one of making as much money as possible.

Perhaps there's another way. A shining example that has come out in the past fifty years, one that casts serious doubt on the Western no-holds-barred style, is the recent development of the principles of Islamic Finance. Based on Sharia law, which derives its authority from the Holy Qur'an, the principles of Islamic Finance have provided a beacon of clarity and common sense in good investment practices which are desperately needed here in the West.

What is at the core of the philosophy of Islamic Finance is the idea of money as a measure of value, and not a real asset in itself. According to the principles of Islamic Finance, profiting from money—including charging interest on loans—is regarded as riba, or nonpermissible investing activity under Sharia law. Instead, what Islamic Finance emphasizes is the idea that the investors should share the risks involved in whatever projects they are investing in, and that they should be investing in real things, whether it's land improvement projects, housing, or helping start up a new business. This represents a glaring difference from daily activities of investment firms in the West, who get huge returns by hacking variations in currency exchange rates, legally manipulating stock prices, and engaging in the kind of risk-spreading and avoiding activities (through an ever-increasing range of derivatives) that have created the huge mess we're in now.

We have to learn to differentiate between the legitimate function of finance, which is to provide money to start and expand a wide range of projects, and the activities that are really disconcerting: The hacking of markets, currency trading, calls, puts, the entropic soup of Western instruments, many of which do nothing, absolutely nothing to help start projects, nothing to help businesses stay afloat during the hard times and expand during the good, nothing to help people buy their first homes or first cars or, yes, even go to college. These do nothing at all except fatten the pockets of the financiers that carry them out. They're skimming off the top of a huge pot of resources made from the commonwealth, from the work of people who make an honest living. And at the end of the day this "skimming" leaves everyone a little bit poorer, with a little bit less left in the pot, and it's a practice that really ought to provoke outrage.

At a time like this we need to start thinking about how to put real principles into the world of finance, ideals that are at the core of Islamic Finance and at the core of human decency.

In my idle time, I dream of the day when I can walk down Wall Street and see coffee shops, music halls, see kids busking on the street, see the hideous cigar store on Broad Street turned into a hangout space for artists and philosophers where they talk about the latest ideas and ideals while on break from the tedious job of handling finance. I dream of the day when flower vines grow over the grotesque naked buildings of the financial districts here and in London and in Tokyo and in Dubai, for the day when finance is again the pulsing heart of the coming Renaissance. I dream of the day when—as one of my friends put it—a tree grows from the New York Stock Exchange.

Joel Daniel Myers is a writer and musician living in Maspeth, New York. He studied economics at Columbia University.

# global 'shi'

Under the capitalistic political system, democracy, freedom, science and technology, consumption and globalization, which are beautiful things in human society, suddenly become great scourges and devour the environment ruthlessly. In 2010, Stephen Hawking, the renowned physicist, made shocking remarks saying that because human genes carried the genetic codes of "selfishness" and "greed," human beings would increase the plundering of the Earth until resources are exhausted little by little and within two hundred years the Earth would be destroyed. Science, democracy and freedom, key concepts of Western society, have simultaneously created splendid civilizations and led humanity into disaster.

In the past two hundred years of the vigorous international communist movement and the ninety years of history of the Communist Party of China, millions of people have sacrificed their lives for the realization of a communist ideal, which has since composed magnificent chapters in the history of mankind. The international communist movement is not defeated by capitalism but defers to develop its own theory. Socialism with Chinese characteristics is still pressing ahead.

Communism demands that all extreme tendencies such as absolute freedom, absolute democracy, absolute fairness, GDP worship and rampant capital are resolutely corrected. Thus, to realize the communist ideal, an implementation scheme is suggested as follows:

Personal consumption will be restricted and prescribed according to the consumption limits that can be borne by the environment and other factors. To be fair, no matter how much wealth a person possesses, each person's consumption is equal.

The size of personal residence will be restricted and prescribed according to the consumption limits that can be borne by the environment and other factors. To be fair, no matter how much wealth a person possesses, the size of each person's residence is equal.

Personal consumption of water, electricity and fuel will be restricted and prescribed according to the consumption limits that can be borne by environment and other factors.

To be fair, no matter how much wealth a person possesses, each person's consumption amount of water, electricity and fuel is equal.

Government finance will be made public. Officials' properties, enterprises' finance situation and personal properties will also be made public.

Investments made by individuals and enterprises will be encouraged while speculation will be restricted. Strict limits on advertising and promotional expense of enterprises will be imposed.

The scheme will train all social members to have lofty communist consciousness and morality. A person can possess wealth but cannot consume entirely and freely, hence, corruption will be meaningless. Personal wealth will be considered as the quantitative indicator of one's contribution to the society. Wealth will give the person noble spiritual enjoyment through social respect but will not increase one's consumption allowances. A Bill Gates or Steve Jobs can still soar and be heroes of civilization and celebrated by all, but they will live just like everyone else with a one-planet footprint. Thus we will guide and transform the whole society from a "selfish" society to a "selfless" society, which is the communist ideal.

By using natural law to guide our practice, understanding and transforming nature from the perspective of nature, our civilization and the future of mankind will be like nature: Eternal!

People of the world, let us unite and strive for the realization of the communist ideal!

Zhou Xifeng has worked as a physics teacher and conference organizer in Shanghai, P. R. China

## FOR THE CHILDREN

The rising hills, the slopes,
of statistics
lie before us.
the steep climb
of everything, going up,
up, as we all
go down.

In the next century
or the one beyond that,
they say,
are valleys, pastures,
we can meet there in peace
if we make it.

To climb these coming crests
one word to you, to
you and your children:

*stay together*
*learn the flowers*
*go light*

Gary
Snyder
"Turtle Island"
New Directions, 74

# A Bill of Rights for Future Generations

We, the people of the future,
like the multitudes who came before us, have the right to air that smells sweet, to water that tastes pure, and to land that is fertile, unspoiled and green.

We have the right to inherit a world free of chemicals, nuclear waste and genetic pollution. We have the right to live alongside nature, some of which is still untamed.

We ask you, the people of the present, not to bequeath us a toxic legacy. We ask that you not gamble with technology that may backfire in the future, and request that you not burden us with the weight of ever-deferred debt. We would like to claim our share of the planet's bounty. Please do not use it all up.

In turn, we promise to grant the same rights and privileges to the generations who follow us, in the sacred hope that the human spirit will live forever.

A curse on any generation who ignores this desperate plea.

**ASK YOUR PROFESSOR:**

**What is the ultimate responsibility of economists? Is it to do no harm? Is it to manage our planetary household in a responsible way ... to make sure the human race survives?**

Time it takes to grow one inch of soil: 1,000 years

professors of the
future will
begin every
lesson with
a minute
of silence...

# time capsule found on the dead planet

I

In the first age, we created gods. We carved them out of wood; there was still such a thing as wood, then. We forged them from shining metals and painted them on temple walls. They were gods of many kinds, and goddesses as well. Sometimes they were cruel and drank our blood, but also they gave us rain and sunshine, favourable winds, good harvests, fertile animals, many children. A million birds flew over us then, a million fish swam in our seas.

Our gods had horns on their heads, or moons, or sealy fins, or the beaks of eagles. We called them All-Knowing, we called them Shining One. We knew we were not orphans. We smelled the earth and rolled in it; its juices ran down our chins.

## 2

In the second age we created money. This money was also made of shining metals. It had two faces: on one side was a severed head, that of a king or some other noteworthy person, on the other face was something else, something that would give us comfort: A bird, a fish, a fur-bearing animal. This was all that remained of our former gods. The money was small in size, and each of us would carry some of it with him every day, as close to the skin as possible. We could not eat this money, wear it or burn it for warmth; but as if by magic it could be changed into such things. The money was mysterious, and we were in awe of it. If you had enough of it, it was said, you would be able to fly.

## 3

In the third age, money became a god. It was all-powerful, and out of control. It began to talk. It began to create on its own. It created feasts and famines, songs of joy, lamentations. It created greed and hunger, which were its two faces. Towers of glass rose at its name, were destroyed and rose again. It began to eat things. It ate whole forests, croplands and the lives of children. It ate armies, ships and cities. No one could stop it. To have it was a sign of grace.

## 4

In the fourth age we created deserts. Our deserts were of several kinds, but they had one thing in common: Nothing grew there. Some were made of cement, some were made of various poisons, some of baked earth. We made these deserts from the desire for more money and from despair at the lack of it. Wars, plagues and famines visited us, but we did not stop in our industrious creation of deserts. At last all wells were poisoned, all rivers ran with filth, all seas were dead; there was no land left to grow food.

## 5

Some of our wise men turned to the contemplation of deserts. A stone in the sand in the setting sun could be very beautiful, they said. Deserts were tidy, because there were no weeds in them, nothing that crawled. Stay in the desert long enough, and you could apprehend the absolute. The number zero was holy.

You who have come here from some distant world, to this dry lakeshore and this cairn, and to this cylinder of brass, in which on the last day of all our recorded days I place our final words:

Pray for us, who once, too, thought we could fly.

Margaret Atwood is a recipient of the Order of Canada, the Governor General's Award and the Booker Prize. From *In Other Worlds: Science Fiction and the Human Imagination*, 2011. © Virago Press, McClelland and Stewart and Random House.

# So, students. Decision time.

You live at what many believe is a bifurcation point in human history. You've seen all the graphs with lines curving up like a ski jump. Human population. Gross domestic product. Species extinction. Carbon emissions. Inequality. Resource shortages. You know that something has to give. You've got an idea that the price isn't right. Maybe you're even suspicious that if the world economy does turn out to be a Ponzi scheme, you or your children are a little bit late to the game.

You therefore stand at a fork in the road. You can take the orthodox route—and risk ending up with a qualification as impressive as a degree in Marxist ideology right after the fall of the Berlin Wall. Or you can take a chance on regime shift by speaking up, questioning your teachers, being open to disruptive ideas, and generally acting as an agent of change.

You can insist that the economy is a complex, dynamic, networked system—and demand the tools to understand it.

You can point out that the economy is unfair, unstable and unsustainable—and demand the skills to heal it.

You can tell the oracles that they have failed.

You can go in and break the machine.

And then you can do something new.

David Orrell, *Economyths*

"Art students demanded the realization of art; music students called for 'wild and ephemeral music;' footballers kicked out managers with the slogan 'football to the football players'; gravediggers occupied cemeteries; doctors, nurses, and the interns at a psychiatric hospital organized in solidarity with the inmates." For a few weeks, millions of people who had worked their whole lives in offices and factories broke from their daily routines and . . . lived.

Paris, Latin Quarter, 1968.

The biggest challenge
in jazz improvisation,
Miles Davis observed, is not to play all the
notes one could play,    but to wait,   hesitate,   to play what's not there.

PLAY

JAZZ

Santiago, Chile, 2011.

A butterfly
  Asleep, perched upon
    The temple bell

**Basho**

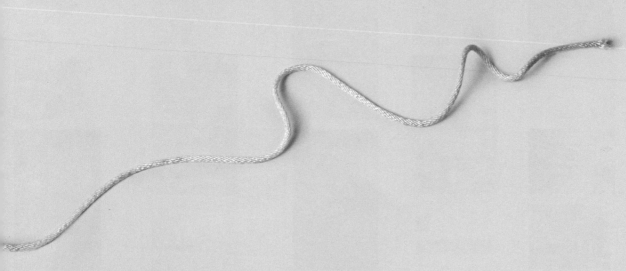

EPILOGUE

# IF THE OLD AMERICAN DREAM WAS ABOUT PROSPERITY, PERHAPS THE NEW ONE WILL BE ABOUT SPONTANEITY ...

KALLE LASN

# COLLABORATORS

This book would not have happened without Doug Tompkins, Robert Halper, Bruce Grierson, James McKinnon, Tom Green, Sarah Nardi, Edward Fulbrook, Justin Hayes, Micah White and all the creative sparks and rabble rousers who have passed through Adbusters Media Foundation over the past 20+ years.

# ARTISTS

**Loe Russell**

**National Geographic**

Photographer unknown. c. 1885–1910
African soldiers presenting arms in front of colonial officials at the railroad station. — Smithsonian Institution

**Craig Cameron Olsen  Loe Russell**
craigcameronolsen.com loerussell.com

**Albert Gea/Reuters**

**El Greco**
*Christ Driving the Money Changers from the Temple*
Presented by Sir J.C. Robinson, 1895 (NG1457). National Gallery, London, Great Britain. © National Gallery, London / Art Resource, NY

**Francis Wheatley**
*Mr. John Howard Offering Relief to Prisoners*
1790

**Ed Kashi / VII**
edkashi.com

**THE BATTLE FOR THE
SOUL OF ECONOMICS**

**Rembrandt Harmensz van Rijn**
*The Syndics* 1662
Collection Rijksmuseum, Amsterdam

**Bedfordshire and Luton Archives Services**

**NASA**

**Daniel Goodman/
Business Insider**
nyceen.tumblr.com

**Bibliothèque nationale de France**

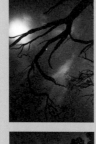

**Steve Morgan**
stevenmorganjr@gmail.com

**Branzino**
*Cosimo de' Medici*

**George Stubbs**
*Lincolnshire Ox*

**Gerald L. Campbell**
flickr.com/photos/
dcnittygritty/

**Sarah Pether**
sarahpether.com

**Mohsen Mahbob**

**Theodore de Bry/AKG-Images Ltd.**
*Port of Lisbon* 1593

**Thomas Gainsborough/National Gallery UK**
*Mr. and Mrs. Andrews*
Bought with contributions from the Pilgrim Trust, The Art Fund, Associated Television Ltd, and Mr and Mrs W. W. Spooner, 1960. (NG6301). National Gallery, London, Great Britanic National Gallery, London / Art Resource, NY

**Mohsen Mahbob**
mohsen.carbonmade.com

**Matthias Quasthoff**
quasthoffs.de/matthias

**Karen Wonders**
firstnations.de

**Bibliothèque nationale de France**

**Marinus Van
Reymerswaele**
*The Usurers* 1540

**Theodore de Bry/AKG-Images Ltd.**
*Columbus* 1596

**© The Trustees of
the British Museum**

Marco Longari/
Newscom

Mario Ruiz/Corbis

Xavier Le Roy
*Self Unfinished 2010*

Doug and Mike Starn
*Take Off Your Skin, It Ain't No Sin 2007*
starnstudio.com

Matthias Ziegler
matzeziegler.de

Mike Mills
*Let's Be Human
Beings 2003*
Photo: Todd Cole

Nina Berman/Noor Images

Mohsen Mahbob

Brian Ulrich
*Chicago, Il 2003 (Cel.)*
notifbutwhen.com

Kim Thue Johnson
From the book *Dead Traffic*
kimthue.com

Michael Bodiam/Millennium Images

Bob Mannseichner
apoplecticpress.org

Wang Ningde
*Some Days — 04,1999*
Courtesy of Wang Nindge and Galerie Paris-
Beijing

**II.**

**PARADIGM LOST**

Ed Buziak
© a la france / Alamy

Stanislav Markov
flickr.com/photos/
garmonique

Paula Bronstein/Getty Images

**III.**

**LOGIC FREAKS**

Xavier Le Roy
*Product of Other
Circumstances 2009,*
xavierleroy.com

Istvan Banyai
*Addicted to Profit*
ist-one.com

Chris Jordan
*Recycling Yard #5 from Intolerable Beauty:
Portraits of American Mass Consumption*

Chris Jordan
From *Midway: Message from the Gyre*

Mohsen Mahbob

Chris Jordan
*Scrap Metal, Seattle 2003*

Mobil Mart

John Goto
*Mobil Mart from Capital Arcade (1997-99)*
johngoto.org.uk

Rafiqur Rahman/Reuters

Brent Humphreys
brenthumphreys.com

Morad Bouchakour
*No Pain No Gain*
moradphoto.com

Robert Longo
From *Men in the Cities
1979-1983*
Courtesy of the Artist
and Metro Pictures
New York

**IV.**

**MEET THE
MAVERICKS**

Georg Gerster/Panos
*A field of strawberries*

Science Faction
*Irrigated Rice
Fields, Bali*

Marious van der Sloot
and Irene Cécile
*Garbage 2008*
mariousvandersloot.com
irenececile.com

Raghu Rai/Magnum

Edward Burtynsky
*Breezewood, Pennsylvania, USA 2008*

Anita Kunz
anitakunz.com

Fred Dufour/Newscom

Elicia di Fonzo, Mohsen Mahbob

Drusaawin Leepalsal
*The Hidden Face*

Nicholas Weissman
weissmanstudio.com

Perfilyev Ilya
flickr.com/photos/mr_Wood

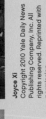

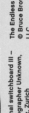

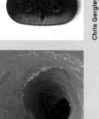

**Reuters**

**Maartje van Caspel**

**Jean-Christian Bourcart**
jcbourcart.com

**Francesca Jane Allen**
francescajane.com

**Adam Ragusea, WBUR Boston**

**Mohsen Mahbob**

**Gil Inoue**
coletivo.org/gilinoue

**Mohsen Mahbob**

**Ferdinand Pauwels**
*Martin Luther's 95 Theses*

**Alex Da Corte**
*Activity #90 2009*
alexdacorte.com

**Stephen Corn, U.S. Geological Survey**

**James Porto**
jamesporto.com

**Mohsen Mahbob**

**The Endless Summer**
© Bruce Brown Films,
LLC

**Jonathan Barnbrook**
barnbrook.net

**Chris Gergley**

**Barry Lewis/Corbis**

**Mohsen Mahbob**

**Nick Whalen**
nickwhalen.com

**Main station of the internal switchboard III –
20 series 47 (1947) Photographer Unknown,
Archiv Siemens Schweiz, Zurich**

**Robert Smithson**
*Glue Pour Vancouver, Canada*
*December, 1969*

**Jim Sugar/Corbis**

**Jean-Noël Lafargue**

**Janine Gordon**
janinegordon.com

**1955 Ford Thunderbird**
Ford Images

**Roy Hancliff**
royhancliff.com

**Bernd Nies**
nies.ch

**Nicholas Haggard**
nicholashaggard.com

**Mohsen Mahbob**

**Charles Peterson**
charlespeterson.net

**Denise Scott Brown**
*Car View of the Strip, Las Vegas*

# V.

**BIONOMICS**

**Uma Partap, ICIMOD**

# VI.

**PSYCHONOMICS**

**Mohsen Mahbob**

**Emmanuel Dunand/Newscom**

**Ruth Skinner**
ruthskinner.com

# VII.

**MEME WARFARE ON CAMPUS**

**Mohsen Mahbob**

# VIII.

**EARLY PIONEERS**

**Rafiq Maqbool**

**Max Temkin**

**Paulo Pinto**
paulopinto.com

**Reuben Cox**
reubencox.us

**Ewen Spencer**
ewenspencer.com

**Soe Zeya Tun/
REUTERS**

**Loe Russell**

**Tess Scheflan/Activestills.org**

**Mohsen Mahbob**

**Axel Corjon**
creaktif.com

IT'S PRETTY AMAZING THAT
EXTRACT OIL FROM THE GROUND
SHIP IT TO A REFINERY
TURN IT INTO PLASTIC
SHAPE IT APPROPRIATELY
TRUCK IT TO A STORE
BUY IT AND BRING IT HOME

The publisher would like to thank all the individuals and photographic libraries, agencies and collections for permission to reproduce their material. Every care has been taken to trace copyright holders. However, if we have omitted anyone we apologize and will, if informed, make corrections to any future edition.

2017

**David Niddrie**

**John McWilliams**
*Graybacks*

**Mohsen Mahbob**

**Michael Simons**

**Kurt Vinion**

**Paul Klee**
*Angelus Novus*
Collection the Israel
Museum, Jerusalem. Photo
© The Israel Museum,
Jerusalem by Elie Posner

**NASA**

**Flore-Aël Surun**

**Patrick Hemingway**

**Gael Turine/Agence Vu**

**Wes Magyar**
*Futility*

**Vinca Petersen**
vinx.co.uk

**Tensta Kontshall**
ABC Trio

**Richard Barnes**
richardbarnes.net

*Candy (Reese's)*

*Candy (M&M's)*

*Chips (Utz)*

*Candy (Twix)*

**Derek Stroup**
derekstroup.com

**Loe Russell**

**Bruno Barbey/Magnum Images**

**Nicholas Burrows**
neverdoingnothing.com

©Andy Goldsworthy
Courtesy Galerie Lelong, New York

**Joachim Tschirner**
From the documentary THE ARAL SEA – Where
the Water ends, the World ends
© by Um Welt Film Produktionsgesellschaft
mbH, Berlin, Germany, www.umweltfilm.de

**Adbusters Art department**

**Mohsen Mahbob**

X.

**A NEW AESTHETIC**

**Yago Hortal**
KL 30

**Paul Cowan**
Untitled, 2010

**Loe Russell**

**Charles Hossein**
© 2012 Artists Rights Society (ARS), New York
/ ADAGP, Paris

**Erwin Pollakoff**

**Janne Lehtinen**
Balloon 2003 from Sacred Bird
gjanne.com

**Brian Ulrich**
Las Vegas, NV 2003 (Cash & Redemption)

**Brian Ulrich**
Medford, NY 2303 (Man with cart)

**Jessica Williams**
jessicawilliams.info

**Carlos Vera/Reuters**

**Heather**
Newyorkshitty.com

# RESOURCES

KICKITOVER.ORG
NEWECONOMICS.ORG
STEADYSTATE.ORG
DEGROWTH.NET
PAECON.NET
THEOILDRUM.COM
INETECONOMICS.ORG
GUY DEBORD
MICHELLE BERNSTEIN
RAOUL VANEIGEM
**BALLARD**
HANS HAACKE
WILDE
SONTAG
GANDHI
AI WEIWEI
ASSANGE
**DADA**
GIL SCOTT HERON
MALCOLM X
ZINN
**TIBOR**
GALEANO
PAZ
BENJAMIN
MARCOS
MARINETTI
BARRIO
GODARD
RESNAIS

PROMIITITT.

David Zinn
zinnart.com

...to be continued